The Crisis of Political
Understanding

Hwa Yol Jung

The Crisis of
Political
Understanding

*A Phenomenological Perspective
in the Conduct of Political Inquiry*

DUQUESNE UNIVERSITY PRESS
PITTSBURGH   1979

Copyright © 1979 by Duquesne University Press

All rights reserved under International and Pan–
American Copyright Conventions.
Published by Duquesne University Press, Pitts-
burgh. Distributed by Humanities Press, Inc.,
Atlantic Highlands, N.J.

Library of Congress Cataloging in Publication Data

Jung, Hwa Yol. The crisis of political understanding

Bibliography: p.
Includes index
1. Political science.   I. Title
JA71.J84   320   78-26938
ISBN 0-391-00861-7

Manufactured in the United States of America

FIRST EDITION

To the memory of my parents,
MAENG KUN JUNG AND HO JUM HWANG,
*who cherished education above all
things in life
and*
JOHN WILD
*who introduced me to the
Tao of phenomenology*

Contents

Foreword

There is today an increasing awareness that the human sciences have lapsed into a situation of crisis. This is becoming more and more evident to the practitioner and the casual observer alike. The various sciences of man have proliferated into a spectrum of separate disciplines, gravitated into an abstract academic insularity, and undergone a veritable conceptual crisis in their methodological designs and definitions of purpose. This has conspired to produce a distressing loss of center. It is no longer evident to the interested and informed layman, nor to the practicing social scientist one might add, how the varied and dispersed human sciences speak about their purportedly central concern—namely, an understanding of the being and behavior of man. Man, as that center around which the several human sciences pivot, is threatened with displacement by the very inquiries which were devised to provide an understanding and explanation of his behavior and socio-historical development. Sadly it must be said that the current human sciences, however notable their achievements in the collection of data and the codification of information might be, stand in danger of losing the humanistic center which first defines them as sciences *of man.*

Since the publication of Edmund Husserl's *The Crisis of European Sciences and Transcendental Phenomenology* both formal philosophy and the specialized sciences have become gradually cognizant of the occlusion of their origins that has followed in the wake of the accelerated objectivization of thought and praxis so characteristic of the late nineteenth and early twentieth century. In *The Crisis* Husserl traces the genealogy of this objectivization of thought and praxis back to the mathematization of nature which emerged from Galilean science and found a congenial home in contemporary positivism. These developments, argued Husserl, led to a virtual breakdown (*Zusammenbruch*) not only of philosophy but science itself. Contemporary philosophy and science alike have succumbed to a lapse into objectivism in which mathematical and cybernetic models have become paradigmatic. Husserl attempted to counter this disquieting state of affairs with a rigorous and radically reflective return to the life-world. It is at the juncture of the concrete deployment of thought and action within a precategorial life-world that the origins of philosophy and science as human activities are to be found, and the new task of phenomenological philosophy becomes that of a careful and disciplined exploration of this rich and variegated life-world.

Professor Jung's analysis and discussion in the present volume receive much of their inspiration from Husserl's seminal reflections on the event of crisis that has settled in on the contemporary intellectual scene. More specifically, Professor Jung develops the theme of crisis as it relates to current developments in political theorizing so as to articulate the expression of crisis as a "crisis of political understanding." In his analysis of this theme some of the more durable procedures and insights of Husserl's philosophy are appropriated; but in the end the pathways of his critical reflection are marked out more by the fundamental ontology of Heidegger and the existential phenomenology of Merleau-Ponty, as well as some recent analyses in social theory. Professor Jung develops his critique of political theorizing out of this background of formative influences. This critique is launched via an attack on political behavioralism and then moves out to a more general and constructive analysis and interpretation of the nature of political knowledge and the world of political intersubjectivity from the vantage point of phenomenological reflection. It is shown in the course of Professor Jung's analysis how the cybernetic model as theory and technique occludes the structure and dynamics of concrete socio-political activities and concerns rather than making them transparent. Cyberneticism is seen as an extension of a *mathesis universalis* geared to a formalization and quantification of the phenomena of the socio-political life-world, with the ironic resultant loss of the life-world itself. It is in this connection that some of the more grievous problems attendant to an isomorphism of natural and social science methodologies are addressed, and a solution that avoids the Scylla of reductionism and the Charybdis of separatism is proposed. In working out the various problems and shortcomings of political behavioralism Professor Jung makes a constant appeal to a radical phenomenological reflection that penetrates the origins of sedimented philosophical and scientific thought and reformulates in a decisive manner the critical question concerning the *possibility* of knowledge. The installation of the requirement for radical reflection constitutes a move beyond the definition of science as a collection of empirical facts and the definition of philosophy as a doctrinal body of knowledge, and sets the demand for a constant vigilance over the origin of fact and the source of all knowledge.

Professor Jung's technical competence in both philosophy and political science is considerable and his general knowledge in these areas is vast and incisive. He is thus well equipped to fill the long-standing need for a disciplined interface of philosophical reflection and socio-political analysis as they pertain to issues concerning the being and behavior of man. The reader will find in the following pages an illuminating and trenchant study of the fabric of the political life of man.

Calvin O. Schrag
Purdue University

Preface

Phenomenology is a revolution or a new paradigm in man's understanding of himself as both knower and actor in the world. It seems to have finally come of age in the social sciences. No doubt the publication of *Phenomenology and the Social Sciences* edited by Maurice Natanson in two volumes in 1973 earmarks a new direction and a turning point in the contemporary philosophy of the social sciences—anthropology, sociology, psychology, linguistics, history, political science, economics, and legal theory. Added to it is the initiation in 1978 of *Human Studies: A Journal for Philosophy and the Social Sciences* edited by George Psathas whose declared aim is to explore phenomenological and existential approaches to the social sciences.

Since the seminal publication of Alfred Schutz's *Der sinnhafte Aufbau der sozialen Welt* in 1932 which was translated into English as *The Phenomenology of the Social World* in 1967, it took four decades for phenomenology to reach its high watermark and perhaps its maturity in the social sciences. Noteworthy is also the fact that in recent years in a concerted effort to find the philosophy of the social sciences alternative to scientism there has increasingly been a critical and engaging dialogue with somewhat competing claims between phenomenology (transcendental, existential, or hermeneutical), structuralism, Marxism, and critical theory in the writings of Maurice Merleau-Ponty, Hans-Georg Gadamer, Jean-Paul Sartre, Paul Ricoeur, Enzo Paci, Kostas Axelos, Calvin Schrag, William McBride, and John O'Neill—let alone the "phenomenology" of Hegel, the psychoanalysis of Sigmund Freud, the sociology of Max Weber, Ludwig Wittgenstein's philosophy of ordinary language-in-use, J. L. Austin's philosophy of language as "performative utterances" or speech acts, the ethnomethodology of Harold Garfinkel and his followers, the symbolic interactionism of George Herbert Mead and Herbert Blumer, and the pragmatism of John Dewey.

Indeed, the possibility of phenomenological thinking has just begun in political theorizing. It was only in 1959 that in his *Political Theory*, which was meant to be a comprehensive analysis of the philosophical and epistemological foundations of twentieth-century political thought, Arnold Brecht made reference to Husserl's phenomenology and noted its limitation for political theory because, on account of its "subjective" method, it is allegedly incapable of overcoming scientific value relativism, that is, establishing the objective, universal, or absolute validity of values. In the third edition (1978) of his *Theories of the Political System*, William T. Bluhm discusses briefly the importance of phenomenology viewed in the tradition of Hegel's "phenomenology" and recognizes the relevance of Husserl's conception of the life-world to the philosophy of the social sciences. *Foundation of Political Science: Research, Methods, and Scope* (1977), edited by Donald M. Freeman, also includes a lengthy account by Maurice Natanson on phenomenology as a philosophy of the social sciences. Although phenomenology has increasingly attracted the attention of political scientists in recent years, I am by no means suggesting here that it has become a steady diet in the household of political theorizing today. Far from it. For example, there is no serious discussion of phenomenology as a possible way of political theorizing in *Political Science: Scope and Theory*, volume 1 of the recent eight-volume survey of the status of political science entitled *Handbook of Political Science* edited by Fred I. Greenstein and Nelson W. Polsby in 1975. The present study is, I believe, the first systematic treatise on phenomenology in political inquiry or the phenomenological philosophy of political science which hopes to introduce phenomenology to those political scientists who wish to be self-conscious of what they are doing.

This work is a critique of political theorizing in the midst of the alleged "post-behavioral revolution" in contemporary political science. By treating phenomenology as the vigilant activity of *reflexivity* that seeks the "origin" of knowledge or truth in the everyday, experiential life-world (*Lebenswelt*), this work attempts to indicate a *radical* approach alternative to the contemporary theories of politics which have been dominated by ontological objectivism and epistemological scientism—particularly by political behavioralism. The epithet "radical" is meant to suggest a break from the dominant modes of political theorizing.

Testing and seeing the full implications of phenomenology as a new way of political theorizing requires, I think, something like a "phenomenological critique of politics" based on philosophical anthropology in which at least three fundamental questions of political theory must be explored systematically from a historical and cross-cultural perspective: (1) theory and practice, (2) the individual and society, and (3) nature and culture in their *dialectical nexus* in the exact sense in which Maurice Merleau-Ponty employs the idea "dialectical" in his *Phenomenology of Perception*. By the dialectic is meant for him the tendency of one existence toward another which denies it and yet without which it cannot be sustained rather than a relationship between contradictory and inseparable thoughts. In short, the dialectic is the existential and conceptual nexus in which one category is related but not reduced to the other—especially the mistaken identification of the part with the whole—in which the inherent ambiguity of the existential and conceptual nexus is recognized, whether it be the nexus of theory and practice, the individual and society, or nature and culture. Therefore, all forms of reductionism are incompatible with the *phenomenological dialectics*. The aim of the present study, however, is limited in scope: it covers primarily one aspect of, or is a prolegomenon to, the phenomenological critique of politics as a new way of thinking. It intends to explore singularly a new "angle of vision" in appropriating the tradition of phenomenology for the conduct of political inquiry which is necessarily metascientific because, strictly speaking, the questioning of political science as a discipline is a conceptual *after*thought or distanciation different from "doing science." By the term "conduct," it should be also noted, I mean to emphasize the *existential* dimension of inquiry in that, not unlike the *pragmatic* mold of Abraham Kaplan's *The Conduct of Inquiry* (1964), the standpoint of inquiry itself is a special way of existing in the world or—to use the technical phrase of Heidegger—a way of "Being-in-the-world" in which "knowing" (epistemology) is always seen in the total context of "existing" (ontology). The model I wish to emulate is set forth by the phenomenological thought of Merleau-Ponty as a ceaseless *interrogation* on an inseparable link between *existence* and *meaning* and all their ramifications. Although it is the central issue of this study, political epistemology must be grounded in phenomenological ontology and the former must never lose the sight of the latter. Without an ontological foundation, it degenerates into methodolatry. All theorizing, both scientific and metascientific, is a "vocation" in the sense Max Weber employed the term which is in need of an existential commitment at least to truth.

I am grateful to Fred Dallmayr for having invited me to teach in the Department of Political Science at Purdue University and tolerated my long-distance commuting during the spring semester of 1975 to present and test the main ideas contained in this work in a graduate seminar on phenomenology and the philosophy of political science. I am also grateful to Fred, Cal Schrag, Dick Grabau, Bill McBride, and Professor Karl-Otto Apel, then visiting professor of philosophy at Purdue, for having discussed engagingly the substance of this work in one of our lively biweekly luncheon gatherings at Purdue. I thank particularly Cal for sacrificing his valuable time and energy to write a Foreword to this work. Without his encouragement, this project might have been never completed or delayed indefinitely. My thanks are also extended to Kay Boals then of Princeton University who originally gave me an opportunity to think of this project by inviting me to read a paper for the Caucus for a New Political Science panel on "Phenomenology as Epistemology" at the Annual Meeting of the American Political Science Association, Chicago, Illinois, August 29-September 2, 1974 and to Herb Reid of the University of Kentucky, the panel's chairperson, Ernie Yanarella of the University of Kentucky and Kazuhiko Okuda then of the University of Toronto, its discussants who made valuable comments. I am especially grateful for Fred and Herb whose ideas have been the constant source of stimulation for me. I also thank Suzann Thomas for checking meticulously the original manuscript. My wife, Petee, has always been patient and willing to be a sounding board for testing my ideas and the manner in which they are presented. The still rugged style of presentation—rugged for those who are unfamiliar with the linguistic terrain of phenomenology—is not due to the failure of her linguistic nerve but is rather a high tribute to a mathematician for comprehending the "tribal language" of phenomenology or, for that matter, political science. Some of the works on which she and I have collaborated are incorporated into chapters 3 and 4 of this book. George J. Benston read most of the manuscript and clarified some of my ideas in it as he had done on many other occasions in the past. In our lively discussions, he is always a happy reminder that lasting friendship does not mean the lack of disagreement. Listening to the sound and resonance of the everyday piano practice of my sons, Michael and Eric, has been a constant reminder of a psychophysical unity in the dexterous movement of their delicate fingers and an indubitable affirmation of the marvelous working of the human body. Last but not least, I am grateful to Mrs. Margaret Boyer who spent many hours in typing and retyping this manuscript from beginning to end so conscientiously, promptly, and expertly, and to Moravian College for having granted me a sabbatical leave during the spring semester of 1978 to complete this book in its present form.

Finally, one thing remains to be said that stands out above all other things. All those whom I cited in the text and many more uncited made me realize more acutely than ever before that both thinking and writing as results of diacritical discourse are an unfinished task, that is, an existential project. Mr. John Dowds, director of Duquesne University Press, understands well what I mean. As *in*completion, this book is only pointing the way to extended reflection and revision.

Acknowledgments

I wish to express my gratitude to Northwestern University Press, D. Reidel Publishing Co., and the editors of the following journals for having given me permission to use my previously published work: *Cultural Hermeneutics,* now called *Philosophy and Social Criticism,* ed. David M. Rasmussen; *Dialectical Anthropology,* ed. Stanley Diamond; *Human Studies,* ed. George Psathas; *The Journal of the British Society for Phenomenology,* ed. Wolfe Mays; *The Journal of Value Inquiry,* ed. James Wilbur; *Man and World,* ed. John M. Anderson, Joseph J. Kockelmans, and Calvin O. Schrag; *Philosophy Forum,* ed. Ervin Laszlo; and *Polity,* ed. Peter J. Fliess. The extent to which I made use of each of my works is indicated in the text.

PART ONE——Introduction

Questioning is the piety of thinking.
—*Martin Heidegger*

Philosophy is not the passage from a confused world to a universe of closed significations. On the contrary, philosophy begins with the awareness of a world which consumes and destroys our established significations but also renews and purifies them.

—*Maurice Merleau-Ponty*

Chapter 1

The Nature of
Phenomenological
Thinking

This work is a phenomenological response to
the crisis of political understanding today.
Those who are familiar with the works of Edmund Husserl, Martin
Heidegger, and Maurice Merleau-Ponty will readily recognize the
genesis of its title. It is with a sense of loyalty to phenomenology that
this response is conceived and formulated—loyalty, when enlight-
ened, being a person's willing and thoroughgoing devotion to a
cause which should not be confused with fanaticism that dogmatism
engenders.[1] In *The Structure of Scientific Revolutions,* Thomas S. Kuhn
perceives of crisis as an interlude in the transition of an old paradigm
to a new one when the puzzle-solving of normal science becomes
enigmatic or anomalous.[2] Phenomenology is a response to the crisis of
political understanding due largely to the failure of scientism to take
into account the experiential vectors of subjectivity in political inquiry.[3]

The title of this work is resonant with Merleau-Ponty who spoke of
"the crisis of understanding" (*La Crise de l'Entendement*) which, in deal-

ing sympathetically with Max Weber's politics of understanding, recognizes the subtle dialectic of ambiguity between the human historical order and the historian who reflects on it.[4] Heidegger is far more daring and sweeping in intention and scope than Merleau-Ponty in sensing the end or death (not just the crisis) of the entire spectrum of Western thought from Plato to Nietzsche.[5] It is Husserl, however, who is most immediately and directly relevant to the themes of our present inquiry when in his last and posthumously published work, *The Crisis of European Sciences and Transcendental Phenomenology,* he "introduced" a new avenue of approach to the theme of the crisis of European thought since Galileo and the revolutionary notion of the life-world (*Lebenswelt*).[6]

The immediate relevance of Husserl's *Crisis* to our present inquiry is twofold. In the first place, the defense of philosophy is *essentially* the defense of man and humanity since it is in itself a human cultural accomplishment. Thus Husserl spoke of the philosopher as the functionary or civil servant of humanity. For Husserl, as philosophy is the "nursemaid" of humanity, the sense of history depends on the sense of philosophy; and the crisis of philosophy *is* also a crisis in human existence.[7] To rescue philosophy and humanity from the quicksand of naturalistic objectivism and positivism, Husserl criticizes them in his *Crisis*: "positivism, in a manner of speaking, decapitates philosophy" and "merely fact-minded sciences make merely fact-minded people."[8] In his criticism of positivism, Husserl asks: "can the world, and human existence in it, truthfully have a meaning if the sciences recognize as true only what is objectively established in this fashion, and if history has nothing more to teach us than that all the shapes of the spiritual world, and the conditions of life, ideals, norms upon which man relies, form and dissolve themselves like fleeting waves, that it always was and ever will be so, that again and again reason must turn into nonsense, and well-being into misery?"[9] In the second place, Husserl attempts to show once and for all the "genesis" of science in the life-world, the most inclusive horizon of meaning and the homeland of common humanity which is presupposed in both scientific and philosophical theorizing.

With some justification it is often said that there are as many phenomenologies as there are phenomenologists. The ongoing "family quarrel" among phenomenologists themselves, especially between transcendental and existential phenomenologists, is well-known.[10] In discussing the relevance of phenomenology to political inquiry, however, we will freely draw conclusions from its core characteristics.

Whatever else phenomenology may be, it is foremost a critique of human knowledge. The term "critique" used often in this text, when properly understood, is not a purely negative endeavor merely to find faults in and discredit the thought of an adversary but is rather a philosophical inquiry into and justification for both the limits and possibilities (i.e., validity) of human thought and cognition in terms of experiential evidence whose schematization is at least as old as the philosophy of Kant.

Phenomenology is neither a school, nor a set of dogmas, nor a method, nor a technique in the same way that mathematics is a technique for the physical and social sciences today. Rather, it is a "movement."[11] Husserl conceived of philosophy as a perpetual beginning, as Socratic ignorance. For the "true thinker" (*Selbstdenker*), philosophy never ceases to be a riddle or enigma, wonder, and astonishment to itself. As a vigilance, philosophy seeks the source or origin of knowledge in the "things themselves" (*Sachen selbst*). Husserl thus sought the *experiential* genesis or origin of logic, judgment, and science in the life-world. So he looked for the origin of conceptual thinking in the original, preconceptual experience to be had in the life-world or what Plato disdainfully called the cave world. Unlike Plato, in seeking the "beginning" Husserl's approach is a "retrogressive" one which descends or plunges into the world of *doxa* in order to found the world of *epistēmē* and to see the "natural light" of ordinary things. Heidegger expresses the true spirit of phenomenological philosophy when he says that "in what is most its own phenomenology is not a school. It is *the possibility of thinking*, at times changing and only thus persisting, or corresponding to the claim of what is to be thought. Phenomenology is not a matter of designation as a school or method, but it will disappear in favor of thinking whose manifestness remains mystery."[12] If phenomenology will ever succeed in political thinking, it will disappear after establishing the possibility of political thinking itself.

The crisis of man and his humanity *is* foremost the crisis of thinking. In our "time of need," what is most needed is a way to think properly. There is interest in thinking today as it is engendered by thought-provoking events. Paradoxically, however, Heidegger rightly observes in *What Is Called Thinking?* that in our age what is most thought-provoking is that we are not thinking.[13] In such an impoverished state of thinking, we must first clarify the conditions of our thought—the primary function of philosophy. The thought-provoking trial in Jerusalem of Adolf Eichmann and his mentality led Hannah Arendt to discover and reflect on the peculiar phenomenon

called the "banality of evil" in which the monstrous deeds of the man
are not caused by his equally monstrous motives or intentions.
Arendt observes:

> I was struck by a manifest shallowness in the doer that made it
> impossible to trace the incontestable evil of his deeds to any
> deeper level of roots or motives. The deeds were monstrous, but
> the doer—at least the very effective one now on trial—was quite
> ordinary, commonplace, and neither demonic nor monstrous.
> There was no sign in him of firm ideological convictions or of
> specific evil motives, and the only notable characteristic one
> could detect in his past behavior as well as in his behavior during
> the trial and throughout the pre-trial police examination was
> something entirely negative: it was not stupidity but *thoughtless-
> ness*.[14]

In caring for the possibility of thinking and the thinking of human
possibilities, Heidegger evokes the "piety of thinking" (*Frömmigkeit des
Denkens*).[15] Pious thinking is the spirit of "questioning" in accordance
with the natural order of the "things themselves"—with Being as
aletheia. It is a holy vision on things both natural and cultural. Thinking as questioning—always with an interrogation mark—is an ever
alert obedience to the advent of what *is*, and ultimately it makes the
questioning activity itself problematical or questionable. Thinking in
accordance with the natural luminescence of things is *interesting* (or
"caring") because "interest" (*inter-esse*) means to *be among* and at the
hub of things. What then is this thinking as interesting? What are the
demands it makes on us as thinking beings? Heidegger defines it in
terms of what it is *not*:

(1) Thinking does not bring knowledge as do the sciences.
(2) Thinking does not produce usable practical wisdom.
(3) Thinking solves no cosmic riddles.
(4) Thinking does not endow us directly with the power to act.[16]

Strictly speaking, then, thinking as autonomous activity is distinguished but not separated from both "knowing" (in an epistemological sense) and "acting" (in a pragmatic sense). For it neither produces
solely epistemological truths nor is merely instrumental to action
whose manifest aim is measured by its pragmatic cash value. Rather,
"knowing" and "acting" presuppose "thinking" or the possibility of
the latter precedes that of the former. Thinking as disclosure of
things (*aletheia*) is presupposed in both knowledge and action.[17]

Authentic and inauthentic thinking may be defined in terms of its piety and impiety to the natural order of things in general. For Heidegger, there is a fundamental difference between "meditative thinking" (*besinnliches Denken*) and "calculative thinking" (*rechnendes Denken*). The mode of the former is characteristic of "poetry" or the poetic (*Dichtung*) which is the mood of "serenity" or "releasement" (*Gelassenheit*) towards things.[18] The latter is characteristic, at its height, of technocentric and cybernetic thinking whose "metaphysical" underpinnings are deeply rooted in the logocentric tradition from the inception of Western thought in Plato and continued in and modified by Descartes and Hegel in modern thought. Heidegger calls for "overcoming" (*Überwindung*) metaphysics with the purpose of initiating a new beginning born out of its ashes.

Calculative thinking "enframes" history by the conceptual net where the body politic is "manufactured" as "power" or reduced to the "framework" (*Ge-stell*) of what Heidegger calls "politology." Although modern "civil philosophy" may be the invention of Hobbes, his political ingenuity succumbed to the Galilean and Cartesian geometric "framework." Hobbes's "civil philosophy" is the harbinger of modern politology or political cybernetics. The "naturalization" of politics is the death of the body politic. Now we must be aware of the unprecedented perils of "making nature" by means of "work" and their effects on "making history," that is, the planetary domination of technology over both "nature" and "history." Technology as man-made is an order of *factum;* however, since the made is now making the maker, technology is indeed an extraordinary category of *factum* in its planetary domination which not only stifles the maker's self-making but also has brought humanity to an unprecedented epoch when we can say that, as the saying of a Hindu epic goes, "I *am* my death."

For Heidegger, calculative thinking abandons or obliterates Being as *aletheia*. The natural luminescence of Being is cast on beings and unveils their whereabouts. Mortal man, earth, sky, and gods are the elemental *topos* of Being—its fourfold unity. Calculative thinking does not see the earth as earth, water as water, air as air, work as work, language as language, etc., when it conceals the earth as a planet, water as a liquid, air as a gas, work as an occupation or productive industry, and language as merely an instrument of manipulation, domination, and lying. According to Heidegger, "making" in Greek as in a work of art is *poiesis,* the poetic; *technē,* both technique and "production," originally meant neither "art" nor "handicraft" but "making" or letting things appear in their own nature. So the "*techne-*

tronic age" has concealed this original meaning of *technē*. The original way of *technē* is then man's reverential receptivity or openness towards the natural order of things.

According to Paul Ricoeur, phenomenology as the *possibility of thinking* unites the following three general theses: "(1) meaning is the most comprehensive category of phenomenological description; (2) the subject is the bearer of meaning; [and] (3) reduction is the philosophical act which permits the birth of a being for meaning."[19] If phenomenology is an archaeology (the *logos* of *archē*) of meanings, it is interested in the quest for a retrieval of the origin or genesis of meaning (*Sinnesgenesis*) in "knowing" and "acting." As a philosophy of experience, as a "radical empiricism," phenomenology insists on direct experience as the homeland of conceptual thought. What is experiential is deeply subjective (or, better, intersubjective). Phenomenology is a *philosophy of subjectivity* as the idea of experience is meaningless without first including the existing subject who experiences. The phenomenological philosophy of subjectivity must be distinguished from either "subjectivism" or "objectivism." For it is a theory of meaning based on consciousness as *intentionality*, that is to say, when the conscious subject encounters an object in thought, imagination, feeling, or perception, there is a meaning or a set of meanings. Meaning then is constituted as a unity of the intending subject and the intended object which are called *noesis* and *noema,* respectively. *Noesis* is the act of intending, while *noema* is its referent. In phenomenology there is no dichotomy between "appearance" and "reality" on the one hand and between "phenomenon" and "noumenon" on the other. This dichotomy is dissolved in phenomenology as a theory of meaning. Insofar as phenomenology is concerned with the problem of subjectivity as an *existing* individual, it encounters the existential philosophy of Søren Kierkegaard; and insofar as the existing individual is a social being, that is, subjectivity implies intersubjectivity, it encounters Marxism. As subjectivity is the existential precondition for both thinking and acting, phenomenology deals with the subjective meaning of everything that man does. As a philosophy of subjectivity, phenomenology is opposed to "objectivism" or "naturalism" as an ontology and "scientism" as an epistemology and a methodology. Objectivism is the philosophical claim that reality is objective in the sense that it is separable or ought to be separated from the realm of subjectivity. It claims that no reality is subjective. Unlike phenomenology, objectivism denies the qualitative differences between what is human—human because it is subjective—and what is merely natural. So methodologically speaking, the objectivist claims that the human or social sciences are amenable to the same treatment of the natural sciences in the name of causal explanation and prediction (i.e., scientism).[20] Political behavioralism as a philosophy of human behavior is objectivism and/or scientism. Insofar as political behavioralism treats political behavior as if it is a physical object and therefore is amenable to the same techniques of the physical sciences, it is both objectivism and scientism, whereas while it maintains the difference between the behavioral and the natural but succumbs nonetheless to the "canons of scientific method," it is committed to scientism. To adopt the convenient terminology of Max Scheler, objectivism is an (ontological) "illusion," whereas scientism is an (epistemological) "error."[21] Thus the philosophy of man may be an illusion and/or an error.

Phenomenology seeks the experiential genesis of conceptual thought. However, the radicality of phenomenology lies also in its insistence on the imperative of philosophy's self-scrutiny, of the *interrogation* of its own meaning and possibility. Phenomenologically speaking, philosophy is nothing but a "set of questions wherein he who questions is himself implicated by the question."[22] The phenomenological notions of "reduction" (*epochē*), "rigor," "presuppositionlessness," and "interrogation" have their common origin in the effort of phenomenology to justify itself as a transcendental or philosphical activity. Although, as Merleau-Ponty rightly asserts, reduction is never complete and absolute, the methodic suspension of practical beliefs and concerns is necessary to justify philosophy as a transcendental activity—as "reflective liberation." Maurice Natanson says that phenomenology is centered in intentionality, that intentionality is opened up by reduction, that reduction involves origin, and that origin is the transcendental clue to existence"[23] and, we might add, Being in general. Insofar as this transcendental activity is grounded in the world of preconceptual or prepredicative experience called the life-world which as such precedes the distinction between *thatness* (the existential) and *whatness* (the essential), phenomenology as interrogation is also a critique of the social world. For the assurance of Being-in-the-truth is one with the assurance of Being-in-the-world.[24] Phenomenologically speaking, then, *the philosophy of the social sciences is also a philosophy of the social world.*[25] In short, phenomenology is *critical* in a twofold sense: it is an interrogation on its own activity *and* a critique of the social world. In this sense, phenomenology is more critical than the "critical theory" of Jürgen Habermas whose philosophy is unthinkable without the *tradition* of Husserl's phenomenology of the life-world and Heidegger's hermeneutic of human existence (*Daseinsanalyse*) along with the Marxian "critique of ideology" (*Ideologie-*

kritik), Freud's psychoanalysis, Dilthey's hermeneutics of the "human sciences" (*Geisteswissenschaften*), and the pragmatics of Charles Peirce. Nonetheless, Habermas is critical of Husserl's notion of phenomenology as transcendental philosophy and his critique of objectivism and scientism. According to Habermas, Husserl is right in criticizing the objectivist illusion of identifying the method of science with reality itself but he succumbs to another objectivism or is unable to extricate himself from the traditional conception of *theoria*. Because he disconnects knowledge from human interests in his critique of objectivism, according to Habermas, it turns against itself: "Contrary to Husserl's expectations, objectivism is eliminated not through the power of renewed *theoria* but through demonstrating what it conceals: the connection of knowledge and interest."[26] For Habermas, then, the task of a critical theory of science is to demonstrate "a specific connection between logical-methodological rules and knowledge-constitutive interests." Only by so doing does it escape "the snares of positivism." By ranking a system of interests as values, Habermas shows his preference for the primacy of *emancipatory* interest. Without the practical interest in emancipation, according to him, philosophy like science ends up with "the illusion of pure theory." So for Habermas, Husserl is caught in the purity of theory. In his attempt to fuse knowledge and interest in one ("knowledge and interest are one") which is the inversion of Platonism, Habermas intends to be faithful to the Marxian view of the unity of theory and practice.[27] He is mistaken, however, to the extent to which he is unaware of ambiguity in the dialectic of theory and practice. Without a phenomenological or hermeneutical "distanciation" or what is often called the "disinterested" function of theory in relation to practice, that is, the *momentary* suspension of practical interest in the world, theory itself becomes a sham; it becomes merely subservient to the emancipatory function of practice. "Disinterestedness" must not be interpreted as "uninterestedness." For above all it means "an interest in cognition," a cognitive interest in practice *from a distance*. As Husserl puts it, it is "that interest which is distinguished from all other interests of practical life."[28] Theory as "reflection" (*reflexio*) means always "turning-back," and in a way practice is always ahead of theory. An unavoidable *distance* between the two is created when the former attempts to catch the latter by the tail. Thus philosophy as theory must recognize its own limitation (as well as its possibility) in relation to practice. By recognizing this ambiguous dialectic of theory and practice, Merleau-Ponty forthrightly calls philosophy a "limping" enterprise.[29] The self-scrutiny of phenomenology as theory is neither a matter of self-indulgence nor an escape from the world. At his best the philosopher *puts* everything he reflects on *out of action* or *keeps* the world of action *at bay:* he becomes "the bridge between the *solitude* of radical reflection and the *community* of human action."³⁰

Without distanciation, without cognition as disinterestedness, philosophy will end up destroying both its own integrity and the autonomy of practice. Without losing sight of the emancipatory function of theory, Paul Ricoeur understands well the notion of distanciation in theory or the dialectic of theory and practice or, as he puts it, the "civilization of the word" and the "civilization of work." In reflection, according to Ricoeur, one assumes the attitude of aloofness. The word is an invitation or incitement for action, precisely because it *signifies* what is to be done. Because it *signifies,* it *influences* rather than directly *produces* action. Ricoeur writes:

> The word has ... a function of *foundation* with respect to all the pragmatic activities of man. It conveys the "theoretical" function in its entirety. There is no technique which is not an applied knowledge, and there is no applied knowledge which is not dependent upon a knowledge which at first repudiated all application. *Praxis* does not give us the whole of man. *Theoria* is its *raison d'être.* This founding *theoria* goes from mathematics to ethics, from physical theory to history, from science to ontology. All radical problems are posed in an attitude which suspends the utilitarian concern and vital impatience. This is why there is no civilization which can survive without some sphere of free play left to disinterested speculation, to research without immediate or apparent applications.³¹

Without theory as distanciation, there is no room even for a critique of science and technology as ideology, as "instrumental rationality," which Habermas wishes to repudiate. Without it, moreover, a critique of society—a critique of "doing" by means of "saying"—is an impossibility. An overzealousness for emancipatory interest even does injustice to the famous or infamous Marx's eleventh thesis on Feuerbach which ends up with making him only a pristine pragmatist: "Philosophers have only *interpreted* the world in various ways; the point is, to *change* it."³² Not unlike his Danish contemporary Kierkegaard, Marx meant to stress the *critical* side of theoretical consciousness rather than being antiphilosophical only by rejecting abstract speculation in an attempt "to supersede the abstractness, isolation, passivity, and powerlessness" of the philosopher.³³ To put it in an existential nutshell, Marx intended to end the alienation of "essence" from "existence" and to claim that ideas are not merely in the "head" of the philosopher but in the living "body" of real life. Thus the Yugoslav Marxist philosopher Mihailo Marković says that Marx's formulation is "an *indirect* form of the unification of theory and practice."[34] The responsibility of philosophy as self-reflection, as interrogation, is achieved not so much in fusing knowledge and interest as in the philosopher's *living* his own philosophy.[35] This is what Kierkegaard called the existential fulfillment of the philosopher as "subjective thinker" in criticizing Hegel's "objective" philosophy which may be able to build a lofty conceptual castle but the thinker cannot live in it. At the moment of self-reflection, at the moment of interrogation, the philosopher becomes his own psychotherapist.

Let us extend our foregoing phenomenological reflection to the nature of political thinking. Political thinking is, as Arendt puts it, "nothing more than to think what we are doing" when we are engaged in political activity.[36] In deference to the very nature of thinking as questioning, with her we must further ask: "What are we 'doing' when we do nothing but think? Where are we when we, normally always surrounded by our fellow-men, are together with no one but ourselves?"[37] Arendt is fond of quoting the sentence that Cicero ascribed to Cato: "Never is a man more active than when he does nothing, never is he less alone than when he is by himself" (*Numquam se plus agere quam nihil cum ageret, numquam minus solum esse quam cum solus esset*)[38]—the selfsame paradox that plagued Plato and Aristotle in the very inception of Western political thought in relating philosophy to politics or discoursing the philosophy *of* politics. In the same spirit, Husserl insisted on losing the world by *epochē* for the universal self-examination of philosophy itself by invoking St. Augustine whose idea is on the same footing as the Delphic motto, "Know thyself" and the above-mentioned dictum of Cato: "Do not wish to go out; go back into yourself. Truth dwells in the inner man" (*Noli foras ire, in te redi, in interiore homine habitat veritas*).[39] The difficulty of political thinking as autonomous reflection, however, arises from the inherent tension between the two aforementioned questions Arendt has raised or the effort to reconcile them. That is to say, the political thinker is not only a solitary individual when he does nothing but think but also a citizen as revealed in the Socratic dilemma between search for "truth" and "political loyalty" or "political responsibility." The difficulty of political thinking—perhaps more than any other type of thinking—is further complicated by its dual function of thinking *of* and *for* the sake of the pragmatic world of politics. To be effective, thinking always wishes to withdraw or distanciate itself from political action; and yet, for the sake of political action, it must dwell in political practices and institutions. *Careful* political thinking is both "remembering" that preserves what has been and "projecting" that creates new possibilities for political practices and institutions. This ambiguous duality inherent in political thinking as thinking *of* and *for* the sake of political action inevitably creates risks and tensions. Hasty intolerance of this ambiguity, I think, is the source of harsh criticism by Herbert Marcuse and Theodor W. Adorno of Heidegger's ontology as social and ethical anesthesiology and as irrelevant "jargon of authenticity," respectively.[40] In the end, the difficulty of political thinking is that of maintaining on an even keel the dialectical nexus or rhythm of withdrawal and distanciation on the one hand and return and involvement on the other. Although thinking philosophically arises from the quest for meaning in ordinary, nonphilosophical experiences and both equally make demands on the function of human reason, the peril of political thinking lies in that it is a *transitive act*. Because it is a transitive act, political thinking lies in the intersecting horizon of the *vita activa* and the *vita contemplativa*. The tension of the visible and the invisible or a judicious resolution of it is manifest in Arendt's *The Human Condition*—a treasure of political thinking in the twentieth century. It is *thinking about* the three fundamental activities of the *vita activa:* "labor," "work," and "action." It is the exemplar or masterpiece of political thinking in the age when political activity has become subordinated to other activities (e.g., economic). *The Human Condition* exalts "action" which measures better than "labor" or "work" what is truly human. Above all, it is a vision of politics, for political activity is "action" *par excellence.*

PART TWO——The Primacy of Ontology

Once Chuang Chou dreamt he was a butterfly, a butterfly flitting and fluttering around, happy with himself and doing as he pleased. He didn't know he was Chuang Chou. Suddenly he woke up and there he was, solid and unmistakable Chuang Chou. But he didn't know if he was Chuang Chou who had dreamt he was a butterfly, or a butterfly dreaming he was Chuang Chou. Between Chuang Chou and a butterfly there must be some distinction! This is called the Transformation of Things.

—Chuang Tzu

Chapter 2

The Phenomenological Ontology of Man

Political theory, like any other theory, is an effort to discover an intimate connection between meaning and existence.[1] Whether or not we theorists recognize it, every conception of politics or political theory presupposes manifestly or latently some conception or image of man. Thus John Wild writes that "political philosophy must begin with some understanding of the being of man, for its many problems developed from an inclusive grasp of man as he is."[2] Because of lack of a better term, the general conception of man will be called the ontology of man or, as it is often called today in the tradition of European philosophy, "philosophical anthropology." Heidegger calls it "fundamental ontology" (*Fundamentalontologie*): it is fundamental because, as man is the shepherd or guardian of Being, the being of man has a privileged status in ontology. The ontology of man is the basis of epistemology, axiology, and hermeneutics. As broadly speaking phenomenology is ontological, epistemological, axiological, and hermeneutical, a phenomenological critique of politics must use Husserl (epistemology), Kierkegaard and Heidegger (ontology), Scheler (axiology), and Hans-Georg Gadamer and Paul Ricoeur (hermeneutics). As a radical empiricism, phenomenology founds all these enterprises on human

17

experience in the life-world which is "not a thing, not any set of objects, but rather an ultimate horizon within which all such objects and the individual person are actually understood in the 'natural attitude' of everyday life."[3]

1. Being Human

For Husserl, as we have already noted, the crisis of philosophy is an aspect of the crisis of humanity—European humanity that has been uprooted from the life-world by the calculative thinking of positive objectivism where the human is defined both ontologically and methodologically more and more in terms of the natural or physical. Thus the task of Husserl's phenomenology in the *Crisis* was twofold: to show the rootedness of science in the life-world and by so doing to rediscover the *telos* of science and philosophy for human existence.

Unlike objectivism, phenomenology is above all an *archaeology* of subjectivity (or intersubjectivity) in relation to both action and thought, which must not be confused with "subjectivism," the opposite of "objectivism." An emphasis on subjectivity in phenomenology is not a denial of "objectivity" but only of objectivism which takes for granted the role of subjectivity in human activity. Thus the cardinal merit of phenomenology lies in its avoidance of both extremes of subjectivism and objectivism or of the dualism of subjectivity and objectivity. The Cartesian dualism of the internal (*res cogitans*) and the external (*res extensa*), whether they be subjectivity and objectivity, mind and body, self and other, man and nature, or thought and action, is rejected by modern physicists like Niels Bohr and Werner Heisenberg. Affirming the complementarity of subjectivity and objectivity in science, Heisenberg declares:

> The old division of the world into objective process in space and time in which these processes are mirrored—in other words, the Cartesian differences between *res cogitans* and *res extensa*—is no longer a suitable starting point for our understanding of modern science. Science, we find, is now focused on the network of relationships between man and nature, on the framework which makes us as living beings dependent parts of nature, and which we as human beings have simultaneously made the object of our thoughts and actions. Science no longer confronts nature as an objective observer, but sees itself as an actor in this interplay between man and nature. The scientific method of analyzing, explaining and classifying has become conscious of its limi-

tations, which arise out of the fact that by its intervention science alters and refashions the object of investigation. In other words, method and object can no longer be separated. *The scientific world-view has ceased to be a scientific view in the true sense of the word.*[4]

If so, then science nullifies its own image as merely an objective enterprise. This affirmation of the complementarity of subjectivity and objectivity has been the hallmark of phenomenology.

As an archaeology of subjectivity or intersubjectivity, phenomenology focuses its attention on the very *act* of experience, whether it be thinking, doing, perceiving, feeling, imagining, etc. It contends that because man is subjectivity what is human is qualitatively different from what is merely natural, the thesis of which is applicable to any science of man whether it be political science, anthropology, psychology, sociology, economics, history, jurisprudence, or linguistics.[5] This thesis, whose full implications on the conduct of inquiry will be discussed in chapter 4, is the backbone of particularly Husserl's phenomenology of the life-world and Heidegger's hermeneutic of human existence (*Dasein*) as Being-in-the-world (*in-der-Welt-sein*) which includes the specific modes of "being-with" others (*Mitsein*) and the social world (*Mitwelt*). Merleau-Ponty describes the significance of intersubjectivity or coexistence in everything we do and think when he says:

> [Our] political task is not incompatible with any cultural value or literary task, if literature and culture are defined as the progressive awareness of our multiple relationships with other people and the world rather than as extramundane techniques. *If all truths are told, none will have to be hidden.* In man's co-existence with man, ... morals, doctrines, thoughts and customs, laws, works and words all express each other; everything signifies everything. And outside this unique fulguration of existence there is nothing.[6]

As the most inclusive horizon of meaning, the world includes (1) the phenomenon of man in interaction with other men (the social world), (2) the phenomenon of nature as it appears to human consciousness (the natural world), and (3) artifacts or things of man's own fabrication in his interplay with nature (the world of technology). Insofar as the human and the natural have the structure of meaning for man, they belong to the structure of "care" (*Sorge*). For care first shaped the creature called man (*homo*). Thus "nature" is a constituent of Being-in-the-world whose existential structure is characterized by care. There are things of nature (*Vorhandensein*) and things of culture or artifacts (*Zuhandensein*). Insofar as "natural" and "artificial" things come under the purview of human care, they have worldly meaning (*vorwissenschaftliche Sinn*). Because care is basically the existential characteristic of man capable of endowing him with meaning which is absent in both natural and artificial things, Heidegger says that the essence of human reality (*Dasein*) is its existence. He is in agreement with Scheler's "personalism" (the ethics of man as person) and with Husserl's critique of "psychologism" (or naturalistic psychology) when he says:

> The person is not a Thing, not a substance, not an object. Here Scheler is emphasizing what Husserl suggests when he insists that the unity of the person must have a Constitution essentially different from that required for the unity of Things of Nature. What Scheler says of the person, he applies to acts as well: 'But an act is never also an object; for it is essential to the Being of acts that they are Experienced only in their performance itself and given in reflection.' Acts are something non-psychical. Essentially the person exists only in the performance of intentional acts, and is therefore essentially *not* an object. Any psychical Objectification of acts, and hence any way of taking them as something psychical, is tantamount to depersonalization. A person is in any case given as a performer of intentional acts which are bound together by the unity of a meaning.[7]

The human mode of Being-in-the-world is radically different from things in nature: because of the structure of care, man alone *exists*. He *stands out from* natural and artificial things and, as an individual, from other individuals.

2. HUMAN ACTION AS PROJECT

The structure of human action as *project* in its broadest sense may be interpreted as a dialectical trilogy of meaning, value, and negation. The project is characteristic broadly of human existence or narrowly of human action. According to Heidegger, the project (*Entwurf*) is characteristic of human understanding or understanding human reality (*Verstehen*). Through understanding, human existence is disclosed as a possibility of Being-in-the-world. Because man is a project or "thrown-off" into a project, he is disclosed as a possibility.[8] As the project is an open possibility, an accent on the project as the essence of human existence is an accent on the future. More narrowly, however, Alfred Schutz defines the project as a structural element of human action.[9] For him, the project is merely a planning or designing stage of action (a "phantasying" or "picturing" of action) independently of the execution and fulfillment of an action.[10] We consider Heidegger's and Schutz's notions of the project as complementary despite their differences, for human reality or existence is foremost a field of action which is characterized as project.

Man is an actor or agent who in his very constitution is capable of creating both meaning and value. The life-world is a sociocultural world which is permeated with meaning and value. Meaning is the most fundamental and encompassing category of phenomenological description as the human subject is above all the bearer of meaning. "Phenomenology," Paul Ricoeur says, "can even claim that it alone opens the space of meaning, and thus of language, by thematizing for the first time the intentional and signifying activity of the incarnate, perceiving, acting, speaking subject."[11] As a sociocultural world, the life-world is also a world of values and disvalues or approvals and disapprovals. For Max Scheler, the human problem defined in terms of the self and the other as conscious subjects is in its most fundamental sense a problem of values both aesthetic and juristic.[12] Raymond Polin goes so far as to claim that as values are central to human action, so the phenomenological theory of values is useless unless it contributes to the theory of human action.[13] The essence or basic constitution of human existence is identified with the order of action or *praxis* which contains in it the order of values. As value is the *embodiment* of action, human existence *is* a moral order. By investigating the meaning structure of human conduct, phenomenology shows the possibility of an ethics or moral order. In the context of meaning, Simone de Beauvoir distinguishes the notion of ambiguity from that of absurdity: "To declare that existence is absurd is to deny that it can ever be given a meaning; to say that it is ambiguous is to assert that its meaning is never fixed, that it must be constantly won. Absurdity challenges every ethics; but also the finished rationalization of the real would leave no room for ethics; it is because man's condition is ambiguous that he seeks, through failure and outrageousness, to save his existence."[14]

Human action has a *meaning* and a *force,* that is, it has an intentional meaning structure and has the body as lived rather than as a merely physical thing, an inert object. Without the structure of the project, human action is merely a form of "behavior"—the reduction of action to its external indication or expression. Without integrating a meaning and a force, that is, without a psychophysical unity, the analysis of human action is incomplete. Both are necessary conditions for the explanation of human action. Man as a conscious subject is capable of endowing his action with meaning and of fulfilling it by means of his body. Thus in human action, the relationship of mind and body is not that of the master and the slave, but they are coeval. One is incomprehensible without the other. As John Wild stresses:

> Human behavior is neither a series of blind reactions to external "stimuli," nor the project of acts which are motivated by the pure ideas of disembodied worldless mind. It is neither exclusively subjective nor exclusively objective, but a dialectical interchange between man and world, which cannot be adequately expressed in traditional causal terms. It is a circular dialectic in which the independent beings of the life-field, already selected by the structure of the human body, exert a further selective operation on this body's acts. It is out of this dialectical interchange that human meanings emerge.[15]

Similarly, Merleau-Ponty contends that the structure of the human organism cannot be adequately understood in terms of physiology and/or biology alone. Rather, it must be understood as meaning which avoids "mentalism" on the one hand and "behaviorism" on the other. The structure of human action as meaning integrates the dialectics of the physical, the vital, and the mental in one.

As the presence of a project gives meaning to action, phenomenology aims to understand human action as the structure of meaning. The unity of an action lies in defining action as projected behavior. For Schutz, therefore, "an action is meaningless as action apart from the project which defines it."[16] Properly speaking, it is essential to distinguish between the "motion" of a physical object and "behavior" on the one hand and between "behavior" and "action" on the other. Action is a unity of meaning through the project and its external, bodily indication or expression called "behavior." When all forms of behaviorism reduce "action" to or infer it from its external indication, that is, when they explain human action in terms of physical causality, they are incapable of understanding the structure of action as project or as meaning. By the same token, phenomenology is also a critique of the attempt to explain man in terms of "instincts" and of "ethology" that attempts to explain man and his action from the observation of animal behavior. For, as Scheler emphasizes, "man can be either more or less than an animal, but never *an animal*."[17]

So what endows action and thus man as actor with meaning is the presence of a project. As an internal plan of operations to map out certain prospective courses of action, the project temporally precedes the actual performance or execution of action, whereas the consummation of action requires both the project and bodily execution. Thus the project is an invitation or prelude to the actual performance of action; the former anticipates the latter. In this sense, the project is as much an *insight* as a *foresight*. In action there is the predominance of future plans over past events as there is predominance of the "in-order-to" motive (*um-zu-Motiv*) over the "because-of" motive (*weil-Motiv*) which, in reference to our motivated behavior, means an intention to attain a preconceived goal in ongoing action and the justification of a motive in terms of past experiences, respectively. However, when the projection of action itself becomes a completed act, the project has the temporal character of pastness. To explain this peculiar temporal structure of the project, that is, its pastness as a completed act and its future as a projective effort, Schutz maintains that the project is thought always in the future perfect tense (*modo futuri exacti*) (i.e., "I shall have done").[18]

As to act is to have a project and to have a project is to choose a goal or purpose, the structure of human action contains in itself the negation of the given or facticity. As Erwin W. Straus emphasizes, "purposive movements are directed toward a goal. A change is anticipated and realized through movements subserving a plan. In action, we reach beyond a given situation into the realm of possibilities; within a temporal horizon, open to the future, we busy ourselves producing a new situation. We do not simply react to things as they are, but we act on them—i.e., we move with the intention of modifying things from an actual to a desired condition."[19] In every action, then, the past or present condition is negated in favor of a future one. As in action as project actuality is replaced by possibility, the actual or bygone situation is but a limitation of possibilities. Hannah Arendt speaks of the unpredictability as well as the irreversibility of action. Because what is already done cannot be undone and is already determined, it is redeemed by forgiving; because what is not yet is to come, it is anticipated by promise. As she says, "the possible redemption from the predicament of irreversibility—of being unable to undo what one has done though one did not, and could not, have known what he was doing—is the faculty of forgiving. The remedy for unpredictability, for the chaotic uncertainty of the future, is contained in the faculty to make and keep promises."[20] As action is by definition *social,* both forgiving and promising are unthinkable without assuming the multiplicity of men. Thus enacted in solitude or isolation they "remain without reality and can signify no more than a role played before one's self."[21]

Because man is an actor he has a project; insofar as action has meaning, in choosing the course of action the project is a conscious search for both *what* (end) and *how* (means) to act, which is to say, it involves both intrinsic and instrumental evaluation. In its fulfillment, in the consummation of conscious planning in advance and bodily execution, value is truly the *embodiment* of action. According to Schutz, "*the meaning of any action is its corresponding projected act.*"[22] Insofar as the project of action is a goal or purpose, action has a "reason" or is purposive and rational. Through the project as a goal, the actor intends to change or modify an existing condition toward a desired one. The project as an evaluation first begins with choosing a goal (i.e., an intrinsic value) and then, if he aims to achieve his goal by means of the body, adopts certain appropriate means (i.e., an instrumental value). The project as meaning is the *logos* of action, whereas the project as value is the *telos* of action. It is the existential psychologist Rollo May who emphasizes the important place of value in human action. Value is an (existential) *act* or evaluation to the extent that the conscious subject commits himself to the fulfillment of his action. Evaluation then implies some conscious choice and responsibility rather than "rote values" such as "habits," "mores," "customs," and "standards." It becomes the unifying locus of a meaning and a force: "*It is in the act of valuing that consciousness and behavior become united.*"[23]

So far we have focused on the structure of human action as a field of meanings and values. Now we shall discuss it as *negation*. As a matter of fact, value itself may be interpreted as a form of negation, that is, as "a pushing forward toward some new form of behavior—goals, ends of life to which we are devoted and toward which we choose to move because we believe them to be more desired ways of life."[24] By virtue of his existence as *ecstasis* and the awareness of his own historicity, man distinguishes himself from Nature—both external nature and his own nature. By negation we mean the act which is capable of reforming, transforming, transcending, or surpassing what it *is*. Reform, revolt, resistance, and revolution are all forms of negation or transcendence (*Aufhebung*). Thus freedom is implied in the very structure of human action as project. The project as freedom is then the possibility of transcending the given or facticity. "[T]he present," Simone de Beauvoir echoes the phenomenological ontologist Sartre, "is not a potential past; it is the moment of choice and action; we cannot avoid living it through a project; and there is no project which is purely contemplative since one always projects himself toward something, toward the future.... "[25] It is no accident that the one-time student of Heidegger, Herbert Marcuse too uses the term "project" so repeatedly because for him it seems to "accentuate most clearly the specific character of historical practice. It results from a determinate choice, seizure of one among other ways of comprehending, organizing, and transforming reality. The initial choice defines the range of possibilities open on this way, and precludes alternative possibilities incompatible with it."[26] In a Kierkegaardian sense, the project as negation or the freedom of surpassing what is given is an "existential leap." To put it existentially, then, man is the only being who is capable of refusing to be what he is: he is a multitude of possibilities. Freedom is the negation of the past in favor of a future possibility, and its test lies not in the continuation of the same past or given but in the negation of it toward transcendence. Herein lies the existential priority of the future over the past and the present in the continuum of time. However, it is a mistake to think that the negation of the given or facticity is a total obliteration of it.[27] For the present has both "an endless *past* behind it" and "an open *future* before it." In surpassing the past, negation also preserves what is given. The past is something already embodied in us or else history is the storehouse of dead events. Thus, according to Simone de Beauvoir:

> To abandon the past to the night of facticity is a way of depopulating the world. I would distrust a humanism which was too indifferent to the efforts of the men of former times; if the disclosure of being achieved by our ancestors does not at all move us, why be so interested in that which is taking place today; why wish so ardently for future realizations? To assert the reign of the human is to acknowledge man in the past as well [as] in the future.[28]

Though he was unaware of the primacy of the future, it was Edmund Burke who understood the inseparable linkage of three temporal dimensions in human relationships when he said that "society is a partnership not only between those who are living, but between those who are living, those who are dead and those who are yet to be born."[29] Temporality is awareness of the flow or passage of events from the past to the present and then to the future—the three specific vectors of lived time. Because temporality is primarily lived time rather than objective time, Husserl calls it "internal time-consciousness" (*innere Zeitbewusstsein*) which in reference to the past and the future from the present moment is "retention" and "protension," respectively. Husserl's phenomenology of internal time-consciousness has been the starting point of Heidegger's "fundamental ontology" (or ontology of man) and Schutz's social phenomenology. For Heidegger, everyday temporality or preobjective lived time is a constituent of human care; the activity of everyday life (or existence) is necessarily of temporal nature. For Schutz, the social world is classified into four types based primarily on temporality and secondarily on spatiality: (1) the world of consociates (*Umwelt*), (2) the world of contemporaries (*Mitwelt*), (3) the world of predecessors (*Vorwelt*), and (4) the world of successors (*Folgewelt*). The first two worlds have the temporal dimension of the present whose essential distinction is based on spatiality, whereas the third and the fourth have the temporal structure of the past and the future, respectively.[30]

Negation inherent in freedom and thus action is the capacity to do what is "unexpected." For Hannah Arendt, "natality," "freedom," and "action" are inseparable terms and imply one another. They are the inalienable *birthrights* of man as human. Natality or birth in the beginning of human time is the initial insertion of man into the world. According to her, "Because they are *initium*, newcomers and beginners by virtue of birth, men take initiative, are prompted into action. . . . With the creation of man, the principle of beginning came into the world itself, which, of course, is only another way of saying that the principle of freedom was created when man was created but not before."[31] With natality freedom and action begin in man: with it man is *invested as* freedom wherein his action *is* its actualization. As birth is itself a "miracle," freedom is the capacity to do what has not happened before or what is unexpected, that is, man is expected to do what is unexpected which is inherent in all beginnings or origins. Because of freedom inherent in natality, man is expected to defy the "overwhelming odds of statistical laws and their probability" or what is "infinitely improbable." Natality as the "origin" of the human capacity to begin something new is for Arendt particularly significant to political theory because, although it is inherent in the other categories of the *vita activa*, i.e., "labor" and "work," it is central to political activity which is action *par excellence* and thus is the "central category" of political thought. To extend Arendt's thinking further, political theory *comes before* metaphysics if political action begins with natality or birth and metaphysics is concerned with mortality or death.[32]

In *Matter and Memory*, Henri Bergson, whose notion of time as *durée* along with Husserl's phenomenology of internal-time consciousness influenced Schutz's phenomenology of social action, considered action as "master of time" in the same measure that perception is "master of space."[33] As perception and action are inseparable, so are time and space in social action. To understand freedom as negation or transcendence, therefore, it is necessary for us to understand the nature of temporality or historicity (*Geschichtlichkeit*) and particularly the *primacy* of the future since "natality" is the beginning of both freedom and action and every moment of action is a rebirth as the capacity to do the unexpected and something new, that is, the beginning of a new beginning. As man's Being-in-the-world or life-world is foremost the everyday world of action, the understanding of temporality, especially the primacy of the future, is indispensable to the phenomenological notion of action (as project).[34] Simone de Beauvoir defines human reality in terms of temporality and the primacy of the future when she says: "For human reality existing means existing in time: in the present we look towards the future by means of plans that go beyond our past, in which our activities fall lifeless, frozen and loaded with passive demands."[35] In history as past there is no freedom because what is done cannot be undone. Because he is accented by the temporal vector of the future, man is characterized as "project" or "transcience" (Heidegger), *homo viator* or being-on-the-way (Gabriel Marcel), the journeying self (Maurice Natanson), possibility (Merleau-Ponty, Sartre, and José Ortega y Gasset), ambiguity (Simone de Beauvoir), and even rebellion (Albert Camus). According to Merleau-Ponty, human existence is not in full possession of itself because "it is action or doing, and because action is, by definition, the violent transition from what I have to what I aim to have, from what I am to what I intend to be."[36] Because the primacy of the future is an accent on openness and indeterminacy, man is defined as a multitude or repertoire of possibilities and, as such, his essence *is* freedom. At the height of its affirmation, freedom is "the source from which all significations and values spring" and, following the existential ontology of Sartre, "value is the lacking-being of which freedom makes itself a lack; and it is because the latter makes itself a lack that values appear."[37] In a sense, freedom is instrumental to the creation of meaning and value by man and it is "the means of all means."[38] However, to view freedom as merely instrumental is to rob it of its intrinsicality with human existence as project or possibility. For the essence of existence *is* freedom itself. As the project is an integral trilogy of meaning, value, and freedom as negation, to lower freedom to its instrumentality is also to lower meaning and value and ultimately the project itself. Ultimately, the death of freedom is the death of man himself.[39]

Because man is a possibility with an accent on the future, Sartre
defines man as a "being which is what it is not, and which is not what it
is."[40] Even in his *Critique de la Raison Dialectique* which was intended to
be a departure from and a replacement of his early "phenomenological ontology" by a Marxist philosophy of *praxis*,[41] Sartre has not abandoned but has only modified the existentialist notion of the project as
a purely subjective one when he comes to the conclusion that Marxism
is "the only *philosophy* of our time" which cannot be surpassed and in
which existentialism is merely the subordinate enclave of an *ideology*.
He defines man as "totalization" (not to be confused with totality)
which is *being* achieved through the dialectic of the internalization of
the external and the externalization of the internal. As long as this
totalization is being achieved or proceeds in the dialectical duplexity
of subjectivity and objectivity or of internalization and externalization,
subjectivity and thus the project must not and cannot be discounted
altogether. Insofar as the project is a structure of human reality,
Marxism and existentialism are not incompatible. For Satre, man is a
projective effort to go beyond a given situation; the project is the
possibility of movement from the given or facticity to transcendence.
As he says, "it is by transcending the given toward the field of possi-
bles and by realizing one possibility from among all the others that the
individual objectifies himself and contributes to making History."[42]
As society is presented to each man as "*a perspective of the future*," the
project becomes a real motivation for the individual's action.[43] Without the individual and his project, then, history in both phenomenology and Marxism has no meaning and thus is an abstraction. Viewed
in this way, history—the arena of human action—is not a dead matter
but is a dynamic one. It is the *sedimentation* of human meanings and
values that affects the men of succeeding generations. To put it differently, history is the sedimentation of transcendence as transcendence itself is never complete. Nor is history as the negation of
the past in favor of the future ever the unqualified movement of
progress from absolute falsity to absolute truth. For Merleau-Ponty,
in a concrete conception of history where ideas are nothing but stages
of the social dynamic, "all progress is ambiguous because, acquired in
a crisis situation, it creates a condition from which emerge problems
that go beyond it."[44] When revolutionary *praxis*, for instance, becomes institutionalized or fossilized, when it is regarded as accomplished, then it is already decadent. Rather, revolution is a permanent
task as man himself is. For it is itself the *moment* "when a radical
negation frees the truth of the entire past and allows the attempt to

recover it" and is an event in which "the scintillation of truth and falsity continues."[45] In affirming the contingency of existence and thus history, we affirm freedom to negate the pastness of both truth and action.

To say that man is the possibility of willing the future is to affirm that, contrary to the traditional view of "human nature," he has no fixed and predetermined properties like a thing: indeed he is *becoming*—not a being that is *always to be*. In other words, viewed in terms of history as abstract universality or scientific causality, all determinism is the denial of the concrete meaning of history. "History," Merleau-Ponty writes, "has no meaning if this meaning is understood as that of a river which, under the influence of all-powerful causes, flows towards an ocean in which it disappears. Every appeal to universal history cuts off the meaning of the specific event, renders effective history insignificant, and is a nihilism in disguise."[46] Determinism denies man as possibility because when the future is homogenized into the past it ceases to be a possibility. Thus to accent the future as a continuous passage from the past and the present to the beyond is to affirm existence as an unfinished task, as the bottomless abyss of a "lack," whereas to accent the past is to confirm existence as an already finished product.

3. THE HUMAN BODY AS SUBJECT

As it has already been stressed, human action has a meaning and a force. If in the structure of human action the project is a planner, the body is its executioner. The unity of an action lies in the intertwinement of the project and the body. The meaning of an action is fulfilled in completing a preconceived plan by means of the body. In action or social action the body constitutes the connective tissue of man and the world. The body defines one's placement in the world and is by its mobility the point of contact with others. We position ourselves uniquely in the world by means of our body. The upright posture of the human body, according to Erwin Straus, is a uniquely human mode of Being-in-the-world.[47] The uprightness of man has a moral as well as a factual connotation. It has come to mean to stand up perpendicularly to the ground, to be just, honest, and right. The moral quality of rectitude, standing up for one's own conviction or righteousness, is admired by others. Thus the upright posture of man is a truly human trait which no other animal species has. It is a specific placement of man's Being-in-the-world. As a spatial concept this upright posture determines one's place, factual and moral, in relation to one's natural, social, and cultural environment.

The body is foremost and necessarily the primitive point of *contact* in human relationships. The social world whose "building blocks" are individual bodies is not a sum of objects but a *field* of intersubjectivity. As long as everything we do has an intersubjective structure, whether it be thinking or acting, it is an embodied activity. The *cogito* is an embodied *cogito* as much as acting involves the external mobility of the body: not only the life of thought but also the life of action is an embodied activity. We think and act in "flesh and bones" (*leibhafte Gegebenheit*). In reference to thinking, as the saying goes, "one thinks on his feet." Therefore, phenomenology rejects the conception of man as two separate substances or entities of the "psychic" and the "somatic." If thinking and acting are embodied activities, then ideas are not the project of mind alone nor is acting a physical response or reaction to the stimulus of the environment. When the body is regarded simply as an "extended thing" (*res extensa*) in contrast to a "thinking substance" (*res cogitans*), it becomes "objectified" and "naturalized": it turns into a thing. The naturalization of the body is the death of the body and ultimately of man himself.

As a philosophy of subjectivity, phenomenology treats the body never as an object but as the *subject* of human activity. This notion of the "lived body" (*corps vécu* or *propre*) or embodiment is one of the fundamental theses of phenomenology, especially of the writings of Husserl, Merleau-Ponty, Marcel, and Sartre. "I *am* my body," Marcel writes, "insofar as I succeed in recognizing that this body of mine *cannot*, in the last analysis, be brought down to the level of being this object, *an* object, a something or other. It is at this point that we have to bring in the idea of the body not as an object but as a subject."[48] In Eugene O'Neill's play, *A Moon for the Misbegotten*, one of its characters, Josie Hogan, in her eagerness to hear James Tyrone, Jr., utters, "So go on about love. *I'm all ears*."[49] To emphasize the oral preservation of history and culture in preliterate societies, it is often said that "ancient things remain in the ears." The body as a living subject is never a purely material thing or a materiality (*Sachlichkeit*).[50] Rather, the body is a measure of natural and cultural things. As Giambattista Vico noted, "words are carried over from bodies and from the properties of bodies to signify the institutions of the mind and spirit";[51] and it is through the bodily metaphor that we animate inanimate things in nature:

It is noteworthy that in all languages the greater part of the expressions relating to inanimate things are formed by metaphor from the human body and its parts and from the human senses and passions. Thus, head for top or beginning; the brow and shoulders of a hill; the eyes of needles and potatoes; mouth for any opening; the lip of a cup or pitcher; the teeth of a rake, a saw, a comb; the beard of wheat; the tongue of a shoe; the gorge of a river; a neck of land; an arm of the sea; the hands of a clock; heart for center (the Latins used *umbilicus,* navel, in this sense); the belly of a sail; foot for end or bottom; the flesh of fruits; a vein of rock or mineral; the blood of grapes for wine; the bowels of the earth. Heaven or the sea smiles; the wind whistles; the waves murmur; a body groans under a great weight. The farmers of Latium used to say the fields were thirsty, bore fruits, were swollen with grain; and our rustics speak of plants making love, vines going mad, resinous trees weeping. Innumerable other examples could be collected from all languages.[52]

It is Merleau-Ponty who develops the most comprehensive phenomenology and metaphysics of the body—especially in his phenomenology of perception which is the basis of both thought and action. It is an insatiable search for the Archimedean "origin" of human consciousness that leads Merleau-Ponty to the phenomenology of perception, which is, *humanly speaking,* always angular. In the body as the sentient subject of perception he reaches the most primitive region of human consciousness—the horizon in which inner consciousness and the outer body intersect. "My body," he declares, "is not an object, but is a medium, an organization. I organize in perception with my body as a visitation [*frequentation*] with the world. With my body and by my body, I inhabit the world. The body is the field within which perception is localized."[53] Thus the problem of the body and perception is one and the same. As an embodied consciousness, perception is a synthesis of the sensible and the sensed and, accordingly, perception is a *catch* of the world while the world is an *impact* on perception.[54] As the zero-point of orientation toward the world, the body furnishes the canon and norm of perception. In *The Visible and the Invisible,* Merleau-Ponty speaks of the "flesh" (*chair*) as, he suggests, there is no adequate designation in traditional philosophy for the "intertwining" of the body sensed and the body sentient, that is, the body as the "sensible sentient" (*sentant sensible*). "To designate it," he says, "we should need the old term 'element,' in the sense of a *general thing,* midway between the spatio-temporal individual and the idea, a sort of incarnate principle that brings a style of being wherever there is a fragment of being. The flesh is in this sense an 'element' of Being."[55] This is to emphasize the notion that the body is a sum of neither "spiritual" substances nor "material" forces: it is a prototype of Being, a "wild" (*sauvage*) being just like water, air, earth, and fire. The two sides of the body have the reciprocal insertion and intertwining of one in the other; they are reversible and exchangeable from the sentient to the sensed and from the sensed to the sentient. In the handshake, for instance, "I can feel myself touched as well and at the same time touching."[56] Every thought, too, which presupposes the infrastructure of vision, must occur only to a flesh. As the flesh is the natural landscape of thought, so is the metaphysic of the flesh or the flesh as "an ultimate notion" presupposed in every theory of truth or knowledge. Thus Merleau-Ponty affirms the "genesis" or "origin" of truth in the primordial world of senses, when he says:

> it is this unjustifiable certitude of a sensible world common to us that is the seat of truth within us. That a child perceives before he thinks, that he begins by putting his dreams in the things, his thoughts in the others, forming with them, as it were, one block of common life wherein the perspectives of each are not yet distinguished—these genetic facts cannot be simply ignored by philosophy in the name of the exigencies of the intrinsic analysis. Thought cannot ignore its apparent history, if it is not to install itself beneath the whole of our experience, in a pre-empirical order where it would no longer merit its name; it must put to itself the problem of the genesis of its own meaning. It is in terms of its intrinsic meaning and structure that the sensible world is "older" than the universe of thought, because the sensible world is visible and relatively continuous, and because the universe of thought, which is invisible and contains gaps, constitutes at first sight a whole and has its truth only on condition that it be supported on the canonical structures of the sensible world.[57]

Perception as embodied consciousness is the most primitive point of complicity between our existence and the world performing a sort of reconnaissance mission for the soul's rationality. To affirm the *primacy of perception* is in no way to belittle rationality. The mission of perception is the primary anchorage for the rationality of both action and knowledge: it is their sentinel. Thus Merleau-Ponty writes:

Evidence is never apodictic, nor is thought timeless, though there is some progress in objectification and thought is always valid for more than an instant. The certainty of ideas is not the foundation of the certainty of perception but is, rather, based on it—in that it is perceptual experience which gives us the passage from one moment to the next and thus realizes the unity of time. In this sense all consciousness is perceptual, even the consciousness of ourselves. . . . The perceived world is the always presupposed foundation of all rationality, all value and all existence. This thesis does not destroy either rationality or the absolute. It only tries to bring them down to earth.[58]

Although perception as a preobjectifying performance is the birthplace of all action and knowledge, this does not mean that it is not informed or fashioned by the already established institution of culture—the cultural dilatation of perception. Nonetheless, Merleau-Ponty maintains that "there is an informing of perception by culture which enables us to say that culture is perceived."[59] Certainly, perception is open to the environmental milieu (*Umwelt*), but in its primitive state it is ignorant even of itself as an act, as latent intentionality.

Although the mode of perceiving has a multiplicity of angles, perspectives, or adumbrations (*Abschattungen*), it is not "a mental alchemy"; it is global and total. "The 'I can' [*Ich kann*]," according to Merleau-Ponty, is "the power to organize certain revelations [*déroulements*] of perceptual appearances at each step."[60] Perceptual consciousness being the primordial infrastructure of all rationality in thinking and acting or the "nascent *logos*" of *praxis*, it is misleading to say, as does Enzo Paci, that "perception itself is praxis. Thus, the world emerges as the horizon of possibility of every 'I can.' The horizon of the human world finds praxis at its base as its fundamental structure."[61] On the contrary, more basically it is perception rather than *praxis* that is the foundation of the world. For *praxis* which is a form of rationality is founded upon perception as an embodied consciousness. Phenomenology is an attempt to discover a unique characteristic of the human order under "the spell of the body" as living subject in the life-world. The body is the specific *placement* of man in the world both social and natural. Erwin Straus, Helmuth Plessner, F. J. J. Buytendijk, and Stephan Strasser discovered the uniqueness of the human order from the study of man as a living, bodily organism, whether it be the study of senses, crying and laughing, pain, or feeling.[62] According to Straus, as we have noted earlier, the "upright posture" of the human body is uniquely a human mode of Being-in-the-world. For Plessner, the uniqueness of man lies in the body as expressivity, the various manifestations of which are gestures, mimes, postures, speeches as well as laughing and crying. Bodily expressivity based on a reciprocity of perspectives defines man's *eccentricity* in relation to the world.[63] It is not just having eyes, mouth, nose, chin, and forehead as such that makes up the human face as an expression. But, on the contrary, it is the sense of an expressive unity of the face that makes the human body unique from other animals. When as "the window of the soul" sight or look *catches* the glances of others or the world, it opens up "the vistas of the world."[64] The human order is constituted not only by the dualism of joy and sorrow or pleasure and pain but by the dialectical interchange or duplexity of the seemingly two opposite expressions: we not only laugh for joy and cry for sorrow but we also cry for joy and laugh for sorrow.

Expression is the meeting of the inner and the outer, of an intention and a bodily configuration. "Expression," Plessner says, "is a fundamental trait of mediated immediacy and, like the instrumentality of the body or the objectivity of knowledge, corresponds to that tension and entwinement which we are always having to adjust, between being a body and having a body. Expressivity is a fundamental way of coming to terms with the fact that man occupies a body and yet is a body."[65] Expression then is a fusion of what Merleau-Ponty calls the phenomenal or lived body and the objective body as a structure of meaning. Inasmuch as it *is* a meaning, it is a mode of the flesh. The gesture, for example, is an expression or an expressive language where the body speaks without words ("saying some*thing*").[66] It is a "conversation" without spoken words. For that matter, violence, too, is an essential element of the "body politic." It is a political act even if it is wordless or speechless. For, as a wordless speech, violence is an expressive assertion and insertion of the body in the political life-world. Because violence is a bodily expression and all politics imply violence, Merleau-Ponty forthrightly says:

> we do not have a choice between purity and violence but between different kinds of violence. *Inasmuch as we are incarnate beings, violence is our lot....* Violence is the common origin of all regimes. Life, discussion, and political choice occur only against a background of violence.... He who condemns all violence puts himself outside the domain to which justice and injustice belong. He puts a curse upon the world and humanity— a hypocritical curse, since he who utters it has already accepted

the rules of the game from the moment that he has begun to live.[67]

However, the utility of violence is not equivocal, unqualified, and unmitigated for the following reasons. First, it must justify itself at every moment it is put to use whether it is directed against man or nature. Second, there is an inherent proneness in violence to perpetuate itself even if it is progressive in aim. Merleau-Ponty also recognizes the inherent paradox of revolutionary violence: "Revolution as continued self-criticism needs violence to establish itself and ceases to be self-critical to the extent that it practices violence."[68] Third, nonviolence challenges uncompromisingly the quicksand of violence as the equally efficacious order of making history and re-ordering politics: the advocates of nonviolence assert not only that it is not a form of nondoing or social indifference but also that violence does not monopolize the order of political action and the act of making history.[69]

Language or speech is human expressivity *par excellence* and the exemplar of humanity itself. Man is indeed *the language animal.*[70] Language constitutes the basic grammar of both intersubjectivity and the life-world or, as Enzo Paci puts it, "the *Sprachleib* of humanity."[71] This is why from Vico and Wilhelm von Humboldt to Ferdinand de Saussure and Noam Chomsky, language has been claimed to be not just a tool for intersubjective communication but the innermost need of man himself. For Vico, "Ideas and language accelerate at the same rate"[72] and languages are the "most weighty witnesses" of human customs, conventions, affairs, and institutions. As the aim of *autopsia* is to seek the "evidence of the senses," so is the aim of linguistic autopsy to discover language as the embodiment of human practices, events, and institutions. It was Humboldt who emphasized the intrinsicality of language to the humanity of man and the "generation" of humanity: for man to be human language is intrinsic to him.[73] Merleau-Ponty too maintains that the life of language is to thought as the life of the body is to consciousness. As thought inhabits language and language is its body, language makes thought as much as thought makes language. Thus, if we succeed in getting close to language, we would also succeed in finding the mediation between the inner and the outer, between the subjective and the objective, which is also the key to unlock the mystery of history since for Merleau-Ponty as for Vico men make their history as they make their language.

Philosophy is necessarily a critique of language as *Sprachleib* insofar as it aims to define the possibilities and limits of the human condition

in terms of linguistic experience. With the advent of language or
speech we elevate the human world from mere energetics to hermeneutics. Thus in the phenomenological movement the philosophy
of language occupies an important role, and its relevance to the conduct of political inquiry will be fully explored in chapter 4. Heidegger,
Merleau-Ponty, H. -J. Pos, Mikel Dufrenne, Georges Gusdorf, Paul
Ricoeur, Hans-Georg Gadamer, Jacques Derrida, and others have
been absorbed in it. Speaking of the fourfold unity of Being, language, thinking, and man, Heidegger writes in *Letter on Humanism*:

> Thinking accomplishes the relation of Being to the essence of
> man. It does not make or cause the relation. Thinking brings
> this relation to Being solely as something handed over to it from
> Being. Such offering consists in the fact that in thinking Being
> comes to language. Language is the house of Being. In its home
> man dwells. Those who think and those who create with words
> are the guardians of this home. Their guardianship accom-
> plishes the manifestation of Being insofar as they bring the man-
> ifestation to language and maintain it in language through their
> speech.[74]

Similarly, Wittgenstein too was obsessed with the "bewitchment" of
language and philosophical problems arising from it when it "goes on
holiday."

What distinguishes the phenomenological view of language or
speech from all other views is its *subjective* standpoint, which is to say
that phenomenology focuses its attention on the problems of language from the standpoint of living human subjects who by means of
their bodies speak, experience, and communicate with others in the
life-world. As the analysis of speech that forgets the speaking subject
(or speaker) is an abstraction, the knowledge of language must presuppose the activity of the speaking subject. Thus there is a legitimate
distinction between language as a sedimented, codified, and structured institution (*langue*) and language as living, dynamic, and fluid
speech (*parole*). There is the linguistics of speech as well as that of
language, and the former is presupposed in the latter.[75]

If linguistic expression is a dialectic of the inner and the outer, of
the "subject" and the "structure," speech (*parole parlante*) is "a body
through which an intention appears":[76] It is an embodied meaning.
As verbal expression, speech is the meeting of an intention and a
bodily configureation. In this sense the sound or phoneme is the
original embodiment of speech (as verbal expression). As the body is
to consciousness, the voice is to speech. The voice is for man "a primal

sounding board for expression" and "the medium of development from the internal to the external." [77] By the same token, for Merleau-Ponty language originally began with "singing" rather than "saying" words. In sum, then, it is not simply an abstract system or string of words alone but is indeed the embodiment of meaning.

In exploring Merleau-Ponty's idea of "singing" the word as the primordial form of language or *Sprachleib*, we can say that every word is originally a song: phonemes and words are initially songs. As the "first word" is spoken by singing, singing and speaking are homogeneous. The infancy of speaking begins with singing a monosyllable—the "verbal melody" of "ma" or "pa" which is in itself a world. "The initial form of language," Merleau-Ponty conjectures, "would have been a kind of song. Men would have sung their feelings before communicating their thought. Just as writing was at first painting, language at first would have been song, which, if it analyzed itself, would have become a linguistic sign. It is through the exercise of this song that men would have tried out their power of expression." [78] What is so important for our consideration here is that "singing saying" is the "first act" of embodied, linguistic expression. For Merleau-Ponty as for Vico, the body is not simply the medium of expression but *is* already a polymorphic mass of mute expressions. "Smiling," "going red or pale," "stamping the foot," or "hissing" is an embodied albeit wordless expression. Insofar as the body is a natural property common to all of us humans, singing remains the "first act" of linguistic expression and "higher" conduct is built on the intially "lower" working of the body; and all bodily expressions themselves are different ways of expressing—and thus existing in—the world. Therefore, it would be a mistake to say that bodily expressions are natural, while words are invented. Bodily conduct is also invented as are words or scripts. As Merleau-Ponty writes, "It is no more natural, and no less conventional, to shout in anger and to kiss in love than to call a table 'a table'." [79] Words inhabit and don things in the world. For the "first man" (child or primitive man) the thing is known by virtue of naming. Naming which brings a thing to exist and changes it is on the same natural footing as its color and form. [80] In this process of exchanging naming and a thing in nature, language becomes "the very voice of the things, the waves, and the forests." [81]

By the same token, bodily motion is no less an institution than the invented system of words and scripts. It was the ethnologist Marcel Mauss who argued that the "techniques of the body" are interesting topics for anthropology and sociology because they are expressive extensions of a given social system. As an institution, they are never

simply natural but are subject to the constraints of social mores, customs, and conventions: the "body social" constrains the "body
natural."[82] So everything is both natural and invented in man. The
mutual linkage between the two is "a genius for ambiguity" which
defines the human condition. Not only is there no dualism between
mind and body, but also the body reaches out to nature. Nature and
culture narrow their gap at the edge of the latter's origin. So the
"scatological lyricism" of Mao Tse-tung no less than that of Martin
Luther and Jonathan Swift is as "natural" as the "spiritual" culture of
their revolutionary politics, theology, and literature. In *The Survivor,*
Terrence Des Pres so graphically describes the phenomenon of survival in the "death camps" where symbolism as symbolism loses its
autonomy, that is, in the extremity of the situation the symbolic or
spiritual becomes actualized in the bodily or "excremental assault":

> In extremity man is stripped of his expanded spiritual identity.
> Only concrete forms of existence remain, actual life and actual
> death, actual pain and actual defilement; and these now consti-
> tute the medium of moral and spiritual being. Spirit does not
> simply vanish when sublimation fails. At the cost of much of its
> freedom it falls back to the ground and origin of meaning—
> back, that is, to the physical experience of the body. Which is
> another way of saying that, in extremity, symbols tend to ac-
> tualize.[83]

However, all this does by no means endorse naturalism which is the
opposite of intellectualism. For there is a way of appreciating natural
things—the "body natural" and "natural symbols"—both without de-
grading rationality and without getting caught by the linchpin of
naturalism.[84]

When speaking or the word is viewed as an act of the embodied
subject in the life-world, the understanding (*sous-entendu*) of language
as well as our own body and the gestures of others is primarily not a
cognitive operation or an act of intellectual interpretation but is an
existential act in the process of expressing. Both the intellectualist and
the behavioralist are incapable of understanding the dialectic of
speech and thought, if by "dialectic" (or "dialectical") we mean the
mutual relatedness of two or more phenomena in which one is not
reduced to or lost in the other (i.e., their mutual irreducibility). For
the intellectualist reduces speech to thought, to intellectual consciousness, whereas the behavioralist reduces both speech and thought to
the conditioning of the environment. "Speech," Merleau-Ponty
writes, "is not a simple automatism in the service of thought. It is the

instrument of actualization of thought. Thought is truly realized only when it has found its verbal expression [i.e. speech]."[85] The gesture of others is grasped or understood "as if the other person's intention inhabited my body and mine his"[86] which we call intersubjectivity. To understand speech properly, then we must focus on the intersubjective act of speaking by the embodied subject, on the "speech act." Because Wittgenstein focused on the *use* of ordinary language, on the way it is being spoken in the everyday life-world, he was able to see language as a "form of life" (*Lebensform*).[87] J. L. Austin, too, who once reluctantly spoke of "linguistic phenomenology" as a "mouthful" phrase referred to linguistic utterances as "performative."[88] Whether the word is locutionary, illocutionary, or perlocutionary, it does not merely describe or represent something *else* but is an act of performance. Following Heidegger, Jacques Derrida focuses on the "rhetorical force" of language, on the role that linguistic expressions play in human activities.[89] To understand "politics as symbolic action,"[90] we must first *under*stand language or speech as the existential act of the embodied, speaking subjects. As "speech" (*parole*) is prior to "language" (*langue*), the speech of ordinary political man must precede the technical language of political science. The objectified language of political science must *catch* the living prose of political man.

To view language simply as the fixed sedimentation of meaning is to deprive it of its creative aspects. Thus Hans-Georg Gadamer writes that "Language is not its elaborate conventionalism, nor the burden of pre-schematisation with which it loads us, but the *generative* and *creative* power unceasingly to make this whole fluid."[91] The learning of how to speak by the child would be merely an "imitation" of the already structured and ready-made meanings and his cognition would be simply a "copying." This is why the philosophy of language which focuses on the algorithms of logical, semantic, and syntactical meanings is an insufficient and inadequate philosophy. At its creative moment, at the moment when speech becomes an embodied expression, language becomes a "fold" in the flesh.[92] It is "constituting language" that gives birth to "constituted language." In this sense, then, before becoming "the symbol of a concept" the word is "first of all an event which grips my body, and this grip circumscribes the area of significance to which it has reference."[93] Language is to the word as the body is to a gesture.

The flesh of language is an intertwining of the speaker and the listener or "to speak" and "to be spoken to": language is inextricably an intersubjectivity, the "unique fulguration of existence." Intersubjectivity is the hinge, as it were, that catches everything—language, thought, speech, history, and politics. Because language is intersubjective, Karl Marx and Frederick Engels thought that "language is as old as consciousness" and like the latter the former arises only from man's "intercourse with other men."[94] As an intellectual exercise philosophy seeks to get close to intersubjectivity by getting close to language. A critique of knowledge is always a critique of language and thus of the social world. Thus philosophy is necessarily a critique of language: it is hermeneutics. Inasmuch as philosophy is a critique of language, it is also a *social* philosophy.

Chapter 3

Toward a New Humanism

*The Social Principle of Man and Nature
as the Politics of Civility*

The ecological crisis, as we know it today, has been a sobering experience for humankind.[1] To put it in a Freudian nutshell, it looms as the struggle of Eros and Thanatos or, better, the struggle of life against death. Despite the development of science and technology in their holy alliance, characteristic of our age and history and couched in the faith of unlimited progress, humankind has come gradually but surely to the realization that there is only one earth and the earth itself is finite. As far as the humanness of man is earth-dwelling, beyond the earth there is nothing but the abyss of the void. Thus any realistic ethics must come to terms with this unalterable fact. Man *dwells* on earth. The earth is—to borrow Arendt's phrase—"the very quintessence of the human condition."[2] It provides human beings with a habitat. Today we sense more keenly than ever before the urgency that the problem of external nature is the problem of human life itself. That technology which is the supreme artifact of man is a human, social problem involving man's total system of beliefs, values, and actions. In a time of crisis, when "a Copernican revolution of the mind" or "a new philosophy of life" is called for, the philosopher ought to be aware of Hegel, who, reminiscent of Mephistopheles' words on the greyness of all theories, said that "the owl of Minerva spreads its wings only with the falling of the dusk."[3] In this spirit we must rethink the interwoven nexus of

41

relationships not only between man and man but also between man and nature.

This chapter deals with a basic topic in philosophical anthropology, that is, it attempts to outline a phenomenology of the ecological conscience. It is concerned with the question of *how to dwell rightly* on earth. It is a phenomenological reflection on the ecological conscience as both simple awareness and moral awakening. By the phenomenology of the ecological conscience we mean no more and no less than a philosophical exploration of that part of our primal experience of *"care"* (*Sorge*) for a myriad of visible and public things both natural and cultural. It attempts to appropriate simultaneously both man-nature and man-man relationships: the realm of the between. What philosophical anthropology learns from ecology—the *logos* of the earth as household (*oikos*) is this: everything is related to everything else.

To be holistic, the philosophy of humanity or humanism must necessarily be ethical. For value or valuation is an all-encompassing category of human thinking and doing. It is the fleshfold of humanity itself. Speaking of what we might call the "politics of civility," Albert William Levi defines its essence as "*the quest for value*: all that opposes the specifically human to a 'transcendence' which is too recondite and a 'nature' which is too neutral and unfeeling; the vital, the organic, and the human, that is, against the merely mechanical; human freedom, fortune, and fate against the operations of an impersonal causality; will against force; value against fact; the humane against the brutal."[4] Thus viewed, the philosophy of humanity is opposed to religious transcendentalism, vulgar naturalism, and harsh scientism.

We propose that the *social* or *dialogical principle* be the foundation of our conception of a new philosophy of humanity or a new humanism. It takes its clues primarily but not exclusively from Heidegger's radical thought.[5] The enemies of our social philosophy of humanity are homocentrism or "speciesism," technological thinking (*la technique*), and possessive individualism, all of which are inseparably related issues. In this chapter, we do not intend to spell out in detail our social philosophy of humanity but wish to indicate a few directional signals.

By the social principle we mean an inextricable *nexus* of relationships *both* between man and man *and* between man and nature. In the history of Western thought there is a wealth of literature that is concerned with the social principle of man and man. However, Western thought seldom addresses itself to the social principle of man and nature. This is particularly true in the history of its social and political thinking. For instance, the sociologist and futurologist Daniel Bell in

The Coming of Post-Industrial Society ventures a forecast for "post-industrial" civilization.[6] In his "ideal constructs," he pictures three historical movements of civilization whose central reality is, first, *nature* where men struggled against the vicissitudes of nature for survival, second, *technics* where man the *homo faber* worked on nature and fabricated durable things by substituting the order of technology with the order of nature, and third, *social* reality which, unlike the reality of nature and technics in the two preceding stages, orders primarily a web of the reciprocal consciousness of self and other (i.e., interhuman relations). In the "post-industrial society" men turn their backs on nature and technics, that is, they live "more and more outside nature" and "less and less with machinery and things." In short, they encounter and play "games" with one another. In ordering social reality, "men can be remade or released, their behavior conditioned or their consciousness altered. The constraints of the past vanish with the end of nature and things."[7] So the task of the coming civilization is to realize the ideal that makes the construction of social reality "a work of art." Although he makes an important point of re-ordering man's consciousness and social reality either by behavioral engineering or by consciousness-raising, by social reality Bell means the ordering only of *interhuman* relationships *outside* nature and *beyond* technics. So his attempt to reconstruct social reality is the ideal confined to the relationships of man and man—the games people play with one another.

Aristotle exalted the virtue of man as a *political* animal. For him, as man is by *nature* (*physis*) a political animal, the art whose concern is the life of men in the *polis* is the most authoritative art or the master art. Man's life in the *polis* is prior in nature to both the individual and the family. If man is not a political animal or is not destined to live a life in the *polis,* he is either superhuman or subhuman: a god or a beast. Since good or happy life is the life of self-sufficiency—self-sufficiency being defined as "that which when isolated makes life desirable and lacking in nothing," for man to be self-sufficient or completely happy he must live a political life. However, for Aristotle, political life and productive life are not the same as the "political economy" of today. The life of production, that is, economics, is merely the management of the household which is only supportive of political life. Although the activity of production or the art of acquisition is not action in the strict sense of the term—only political activity is privileged to deserve that name; it is in Aristotle that we see a close link between economics, politics, and ecology when ecology, as we define it today, is the management of the earth as a household (*oikos*). It is in Book 7 of *Politics* that Aristotle discusses the planning of the *polis* or city which includes its physical conditions or "ecology" such as the optimal population and territory. Speaking of the "health" of the city as the most indispensable element of an ideal city, Aristotle includes clean ("good") water and air. However, for him the idea of "nature" (*physis*) is the governing or normative principle only of *human* relationships or of relationships between man and man, which has been one of the cornerstones of Western social and political thought for many centuries.

In recent centuries, Ludwig Feuerbach in his *Principles of the Philosophy of the Future* enunciated a social principle when he says: "The true dialectic is not a monologue of a solitary thinker with himself; it is a dialogue between I and thou."[8] This "Copernican revolution" of Feuerbach had a great influence on Karl Marx and Martin Buber. The philosophical radicalism of Buber lies in his ontology of the betweenness which is extended to the realm of man and nature as well as the realm of the interhuman (*das Zwischenmenschliche*).[9] For Buber, the twofold attitude of man toward the world creates the twofold, primary relations: "I-Thou" and "I-It." The "I" of man in "I-Thou" (man and man or man and nature) is basically different from the "I" of man in "I-It." Man's image of himself is reflected differently in each of the two basic relations: by objectifying the other, man in fact objectifies himself. Accordingly, by transforming his attitude toward nature, from "I-It" to "I-Thou," man changes his own image, too. Buber's dialogical philosophy *is* a *social* philosophy of humanity. Buber goes beyond Marx. With Marx we say that to be radical is to get at the root of things and the root of man is man himself. However, for Buber, the root of things is the social principle which refers to not only Marx's notion of man as an ensemble of social relations but also the relationships of man and nature: where there is no sociality there is no reality.

Man is bound by time and space. He is called a mortal and an earthly being. Because he is the only being who is aware of his own mortality, he is the most mortal of all mortals. Man is also an earth-dweller, and *homo* is rooted in *humus*. The essence of man as an earth-dweller is revealed in the following ancient Latin fable Heidegger cites:

> Once when 'Care' was crossing a river, she saw some clay; she thoughtfully took up a piece and began to shape it. While she was meditating on what she had made, Jupiter came by. 'Care' asked him to give it spirit, and this he gladly granted. But when she wanted her name to be bestowed upon it, he forbade this,

and demanded that it be given his name instead. While 'Care' and Jupiter were disputing, Earth arose and desired that her own name be conferred on the creature, since she had furnished it with part of her body. They asked Saturn to be their arbiter, and he made the following decision, which seemed a just one: 'Since you, Jupiter, have given its spirit, you shall receive that spirit at its death, and since you, Earth, have given its body, you shall receive its body. But since 'Care' first shaped this creature, she shall possess it as long as it lives. And because there is now a dispute among you as to its name, let it be called '*homo*', for it is made out of *humus* (earth).[10]

Man dwells on earth with other mortals and things living and nonliving. Things, no less than men, populate the world—they together make up or build the stuff of the world. Man is a species-being precisely because he is aware of his bond not only with his contemporaries but also with his successors (the unborn) and his predecessors (the dead). This "knot" of all beings and things may be called the *social principle of reality*: where there is no social principle there is no reality. Heidegger calls this social principle the principle of *appropriation*. To appropriate is to belong together. To be is to dwell and to dwell is to belong together among all beings and things. To think ecologically is to think *carefully* about how human beings belong together and how they belong together with other beings and things. Thus the ethical implication of Heidegger's notion of *care* is obvious: the *conviviality* of man and man on the one hand and the *connaturality* of man and nature on the other. Henry Bugbee refers to this selfsame imperative of planetary coexistence when he says in *The Inward Morning*: "We all stand only together, not only all men, but all things."[11] As R. D. Laing puts this social principle so succinctly:

> All in all
> Each man in all men
> All men in each man
>
> All being in each being
> Each being in all being
>
> All in each
> Each in all[12]

Togetherness is a "gathering" of many.[13] It is not the seamless sameness of all the identical but is a unity of the differentiated. The primal aim of ecological thinking is to disclose this social nexus of beings and things as they belong together in the household called the earth, only one earth. This principle of appropriation as "belonging-together-ness" may be called "harmony." Harmony is the essence of the "belonging-togetherness" of man and man on the one hand and of man and nature on the other. So sociology and ecology belong together. In harmony there is an affinity between the aesthetic and the moral: the beautiful and the good are synonymous. Just as the aesthetic is the harmony between man and nature, so is the ethical the harmonious relationship between man and man: not only is the ethical grounded in the aesthetic, but also harmony is the unifying theme of the aesthetic and the ethical. Harmony, therefore, is the essence of both the aesthetic and the ethical.

With Lucien Lévy-Bruhl who discovered the "law of participation" in the unique logic of primitive mentality or the "savage mind," the idea of primitivity has gained a positive evaluation in the human sciences today—especially in the writings of Mircea Eliade, Claude Lévi-Strauss, and Stanley Diamond. Primitive people not only are "anthropological specimens" but also serve as "models" for remedying the ills of modern civilization. Heidegger, too, thought that the study of "primitive" mentality has a positive note for understanding the ontological structures of human reality because it is less concealed and complicated and more directly absorbed in the events and things it encounters than "civilized" mentality.[14] It is Stanley Diamond "in search of the primitive" who finds a critique of modern civilization.[15] For him, primitivity is characterized by the idea of holism, personalism, and communalism. That is to say, it affirms what we call the social principle of man and nature as well as of man and man. Standing at the center of a holistic universe of concrete activities, the primitive does not conceive himself as divided into "religious man," "economic man," "political man," and so on. Primitive society has no elements of an "acquisitive society." For economics or the activity of production is neither competitive and profit-motivated nor an end in itself. Rather, it is "for use or pleasure." Speaking of personalism as the most significant characteristic of primitive life, Diamond says that it "extends from the family outward, to the society at large, and ultimately to nature itself. It seems to underlie all other distinctive qualities of primitive thought and behavior. Primitive people live in a personal, corporate world, a world that tends to be a 'thou' to the subjective 'I,' rather than an 'it' impinging upon an objectively separate, and divided, self."[16] In his phenomenological study of primitive religion(s), *The Myth of the Eternal Return*, Mircea Eliade shows that by making history independent of nature modern man has replaced the "imitation of nature" with the "terror of history."[17] The intimate relationship of man with nature in the felt harmony, that is, their social principle, is characteristic of the archaic ontology of primitive man. This felt intimacy of man with nature and the cosmos is embodied in the "sacred" myth of the eternal repetition and the psychology of participation. The closeness of man to nature is vindicated by the simple fact that an ordinary natural object or thing becomes "sacred," whereas modern man worships only the objects of his own creation, the objects made by his own labor, work, and industry. For primitive man nature is "sacred," whereas for modern man nature is "profane." In primitive ontology, man is inextricably bound up with nature and Mother Earth. The periodicity of time is a mere imitation of the cycle of seasons, an occurrence of nature.

Homocentrism is a negation of the social principle of man and nature. For by regarding man as the "noblest creature" or the "cantor" of the earth, it leads to the ontological and ethical thesis that man is superior to nature. In *The Vocation of Man,* Fichte exemplifies homocentrism when he writes that "I will be the lord of Nature, and she shall be my servant. I will influence her according to the measure of my capacity, but she shall have no influence on me."[18] Here the "spirituality" of man—male as opposed to female—is pitted against the "materiality" of nature resulting in the dualism or polarization of the two. In this light, the "Copernican revolution" of Kant's philosophy too is slanted to a radical separation of history, the arena of human freedom, from nature which has left lasting imprints on later thought. Particularly for Hegel, nature or inert matter is the negation of history, active spirituality—the radical dichotomy of the "for-itself" (*für-sich*) and the "in-itself" (*an-sich*).[19]

To affirm the social principle of man and nature and to criticize the homocentric tendencies of Western thought, however, is not to deny or belittle the historicity of man or to relapse into the dark alleys of vulgar "naturalism." Indeed, man is the unique being that is conscious of the fact that he is a subject of history. Our only hope lies in the recognition and affirmation of this fact. Man dwells on earth uniquely. As he *exists,* the manner of his dwelling and building is radically different not only from other men but from other beings and things. Heidegger characterizes this uniqueness of being human as the possibility of "care." Indeed, there is something very attractive in the metaphysics of naturalism in an age when man's absolute mastery and sovereignty over nature, that is, his obsessive arrogance, has gone so long unchallenged. However, when man is regarded as a mere part of nature or merely "a child of nature," naturalism ignores the *differentia* between mere nature and man as historicity or care. So, as Merleau-Ponty puts it, "there is a truth in naturalism. But that truth is not naturalism itself."[20]

Technological thinking, the *metaphysics* of the modern age, is necessarily homocentric. It is indeed the apex of homocentrism whose "banality of evil" is *domination* in the realms of the natural environment and the social order. In *The Invisible Pyramid*, Loren Eiseley superbly depicts the technological warrior in the space age who epitomizes the legend of the restless soul of Faust in search of the Holy Grail, threatening to alienate himself completely from his natural habitat—the earth.[21] Insofar as science and technology have dominated not only Western thought but also the modern world, homocentrism has become the steady diet of modern thought everywhere. As knowledge is power, science and technology constitute the pillars of building the modern "pentagon of power"—industrial, economic, political, and military. Husserl rightly observed that "the result of the consistent development of the exact sciences in the modern period was a true revolution in the technical control of nature."[22] Despite the polarization of man and nature and the alleged claim of man's mastery over nature, what is so paradoxical about the intellectual climate of our time is that the being of man is defined and understood more and more in terms of physical realities. This physicalism permeates the human sciences as well as the natural sciences. Today the cybernation of man and society is no doubt the *acme* of technological rationality in which technology makes man—that is, man is created in the image of the machine when it is said with great pride that man is the only machine that thinks! According to Heidegger, the cybernetic model of man is the *exemplar* of today's Western thinking that is dominated by logistics, calculation, and technology. He is beyond doubt the most "radical anthropologist" of our time. For he aims to *destruct* (de-struct) Western metaphysics, the "theo-onto-*logic*" way of thinking from Plato to Nietzsche, the long chain of which has also bonded the technological thinking of our day. Heidegger writes that it is "technology that devours the earth in the exhaustion and consumption and change of what is artificial. Technology drives the earth beyond the developed sphere of its possibility into such things which are no longer a possibility and are thus the impossible ... [T]he conquests of technology even make the impossible possible."[23] This is the authoritative verdict of Heidegger on technology, "the highest form of rational consciousness" today. Technology permeates "all the areas of beings" including objectified nature, the earth already converted into things of utility or a gigantic gas station, and politics "manufactured" as "power."

Thus machine technology for the domination of nature by man has now been extended to the domination of man by man. Technology has turned into a social and political problem—that is, the problem of technocracy (*la technique*). It is Marcuse in his famous *One-Dimensional Man* who, armed with the philosophical, psychoanalytical, and sociological insights of Hegel, Heidegger, Freud, and Marx, has attempted to show that technology now provides both concepts and tools for the domination of man by man. "Today," Marcuse writes, "domination perpetuates and extends itself not only through technology but *as* technology, and the latter provides the great legitimation of the expanding political power, which absorbs all spheres of culture."[24] Marcuse's student William Leiss, too, forcefully argues in *The Domination of Nature* that the idea of mastery over nature is "a fundamental ideology of modern society." He further argues that "science itself becomes ideological when a particular method of arriving at scientific knowledge succeeds in establishing a claim to be the only valid entry into the entire realm of objective understanding."[25] In this sense, science has lost its *critical* distance and power. Having lost its critical dimension, the "instrumental rationality" of science (and technology) becomes subservient to the political elite in power.[26] Thus the irony of technological rationality is its irrationality: "The chaotic and frightening aspect of the contemporary technological civilization has its origin neither in the concept of civilization nor in technology as such, but rather in the fact that technology has assumed a specific structure and position in modern society, which stands in a highly disrupted relationship to the needs of human beings. It is not the rationalization of the world which is to blame for the evil, but the irrationality of this rationalization."[27]

Although from Feuerbach to Marx and Marcuse there is a breakthrough in the conception of man as a natural, sentient, and embodied being, Marx and Marxists were not able to free themselves from the homocentric tradition of the West. Marx saw that nature is the material for human activity. Thus, he thought that "Feuerbach's man does not emerge as an independent productive force but remains bound to pre-human nature."[28] In short, nature attracted Marx mainly as a constitutent element of human *praxis*. It is true that the young Marx spoke of his "future society" as "the union of man with Nature, the veritable resurrection of Nature, the realized naturalism of man and the realized humanism of Nature."[29] However, in the most comprehensive study of Marx's

concept of nature, Alfred Schmidt comes to the conclusion that the
mature Marx "no longer wrote of a 'resurrection' of the whole of
nature. The new society is to benefit man alone, and there is no doubt
that this is to be at the expense of external nature. Nature is to be
mastered with gigantic technological aids, and the smallest possible
expenditure of time and labour. It is to serve all men as the material
substratum for all conceivable consumption goods."[30] As a result, nature turns into a "giant workhorse." Due to his optimism in technology as an instrument to improve man's lot on this earth, Marx was
oblivious to what many now speak of as the cunning "revolt" or "re-
venge" of nature—technology's boomerang effects on men.

Following Hegel and Marx, Marcuse, too, never doubts the mastery
of history or the historical project of man over nature, although he
has recently become critical of the mature Marx's conception of nature. For Marcuse, the decisive question is not whether there should
be man's mastery over nature but whether this mastery, *humanly*
speaking, is a repressive or a liberating one. For Marcuse as for Hegel,
History is the negation of Nature. Marcuse writes:

> What is only natural is overcome and recreated by the power of
> Reason. The metaphysical notion that Nature comes to itself in
> history points to the unconquered limits of Reason. It claims
> them as historical limits—as a task yet to be accomplished, or
> rather yet to be undertaken. If Nature is in itself a rational,
> legitimate object of science, then it is the legitimate object not
> only of Reason as power but also of Reason as freedom: not only
> of domination but also of liberation. With the emergence of
> man as the *animal rationale*—capable of transforming Nature in
> accordance with the faculties of the mind and the capacities of
> matter—the merely natural, as the subrational, assumes negative
> status. It becomes a realm to be comprehended and organized
> by Reason. . . . All joy and all happiness derive from the ability to
> transcend Nature—a transcendence in which the mastery of Na-
> ture is itself subordinated to liberation and pacification of exis-
> tence.[31]

Marcuse has most recently stated that "not appropriation but rather
its negation would be the nonexploitative relation: surrender, 'letting
be,' acceptance. . . . But such surrender meets with the impenetrable
resistance of matter; nature is not a manifestation of 'spirit,' but
rather its essential *limit*."[32] So in Marcuse's philosophy there is no
genuine social principle between man and nature. The only issue is
whether the achievements of science and technology should be used

for liberating man (and nature!) rather than for the service of human repression and exploitation. From a perspective of harmonizing man and nature, that is, of the social principle of them, Marcuse's proposals for the cultivation of aesthetic sensibility is far less radical than they appear to be at first glance. Moreover, he sees the violation of both nature and aesthetic sensibility only as cardinal sins of the economy of capitalism; and unfortunately he is unwilling to speak out on, as far as we can determine, the aesthetic insensitivity and ecological ills of its counterpart, the economy of socialism.

When the uniqueness of being human as the possibility of *care* is unduly stressed, that is, misconstrued, there occurs man's "self-assertiveness": "individualism" in defining the relationships of man and man and "homocentrism" in defining those of man and nature. When individualism and homocentrism are put together, there is the birth of Lockean "possessive individualism." Inasmuch as Americans inherited this Lockean tradition—Louis Hartz calls them "born Lockeans" for good reasons—they are guilty of possessive individualism. With Hobbes the "natural law" of political obligation originally is shifted to the "natural rights" of individuals—the doctrine which characterizes "modern" political thought.[33] He is truly a *modern* thinker—as a matter of fact, the "founder" of modern political thought—in another sense: insofar as mathematization characterizes the nature of modern thought, Hobbes mathematizes the "body politic" after the fashion of Galileo. Hobbes exalted "artificial" man pitted against "natural" man. In "the state of nature," according to him:

> there is no place for industry; because the fruit thereof is uncertain: and consequently no culture of the earth; no navigation, nor use of the commodities that may be imported by sea; no commodious building; no instruments of moving and removing, such things as require much force: no knowledge of the face of the earth; no account of time: no arts; no letters; no society; and which is worst of all, continual fear, and danger of violent death; and the life of man, solitary, poor, nasty, brutish, and short.[34]

What is so tragic about possessive individualism is the fact that it never transcended the Hobbesian state of nature. It is interesting to note here "romantic" Rousseau's critique of Hobbes's depiction of natural man which has long been forgotten in the literature of political thought. Rousseau's refutation of Hobbes, whatever its worth, rests on the threefold ground of "method," "fact," and "logical inference."[35] As for method, Rousseau contends that while Hobbes sets out to describe what the nature of man in his primitive state *was*, he ends up answering what the nature of man in the civil state *is*. As for fact, Rousseau criticizes Hobbes for confusing natural man with the man he observed in his own time and for making him a "madman." As for logical inference, Rousseau thinks that even if the initial assumptions of Hobbes are assumed to be true—though they are manifestly false, the inferences and conclusions he draws form them are absurd and even if man is as self-centered as Hobbes portrays him to be, he would not be in the state of war of everyman against the other (*bellum omnium contra omnes*).

However, it is Locke who must be credited with inventing the thoroughgoing theory of possessive individualism, of *homo economicus* or "economism." In the first place, Sheldon S. Wolin argues that the very decline of political philosophy itself is hastened by the ethos of liberalism—from which, for Wolin, Hobbes is excused—in which the distinctiveness of the political is usurped by economics when it becomes the proper study of humankind and "economic man" becomes its proper end.[36] Thus, for Wolin, the politics of civility is a task of making both the art and the knowledge of politics "integrative" for "a life of common commitments." The "poverty of liberalism"—to borrow the title of Robert Paul Wolff's book[37]—lies in the privatization and fragmentation of the political and a loss of the sense of community by creating "the fetish of groupism." In the second place, Victor C. Ferkiss argues in *The Future of Technological Civilization* that the ideology of Lockean liberalism with its philosophical foundation already laid out by Hobbes promotes the ethos of technological civilization based on the subjugation and negation of nature by labor and industry which builds the society of acquisitive "economic men" who are the infinite proprietors of both his own and others' capabilities.[38] For Locke, the accumulation of private property, the protection of which is the sole function of civil government, is to increase "the comforts of life" or happiness. Things acquire their "value" on account of labor and industry: as Locke writes, "when anyone hath computed, he will then see, how much *labour makes the far greatest part of the value* of things, we enjoy in this World . . . Land that is left wholly to Nature, that hath no improvement of Pasturage, Tillage, or Planting, is called, as indeed it is *wast* [waste]; and we shall find the benefit of it amount to little more than nothing. This shews . . . that the increase of lands and the right of imploying of them is the great art of government."[39] So, in the final analysis, Locke's liberal ideology is "a cosmic orgy of boosterism"[40] which is also the ethos of technomorphic culture. However, the liberal is not necessarily a Lockean. Whatever the liberal tradition he inherited, which was a great deal, John Stuart Mill in *Principles of Political Economy* in 1848, which preceded Marx's *Das Kapital* by nineteen years, disdained the acquisitive society and the ethics of labor and work and disclaimed the unlimited spiral of wealth and advanced the idea of "the stationary state" of political economy. Speaking against the ethos of the acquisitive society of his own time, Mill wrote: "I confess I am not charmed with the ideal of life held out by those who think that the normal state of human beings is that of struggling to get on; that the trampling, crushing, elbowing, and treading on each other's heels, which form the existing type of social life, are the most desirable lot of human kind, or anything but the disagreeable symptoms of one of the phases of industrial progress."[41] In this sense, Mill was far ahead of his time and may be called the founding father of the idea of "no-growth society," although he justified it on the ground of human, utilitarian ethics rather than on the ground of the earth as a finite planet. R. H. Tawney echoes and extends Mill's argument when he proposes that, contrary to the doctrine of "acquisitive society," man must regard economic interest as only one element rather than the whole of his life: society "must persuade its members to renounce the opportunity of gains which accrue without any corresponding service, because the struggle for them keeps the whole community in a fever. It must so organize industry that the instrumental character of economic activity is emphasized by its subordination to the social purpose for which it is carried on."[42]

Marx was well aware of the problem of "breaking the habit" of the old social order (i.e., capitalism) in the creation of a new one—the new social order which is "in every respect, economically, morally and intellectually, still stamped with the birthmarks of the old society from whose womb it emerges."[43] The true vision of Marx, however, is blurred because of his *primary* emphasis on the society of "producers." In this context, Karl R. Popper might very well have a message for today's Marxists when he says in reference to Marx's own eleventh thesis on Feuerbach: "The Marxists have merely *interpreted* Marxism in various ways: the point, however, is to *change* it."[44] In this spirit, we must appreciate Charles Taylor who advances a revisionary theory of socialism that depicts "the agony of economic man" and his civilization in pursuit of the "cult of production" for economic development and consumption, one of the effects of which is the precipitation of an ecological crisis. Taylor emphasizes the creative and humane purposes of socialism that may put an end to the orthodox Marxist theology of productive, industrial, and technological developmentalism.

He writes:

> The economic model has as its centre the notion of man as
> producer, as transformer of nature. Man is pure agent. Its Achil-
> les' heel is that this offers men a goal which is ultimately empty.
> The drive to increase production starts with certain goals—to
> overcome poverty, to provide education for the masses and
> freedom of choice. But as the production-oriented society takes
> over, it sets its own priorities, and these end up being those of
> production for its own sake, a glorification of the products.
> When the hold of this image wanes men have the feeling that
> this vast and diversified activity is to no purpose, that it is all
> dressed up with the most prodigious means, yet with nowhere to
> go. Hence the dominant feeling in this period of decline of the
> economic image is one of emptiness. The challenge to the cur-
> rent model is coming from young people who cannot find a
> satisfactory identity in its vision of the future. It offers no form
> of life which makes sense.[45]

Technological thinking which is the driving force and backbone of
modern industrial and acquisitive civilization spurred by the main-
stream of Western thought—not the least by Marxism, Christianity,
and liberalism—is necessarily utilitarian, instrumental, exploitative,
and manipulative. The man of work or *homo faber* is the "producer,"
"fabricator," and "manufacturer" of durable goods and commodities who is also a "consumer." For him, nature's things have
no intrinsic value of their own but only "cash value" to satisfy his
acquisitive and consumptive self-assertiveness. They have only utilitarian and instrumental values. "Being" or desire to *be* is now dominated by "Having" or desire to *have*. In *The Human Condition*, Hannah
Arendt analyzes in a penetrating way the instrumental and utilitarian
rationality of *work* that is the essence of the modern age, the age of
industrialization, machine technology, and consumption. The modern
age is the age of artifacts, the artificial paradise where *homo faber*,
unlike the *animal laborans*, fabricates and builds the world of durable
goods and objects for use, which is distinguishable from what
is strictly natural and human. Preoccupied with utility, modern man
as *homo faber* sees everything in terms of its extrinsic rather than
instrinsic value and therefore becomes homocentric. This is reflected
internally in his egocentricity. The difficulty of the utilitarianism of
homo faber, as Arendt points out, is its innate inability to understand
the distinction between utility and meaningfulness in which all ends
are bound to have a short duration and to be transformed into means

for some further ends. "The perplexity of utilitarianism," she writes, "is that it gets caught in the unending chain of means and ends without ever arriving at some principle which could justify the category of means and end, that is, of utility itself... [I]n other words, utility established as meaning generates meaninglessness." [46] The utilitarianism of *homo faber* breeds meaninglessness when it becomes the ultimate standard for everything we do in the world of other men. As such, Arendt further reasons:

> This generalization is inherent in the activity of *homo faber* because the experience of means and end, as it is present in fabrication, does not disappear with the finished product but is extended to its ultimate destination, which is to serve as a use object. The instrumentalization of the whole world and the earth, this limitless devaluation of everything given, this process of growing meaninglessness where every end is transformed into a means and which can be stopped only by making man himself the lord and master of all things, does not directly arise out of the fabrication process; for from the viewpoint of fabrication the finished product is as much an end in itself, an independent durable entity with an existence of its own, as man is an end in himself in Kant's political philosophy. [47]

We can generalize further: in the utilitarianism of *homo faber,* in the endless chain of means and ends, not only does technology gain a life of its own independently of man who fabricates it but also in the process man himself gains the unwanted status of a use object—which Marx called alienation. [48] To liberate ourselves from the "necessity" of labor and the "utility" of work, according to Arendt, we must direct ourselves to the world of action, political action: the world of the "public realm" beyond the prepolitical phenomena of labor and work. The politics of civility, as we might properly call it, promises to deliver us from the privatization of meaning and value, from the "private realm" and to guarantee the civilizing web of human relationships which is conditioned by organic nature and fabricated things.

In conclusion, our vision of a new humanism is founded on the politics of civility that cultivates the *social principle* based on *care* as the essence of that which governs the conduct of man in his relationships with fellow-men and with other beings and things on earth. Only by this social principle can we avoid "homocentrism" in man's dealing with nature and "individualism" in man's dealing with other men. The great disclosure of Heidegger's thought is that "care" is the basic existential character of being human. Properly understood, caring is letting things be as they are and appreciating their intrinsic value. It is reverential in that it respects the natural way of worldly things. To care means to preserve and conserve, that is, to let worldly things perdure rather than to dominate, exploit, use them up, and ultimately make them perish. To dwell with care is for man to spare and save worldly things. Saving, however, is more than an insurance policy that can be used for a future need. Were it simply that, it would not be caring. In the end, to dwell on earth with care is to belong together (i.e., appropriate) and to celebrate the sacrament of planetary coexistence among all beings and things. To think ecologically is to celebrate this social principle. When man himself is an endangered species, we must pay special attention to extending this social principle to the existence of human beings and their mutual relationships in society. Viewed in this way, this social principle coincides with love, friendship, kindness, compassion, and justice which amounts to the celebration of community. Today too many speak of such things as birth or population control, family planning, and the use of coercion for survival without considering compassion and care but too few are willing to listen to the dire voice of the deprived and oppressed. What we need is indeed the education and conscientization of both oppressed and oppressor, the have-not's and the have's. In the end, our "ultimate concern" in *gathering* our thoughts together consists in setting in motion the politics of civility in defense of people as well as the earth. For they, people and the earth, belong together in a caring way. Only this caring way of politics of civility will end the "civilized" man's long journey into the night.

PART THREE——A Phenomenological Critique of Political Knowledge

The fish trap exists because of the fish; once you've gotten the fish, you can forget the trap. The rabbit snare exists because of the rabbit; once you've gotten the rabbit, you can forget the snare. Words exist because of meaning; once you've gotten the meaning, you can forget the words. Where can I find a man who has forgotten words so I can have a word with him?

——*Chuang Tzu*

Chapter 4

The Life-World, Language, and Human Knowledge

Toward a New Paradigm in the Philosophy of the Sciences

1. THE LIFE-WORLD AND HUMAN KNOWLEDGE

To follow up our arguments in part 1 on the primacy of ontology, epistemology presupposes ontology. In the context of this work, this means that a critique of political knowledge presupposes a phenomenological ontology of man. In other words, *how to know* human action must be based on *what human action is*. Otherwise, methodology becomes a "methodolatry" and science a "scientism." Therefore, a critique of political knowledge must be understood in terms of the description of human action as the structure of meaning which, as we have outlined in chapter 2, has temporal, projective, bodily, and expressive dimensions. In contemporary sociology, it is the "reflexive" sociology of Alvin W. Gouldner which emphasizes that sociological theorizing is more than a matter of technique, for sociology does not simply study society but conceptualizes and orders it. By means of conceptual ordering, it aims at the reconstruction of society.[1] If theorizing is not an empty abstraction but is a part of the common situation of man and humanity, it changes the world by changing the conceptualization of it. For the world is a mixture of both what is experienced and what is constructed (in conceptualization as well as in imagination).

For our present discussion, the importance of Husserl's *Crisis* lies in its seminal and momentous discovery of the descriptive ontology of the life-world as an ultimate horizon of meaning in which all persons, all natural things, and all cultural artifacts are understood in the perceptual and common-sensical attitude of mundane everyday life, if we mean by attitude (*Einstellung*) "a habitually fixed style" of orienting the human will and interests to achieve certain goals both theoretical and nontheoretical. The relevance of the life-world to the social sciences is essentially twofold. First, it is the straightforward, practical field of social action in a historical and cultural setting. As such it is the world of what "we live through" (*pragmata*) rather than what "we think" (*cogito*). Second, the life-world is the presupposed foundation of *all* conceptualization or theorizing as a human activity. As the presupposed foundation of science, the everyday life-world is prescientific. It is the world of the common-sense understanding of political actors themselves prior to scientific theorizing.

The life-world is the most comprehensive and inclusive horizon of all actual and possible experiences. Its ontology is a *philosophical anthropology par excellence* to the extent that it is a disciplined way of analyzing man and his total activities.[2] For our purposes here, however, it is most appropriate to adopt Alfred Schutz's rendition of the life-world as "social reality" which is defined by him as "the sum total of objects and occurrences within the social cultural world as experienced by the common-sense thinking of men living their daily lives among their fellow-men, connected with them in manifold relations of interaction."[3] From a phenomenological perspective, the aim of the social sciences is to organize in a disciplined way the knowledge of this social reality as a whole.

The importance of describing the life-world as social reality, first, lies in its emphasis on sociality as the pragmatic network of man's total interactions and transactions with other men and, in turn, the consequences of his relationships with other things both natural and cultural on his social action. For sociality is an ontological "datum" (*Gegebenheit*) of the life-world. The basic grammar of this social *a priori*, as we might call it, is not a matter determined by a genealogy of logic, an empirical sociology of knowledge, or a historical semantics. Rather, it is fundamental because all human practice and conceptualization (i.e., transcendental activity) presuppose it. This is why transcendental subjectivity is also intersubjectivity. Second, the term "reality" is not a metaphysical concept, but rather it refers to the total order of meaningful experience (*Erfahrung*) both actual and possible. Thus what is experienced is real, and, conversely, what is real is experience-able. Reality always as experienced has a multiplicity of meaning structures—as Schutz calls it "multiple realities." The horizon of each is distinguishable from that of another. The world is divided into subworlds: the world of work, the world of theory, the world of dreams, the world of imagination, the play world of the child, the world of the insane, etc. Schutz thus speaks of these subworlds as "finite provinces of meaning," which has "a specific accent" in its own unique or autonomous way; and there are also "enclaves" which are the intersecting domains of more than one province. However, the world of "work" in our wide-awake consciousness is called the "para-mount reality" because it sets the standard to judge all other subworlds.

This social world also has temporal and spatial dimensions. As we have already noted, Schutz divides it into four regions according to a temporal sequence and a spatial distance: (1) consociates, (2) contemporaries, (3) predecessors, and (4) successors. The world of contemporaries is particularly relevant to the social sciences because it is a world in which persons are typically understood in terms not of "individuals" with proper names but of their "roles" or "typified" performances (performatory matrices), that is, the matrix of the *functions* they perform: "phenomenologist," "political scientist," "politicians," "citizens," etc. Maurice Natanson speaks of the phenomenology of the life-world as an "ontology" of social roles. Phenomenologically speaking, the matrix of social roles transcends the dichotomy of "anonymity" (or alienation) and "recognition." They are two contrasting modalities of sociality in which the former may be defined as its "structural deformation."[4]

Phenomenology does not provide a practical handbook that directly aids empirical research or scientific experimentation. Rather, its primary aim is to clarify the presuppositions the empirical sciences make and to examine and justify the aims of science.[5] For the purpose of disciplinary inquiry as a metascientific activity, the importance of the life-world lies in its status as the *funding* as well as *founding matrix* of all the sciences—the ultimate foundation of all objective knowledge. In phenomenology as the "science of the life-world" (*Lebensweltwis-senschaft*), Enzo Paci finds the idea of "a new science" in the established tradition of Vico: "It is demanded by the necessity of basing the sciences on the operations that we perform in time. We can know these operations in temporal reflection which is both history and the foundation of its meaning of truth."[6] Phenomenology as a philosophy performs the function of clarifying the nature of science as a human activity on the basis of the life-world as the infrastructure of science. For, as Heidegger says, "Physics as physics can make no assertions about physics. All the assertions of physics speak after the manner of physics. Physics itself is not a possible object of a physical experiment. The same holds for philology. As the theory of language and literature, philology is never a possible object of philological observation. This is equally the case for every science."[7] By the same token, the aim of phenomenological philosophy in political inquiry is to clarify the common-sense world of political actors as the *funding* and *founding matrix* of theoretical activities in political science. The conceptual "geography" of politcal science presupposes the existence of the "natural landscape" of politicians and citizens. "It is this *universal ground of belief in a world*," Husserl writes, "which all praxis presupposes, not only the praxis of life but also the theoretical praxis of cognition. The being of the world in totality is that which is not first the result of an activity of judgment but which forms the presupposition of all judgment."[8] The primary task of the phenomenology of science is then to discover the genesis of meaning in the life-world itself. Accordingly, the phenomenological task of political science too is to discover the genesis of meaning in the immediate, experiential, and common-sense knowledge of political actors. Merleau-Ponty echoes Husserl so clearly when he says: "To return to things themselves is to return to that world which precedes knowledge, of which knowledge always *speaks*, and in relation to which every scientific schematization is an abstract and derivative sign-language, as is geography in relation to the countryside in which we have learnt beforehand what a forest, a prairie or a river is."[9]

To understand the phenomenology of the life-world as an archaeology of science and a "new theory" of knowledge and its relevance to the epistemology of the social sciences, it must also be seen as a critique of scientism which claims to be the absolute paradigm for all knowledge—including political knowledge. In *under*standing scientism, phenomenology aims to be *therapeutic*. Scientism has an ontological implication in that in meeting the conceptual and methodological requirements of the physical sciences, it determines the order of human reality in terms of physical reality. By reifying the order of human reality or social reality in terms of that of physical reality, scientism in the social sciences commits in fact an "empiricide." This kind of conceptual reification or empiricide in which conceptual thought forgets its rootedness in the direct immediacy of everyday experiences has been criticized by various modern philosophers (e.g., William James and Ludwig Wittgenstein). However, none is so succinct as Alfred North Whitehead who characterizes it as "the fallacy of misplaced concreteness."[10]

In the *Crisis*, Husserl shows the conceptual fallacy of scientism in the modern age since Galileo's mathematization of nature where the prestige of the scientific abstraction of nature is indicated in the universal acceptance of it as *"natural"* in replacing the experiential strata of the life-world itself (i.e., the "natural attitude"). "World facts" are replaced by "scientific facts" or the latter "occluded" the former. Husserl calls this "occlusion" of the life-world in Galileo's mathematized idealization or abstraction of nature the "garb of ideas" (*Ideenkleid*). This mathematization of nature or nature as a mathematical manifold, which revolutionized in the modern age the technical control of nature, is propounded by Galileo in his famous passage: "Whoever wants to read a book, must know the language in which that book is written. Nature is a book and the characters in which it is written are triangles, circles, and squares."[11]

The garb of scientific ideas not only deforms human reality but also—as discussed in chapter 3—alienates man from nature which remains no longer the same nature unveiled in naked experience and sensibility but becomes a mathematical bundle which in turn leads to the technological domination of man by man. In this sense, the liberation of man from man is implicated in the liberation of nature from the domination of man. Although the order of nature is susceptible to mathematical formalization which aims to yield the exact knowledge of nature, phenomenology views the mathematical conception of nature as only one way of understanding it. Aron Gurwitsch argues not only that in our direct experience nature is not presented as a mathematical system but that the mathematization of nature is not even essential to the human mind. He speaks of the "ever growing alienation of the universe of physics from the world of perceptual experience" in which "visualization" has given way to the constructs of "a totally abstract nature" formalized according to "algorithmic rules of operation" alone.[12] Nature as *perceived* in our direct experience is radically different from nature as conceived in the theoretical constructs of mathematical formalization.

The Galilean mathematization of nature into the geometric boxes of triangles, circles, and squares, that is, the *mathesis universalis* or mathematics as a universal science, also became the basis of the formulation by Descartes of his *prima philosophia*. In emulating Galileo's geometry and Descartes's mechanicomorphic philosophy of nature,[13] Hobbes created a new science of politics in the modern age. Hobbes's ambition, as Ernst Cassirer points out, was "to create a theory of the body politic equal to the Galilean theory of physical bodies—equal in clarity, in scientific method, and in certainty."[14] This Hobbesian scientism, as will be discussed in chapters 6 and 7, is consistent with his ideology of individualism and makes him the harbinger of the cybernetic model of political man.

Insofar as mathematical and scientific construction is a product of the human mind, the function of phenomenology is to clarify and show the conditions in which scientism takes for granted the lifeworld as the preconceptual infrastructure of all meaning, that is, scientism is indeed the "garb of ideas." Scientism, according to Husserl, is fallacious because it is foremost a conceptual garb whereby what once was or was intended to be true in the mathematical formalization of nature *as a method* has gradually been taken or indeed mistaken for reality itself. Husserl writes:

> mathematics and mathematical science, as a garb of ideas, or the garb of symbols of the symbolic mathematical theories, encompasses everything which, for scientists and the educated generally, *represents* the life-world, *dresses it up* as "subjectively actual and true" nature. It is through the garb of ideas [*Ideenkleid*] that we take for *true being* what is actually a *method*—a method which is designed for the purpose of progressively improving, *in infinitum*, through "scientific" predictions, those rough predictions which are the only ones originally possible within the sphere of what is actually experienced and experienceable in the life-world.[15]

So the mathematical sedimentation of science since Galileo "is cast upon the life-world so as to conceal it to the point of being substituted for it. What in truth is a method and the result of that method comes to be taken for reality."[16] In *Greek Mathematical Thought and the Origin of Algebra*, Jacob Klein discovers the difference between the ancient and the modern conception of mathematics. He contends that the ancients intended to solve the problem of (mathematical) method on the basis of an ontology of (mathematical) objects. On the contrary, however, the moderns since the sixteenth and seventeenth centuries turned their attention *first* and *last* to method as such, although their scientific thought was inspired by the logocentric framework of the ancients. Like Husserl, Klein argues that in modern science the "generality of the method" (methodology) replaced the "generality of the object" (ontology): modern mathematics determines its objects by reflecting on the way in which mathematical objects become accessible only through a general method.[17] Scientism in the social sciences today is the blind transference of this methodolatry to the study of social reality.

For Husserl, the mathematization of nature and the world since Galileo has maligned European humanity. Inasmuch as science or mathematized science is symbolic of the human condition, it is the crisis of European humanity itself. Thus the search for the meaning genesis of the mathematization of nature and the world is the search for the meaning of humanity: to *under*stand the sedimented garb of ideas and symbols in the life-world as the "substruction" of science is to discover man as the *subject* of knowing and acting hidden in the thickness of scientism. "It was first through Husserl," Ludwig Landgrebe writes, "that we realized that we are not dealing here with a mere theoretical problem that is interesting only to logicians and linguists. Rather this problem stands in a direct connection with the crisis of the modern world resting as it does upon science and technology."[18]

Through mathematical formalization the language of science and philosophy has forgotten the meaning of man himself and ultimately their own *telos*. A phenomenological critique of scientism is a search for the restoration of the *true being* of man and his humanity. The new *telos* of phenomenology aims to heal the crisis of modernity and to eliminate the alienation of science and philosophy from the meaning of human existence by returning to the everyday life-world as the foundation of their meaning and as an encompassing unity of knowing and acting, which is tantamount to the recovery of human subjectivity. Viewed as the recovery of subjectivity in the context of politics, the condition of which Husserl himself experienced and was fully aware in his own time as the background of his philosophical activity, Robert Sokolowski says: "Since political life is acted out within the manifest image of the self and the world, the theoretical problem of the foundations of science is also the political problem of how science and technology can be intellectually related to ordinary public life, to the *Lebenswelt*. Husserl's attempts to restore the theoretical integrity of the self is likewise an attempt to discover the possibility of the scientist as citizen."[19]

Scientism in the social sciences is both ontologically and epistemologically mistaken: it is "illusionary" and "erroneous." The objection of phenomenology to scientism is based on the recognition that there is the fundamental, ontological *differentia* between being human and being merely natural or between human reality and physical reality. This ontological difference itself determines or dictates the choice of methodology in the social sciences: methodology presupposes ontology. There is, therefore, the fundamental methodological difference between what is social-scientific and what is natural-scientific. However, phenomenology is not demanding that there must be two separate orders in the logic of scientific inquiry—one for the social sciences and the other for the natural sciences. Rather, it maintains that the respective "objects" they investigate are qualitatively different. As Schutz contends, "The world of nature, as explored by the natural scientist, does not 'mean' anything to molecules, atoms, and electrons. But the observational field of the social scientist—social reality—has a specific meaning and relevance structure for the human beings living, acting, and thinking within it."[20] Nature does not experience itself; only human beings experience themselves as well as other people in society and other things in nature. Whereas all forms of scientism or scientific epistemology (e.g., logical empiricism and political behavioralism) take for granted this social reality, phenomenology insists that it is the proper observational field of social-scientific investigations. While the natural sciences may legitimately be able to bypass or ignore *as their observational field* this primary meaning layer of the life-world as social reality in their idealizing abstraction of nature, the social sciences cannot for the reason that:

> The thought objects constructed by the social scientist, in order to grasp this social reality, have to be founded upon the thought objects constructed by the common-sense thinking of men, living their daily life within their social world. Thus, the constructs of the social science are, so to speak, constructs of the second degree, that is, constructs of the constructs made by the actors on the social scene, whose behavior the social scientist has to observe and to explain in accordance with the procedural rules of his science.[21]

The phenomenological method used to investigate the life-world as social reality may be called "subjective interpretation" which is in the tradition of Max Weber's "interpretive sociology" (*verstehende Soziologie*), although, according to Schutz, Weber is not totally clear as to whether *Verstehen* is (1) the common-sense knowledge of human affairs, (2) an epistemological problem, or (3) a method peculiar to the social sciences.[22] The very questions concerning "self-fulfilling" or "self-defeating" prophesy, "culture-bound," and the "ideological" dimension of scientific inquiry in the social sciences are *corollaries* of these "subjective" meaning structures and "subjective interpretation." Contrary to a quagmire of the positivist misunderstandings of the operation called *Verstehen,* it is neither mysterious, nor intuitive, nor introspective, nor perjoratively "subjective." *Verstehen,* according to Schutz, is the experiential and common-sense layer of comprehension about our surrounding world. The phenomenological method of "subjective interpretation" is called *subjective* because its goal is first to know what action means for the actor himself (i.e., the participant's view) rather than for his partner or a neutral scientific observer (e.g., a political scientist).[23]

2. A Hermeneutical Accent on the Conduct of Political Inquiry

Since man is *the language animal* and all understanding occurs through the medium of language, it is obvious that the notion of linguisticality is central to the understanding of human reality and thus to the inquiry of the human sciences as well.[24] In the modern history of the human sciences, it was Vico in *The New Science,* as we have noted in chapter 2, who saw, more clearly than anyone else, language as occupying a privileged position in human culture—the totality of human practices, events, and institutions—and linguistic autopsy as the "master key" to unlock the mystery of the cultural and historical sciences.[25] In different ways language occupies a central concern in the development of contemporary philosophy. Correspondingly, therefore, many writers have been concerned in recent years with the problem of language in social and political inquiry— Jürgen Habermas, Karl-Otto Apel, Peter Winch, Quentin Skinner, J. G. A. Pocock, Richard E. Flathman, Hannah F. Pitkin, Murray Edelman, and David V. J. Bell with different philosophical persuasions.[26] We can say with confidence that political inquiry has now made a "linguistic turn." Hermeneutics flourishes in literary criticism and psychoanalysis today, but there is a curious lag in political theory. Despite the natural affinity of the history of political thought and jurisprudential studies to hermeneutics in which the notion of interpretation plays a prominent role and the historical disciplines contributed significantly to the development of European hermeneutics in the past, they are yet to make a hermeneutical turn.[27]

Merleau-Ponty once remarked:

> In the philosophical tradition, the problem of language does not pertain to "first philosophy," and that is just why Husserl approaches it more freely than the problem of perception or

knowledge. He moves it into a central position, and what little he says about it is both original and enigmatic. Consequently, this problem provides us with our best basis for questioning phenomenology and recommencing Husserl's effort instead of simply repeating what he said. It allows us to resume, instead of his theses, the very movement of his thought.[28]

The aim of this section is to draw our attention to the importance of language and to place the notion of linguisticality at the center of political inquiry by using the philosophical insights of hermeneutical phenomenology. We are naturally inspired by Paul Ricoeur's pioneering thesis of considering the meaning of human action as a text. By so doing, he opens up again the possibility of applying hermeneutics to the behavioral sciences such as political science. He states:

> if there are specific problems which are raised by the interpretation of texts because they are texts and not spoken language, and if these problems are the ones which constitute hermeneutics as such, then the human sciences may be said to be hermeneutical (1) inasmuch as their *object* displays some of the features constitutive of a text as text, and (2) inasmuch as their *methodology* develops the same kind of procedures as those of *Auslegung* or text-interpretation.[29]

However, our purpose is not to pursue comprehensively the relevance of hermeneutics in the sense of *Auslegung* to political inquiry but to indicate a directional signal for it. In so doing, we shall focus our attention on Gadamer's seminal work in hermeneutical phenomenology, *Truth and Method*.[30] With the advent of Gadamer's work, the idea of language or linguistically (*Sprachlichkeit*) commands the *first* concern of philosophical inquiry within the phenomenolgoical movement. As the philosopher is a perpetual beginner and philosophy is an infinite task, Gadamer's philosophical endeavor is an attempt to renew rather than merely what Husserl and Heidegger said and thought, that is, Gadamer advances *his* thought in the very movement of *their* thought. Despite the influence of Heidegger's analytic of *Dasein* and Husserl's phenomenology on Gadamer, Gadamer's originality resides in extending Heidegger's ontology and Husserl's phenomenology in terms of the following two points which are of great importance for our present inquiry: (1) he places language or linguisticality at the center of the analysis of man as Being-in-the-world and (2) by so doing, more importantly, he relates his analysis to the inquiry of the sciences of man within and beyond the

European academic tradition of hermeneutics as the art of interpretation from Aristotle to Schleiermacher, Dilthey, Heidegger, and Emilio Betti.[31] Gadamer's hermeneutical view puts the question of "truth" (as the disclosure of human reality) before that of "method," that is, a philosophical clarification of *what it is to be human* in its multiple dimensions prior to the question of epistemology or methodology in the human sciences (i.e., the primacy of ontology over methodology as discussed in chapter 2). In its "ontological turn," therefore, Gadamer's hermeneutical phenomenology is foremost a radical challenge to scientism. Moreover, Gadamer's hermeneutical phenomenology complements Schutz's methodology of the social sciences and contributes—in its transcendental unity of the being of the speaking subject and the being of the spoken world—to the establishment of a new paradigm in the unifying philosophy of the sciences.

The essence of meaning is its linguisticality, insofar as everything in both history and nature—correlatively, therefore, the historical and the natural sciences—has for man a name or linguistic designation, that is, when things are transformed into meaning. Phenomenology, whose function is to explore the genesis of meaning, is in a large measure a philosophical quest for the nature of linguisticality. All meaning, which is a product of noetic and noematic correlates, is linguistic in nature, although there are surely the domains of human experience which are strictly speaking both nonintentional and prelinguistic (e.g., the world of infants before they learn how to speak and the world of perception). However, understanding as a hermeneutical event involves linguisticality in thinking and doing, whether it pertains to private meaning or public utterance or their dialectical relations.

The intrinsicality of language to man and his humanity, as has been intimated in chapter 2, is central to Gadamer's hermeneutical reflection. For human existence is a document of communal life and language is its idiom. To speak of the condition of language is to speak of that of man: language and man are inseparable correlates. For Gadamer, language that discloses a world for man is not an ideal construction but is the natural one that mediates man and world in the life-world. Man, language, and world are together a trinary set. For to have a world for man is to depend on language, and the world is a world for man because of language. The world is instituted linguistically, and the limits and possibilities of our understanding coincide with those of language. Language too has no independent life of its own apart from man and world and the world is no world for man without language: the original humanity of language means the fundamental linguistic quality of man's Being-in-the-world in which we make our language just as we make our history. Although some speak of the relevance of "linguistics" to the "philosophy of mind" (e.g., Noam Chomsky), Gadamer's primary concern is neither linguistics as the science of language nor semiology as the theory of signs. Rather, he is concerned with the disclosure of language intrinsic to man's Being-in-the-world. His hermeneutics defined narrowly as the art of interpreting the text or script is rooted in the basic "ontological" concern of man's historical existence.

For Gadamer, language discloses a world for man or man's Being-in-the-world. As a disclosure, it is a tie between man and his world. He describes the inseparable and interdependent troika of language, man, and world as follows:

> Language is not just one of man's possessions in the world, but on it depends the fact that man has a world at all. For man the world exists as world in a way that no other being in the world experiences. But this world is linguistic in nature. This is the real heart of Humboldt's assertion, which he intended quite differently, that languages are views of the world. By this Humboldt means that language maintains a kind of independent life over against the individual member of a linguistic community and relationship to the world as well. But the ground of this statement is life apart from the world that comes to language within it. Not only is the world "world" only insofar as it comes to language but language, too, has its real being only in the fact that the world is re-presented within it. Thus the original humanity of language means at the same time the fundamental linguistic quality of man's being-in-the-world. We shall have to investigate the relation between language and the world in order to attain the horizon adequate to the linguistic nature of the hermeneutical experience.[32]

Language works like an umbilical cord that connects man and world. To borrow the language of Samuel Taylor Coleridge, language is the "armoury of the human mind" which stores at once both the "trophies" and "weapons" of the mind's past and future possibilities.[33] "Words" do not simply designate "things," as though they are independent entities separable from the world. Rather, they are the *natural luminaries* of things in the world. In short, as has been already noted, words and things are not "heterogeneous substances."[34] For men, things in the world dwell in signs, words, and symbols: they are made visible and animated in the transparency of language.

Although it is not wrong to say that language is an expression of culture and culture is embodied in language and that language serves as the instrument or medium of human communication, this instrumental view of language alone falls far short of doing full justice to the ontological dimension of language as a *hermeneutical event,* that is, as the interdependent dialectics of language, man, and world. Even if language is part of the large entity called "world" (or Being), our focus on linguisticality in linking man and world is justified because the part not only is an expression of but also embodies the whole (i.e., the "hermeneutical circle"). It makes sense to say that a view of language is a view of the world, and *vice versa.*

When we define language as a hermeneutical event, the term "event" means a dialectical mediation of integration of the existential *act* of an individual user (as a member of a linguistic community) on the one hand and a linguistic *system* or *structure* as an objective reality independent of its individual users on the other. This is the way Ricoeur defines the "word" (*mot*) as a mediation between the act and the structure: the phenomenology of language must be "the simultaneous 'birth' of the spoken-being of the world and the speaking-being of man."[35] Thus the hermeneutical question of how language discloses or catches man and the world is the question of how man "participates" in the world by means of language. First, man does not belong to the world as objects or things belong to nature. Second, language itself as speech acts in an interfusion of the subjective (inner) and the objective (outer) horizons: there are the "speaker" and the "listener" in communication in the context of something "spoken" or "listened to." Language has the force that pulls us to the world as the world is pulled to us. Moreover, if for man there is a world at all through language, there is the openness of language to him. Thus Gadamer emphasizes the importance of "hearing" or "listening" to the otherness of language before one "speaks" or "interprets" its text or context. Hermeneutics as the art of interpretation requires the openness of the thing interpreted (text) to the interpreting subject. We do not master or control language but listen to it: we "*surrender*" to it. The technologism of language today whose aim is to master it rather than surrender to it devaluates its quiddity and thus the humanity it embodies: the totalitarian language of politics accompanies the totalitarian politics of language.

Thus hermeneutics as the art of interpretation requires an interfusion of the interpreter as subject and the text as the object interpreted. As the interfusion of the interpreter and the text, interpretation is not just a clever "manipulation" of the text for subjectivity but is a partici-

pation in the text where the subject "hears" or "listens" to what the
text "says"—its message, proclamation, or *kerygma*. It is a *testament* of
the text to the interpreter. It is this "hermeneutical autonomy"—let the
text "speak" for itself—which is indispensable to the art of interpretation. When language is manipulated or "technized," which is to say,
when man ceases to listen to the message of the text or loses its hermeneutical autonomy, speaking degenerates into "image-making."
"Listening" to the text, however, is an act of neither empathy, nor
intuition (a flash of insight), nor discovering the subjective "motives"
and the "intentions" of the author.[36] For Gadamer, moreover, what is
important in interpretation is that it seeks the depth of understanding
man as Being-in-the-world rather than the correctness of knowledge:
fundamentally it is the question not of epistemology (*Erkenntnistheorie*)
but of truth as disclosure (*aletheia*) that the art of interpretation seeks.

To understand Gadamer's hermeneutical phenomenology, we must
further consider his notions of (1) "tradition" based on man's historicity and (2) "prejudice" (*Vorurteil*). The basically Heideggerian
and Husserlian framework of Gadamer rests on the idea that temporality is constitutive of *Dasein* as "project" which has three *ecstatic horizons* of the past, the present, and the future, i.e., a "fusion of horizons"
(*Horizontschmelzung*). Man's historicity is ultimately determined by the
facticity of *Dasein* as finitude: *Dasein* is a being-toward-death. Tradition is an interfusion of the temporal horizons of the past and the
present in view of the future. Like memory that is the retention of the
past in terms of the present, tradition is not a fixed set of principles or
situations. It is a dynamic concept involving active participation. Tradition is then the openness of the past to the present. As it is not
simply the "re-enactment" of the past, through it the past is lived or
relived in the present. In tradition as in historical understanding, the
past and the present are *contemporaneous* (con-temporaneous). In historical understanding just as in reading a text, however, the idea of
horizons is

> to see the past in terms of its own being, not in terms of our
> contemporary criteria and prejudices, but within its own histori-
> cal horizon. The task of historical understanding also involves
> acquiring the particular historical horizon, so that what we are
> seeking to understand can be seen in its true dimensions. If we
> fail to place ourselves in this way within the historical horizon
> out of which tradition speaks, we shall misunderstand the sig-
> nificance of what it has to say to us.[37]

Unlike the concept of *sola scriptura*—understanding the scripture
on its own basis rather than on tradition—the concept of tradition as

the disclosure of the past to the present tells us that "truth" is not a blind acceptance of what authority says it is, whether it be a person or an institution. In the advent of meaning, then there is the dialectic of "transmitting" and "renewing" at the same time. Just as there is a temporal continuum of the past and the present, so do tradition and interpretation go hand in hand. As Ricoeur says so succinctly, "tradition . . . , even understood as the transmission of a *depositum,* remains a dead tradition if it is not the continual interpretation of this deposit: our 'heritage' is not a sealed package we pass from hand to hand, without ever opening, but rather a treasure from which we draw by the handful and which by this very act is replenished. Every tradition lives by grace of interpretation, and it is at this price that it continues, that is, remains living."[38] Defined in terms of tradition replenished by interpretation, truth is itself a dialogue. This is why the dialogical structure of Platonic dialogues is so important to Gadamer's hermeneutics. We may even say that the world itself has a tradition, that is, a historical sedimentation of meanings. The word is always already meaningful. The text is a text insofar as it is a historical document. To put it differently, history is "a language-net cast backward."[39]

Another crucial idea related closely to tradition is "historically operative consciousness"[40] (*wirkungsgeschichtliches Bewusstsein*). It is the way in which historicity works, operates in, or effects hermeneutical experience and the art of interpretation. To recognize the effectiveness of history is not to take it as the passive other. As an active participation, understanding is a historically effective operation, i.e., it is hermeneutical. When understanding is historically operative, it is a mixed fusion of the interpreter and the text, where the latter has its own tradition (already meaningful) and the former itself is situated in time and place—whether the interpreter be a literary critic, an art critic, a sociologist, or a political theorist.

For Gadamer, moreover, the idea of "prejudice" (pre-judgment) has an unusual meaning; it is a morally neutral term. It is neither desirable nor undesirable. Like the factual constitution of *Dasein* as Being-in-the-world, it *is there* with us and with the art of interpretation. For Gadamer, prejudice is something not to be gotten rid of but to be *accounted for* or reckoned with. Thus, according to him, the art of interpreting the text or hermeneutical act is "the conscious assimilation of one's own fore-meaning and prejudices. The important thing is to be aware of one's own bias, so that the text may present itself in all its newness and thus be able to assert its own truth against one's own fore-meanings."[41] Take the Enlightenment's supposition of Reason as capable of uprooting and emancipating man from tradition. Gadamer comments that "This recognition that all understanding inevitably involves some prejudice gives the hermeneutical problem its real thrust. By the light of this insight it appears that historicism, despite its critique of rationalism and of natural law philosophy, is based on the modern enlightenment and unknowingly shares its prejudices. And there is one prejudice of the enlightenment that is essential to it: the fundamental prejudice of the enlightenment is the prejudice against prejudice itself which deprives tradition of its power."[42] For Gadamer, there is no dichotomy between "tradition" for the sake of preservation and "reason" in pursuit of "emancipation." For tradition itself is the dialectical appropriation of transmission and renewal. Because of the *privileged* position of language which embodies or mediates the dialectical nexus of man and world, Gadamer's hermeneutics has advantages over other theories—Habermas's theory of interests notwithstanding. In reply to Habermas's commentary on his *Truth and Method,* Gadamer asserts that Habermas's theory of interests is an aspect of hermeneutical reflection. Habermas's critique of Gadamer's hermeneutics as the "idealism of linguisticality" that allegedly ignores the concept of *praxis* (work and politics) is mistaken. A critique of ideology (*Ideologiekritik*) in the Marxian tradition, to be sure, is an aspect of the hermeneutical critique of "prejudice." As Gadamer himself contends, it is absurd to suggest that the concrete factors of work and politics (the material being of life-practice) has nothing to do with hermeneutical reflection that takes the notion of "prejudice" as the *positive* conditionedness of all practice and all reflection. A critique of ideology which intends to unmask the "deceptions of language" too is, of course, a linguistic act of reflection. What hermeneutical reflection as "effective reflection" shows here is not that linguisticality determines all *praxis* but rather that there is no practical, societal reality that is represented in consciousness without ever being formulated and articulated linguistically: all reality, Gadamer insists, happens *within* language. A critique of ideology, however critical and effective it may be in unmasking the material, practical, or societal "prejudices" behind the veil of language, is a particular form of hermeneutical reflection on "prejudices" because nothing is "prejudice" without being unveiled in language or articulated linguistically. As a particular form of hermeneutical reflection on "prejudices," therefore, a critique of ideology is a delimiting concept in more than one way.[43]

It is Dilthey who is best known for his effort to apply hermeneutics to the methodology of the human sciences. His thought has had a pervasive influence on and an affinity with the phenomenological movement—including Husserl, Heidegger, Scheler, Schutz, and Gadamer—and the "interpretive sociology" of Weber.[44] With Dilthey in mind, it should be made clear from the outset that as his concern is the primacy of "truth" over "method," Gadamer's *Truth and Method* is not a treatise on the methodology of the human sciences. In his Foreword to the second German edition of this work, Gadamer says in no uncertain terms: "My real concern was and is philosophic: not what we do or what we ought to do, but what happens to us over and above our wanting and doing. Hence the methods of the human sciences are not at issue here."[45] To emphasize this "philosophic" concern of Gadamer, we have thus spoken of an "ontological turn" in his thought. In contrast, Dilthey considered hermeneutics as "the methodology of the understanding of recorded expressions" whose epistemological concern led him to regard language as a tool for hermeneutics. Well aware of the lack of scientific parity in the human sciences with the natural sciences, his aim was to make the knowledge of the former as rigorous as the latter. That is to say, his chief aim was to construct a (hermeneutical) model alternative to the scientific model in order to yield a certainty of knowledge in the human sciences comparable to that of the natural sciences. This is his main accomplishment in and contribution to the sciences of man. In accounting for a hermeneutical foundation for the human sciences, Dilthey belongs to the tradition of Vico's anti-Cartesian and anti-Galilean "new science" where "history" rather than "science" is paradigmatic to epistemology. Because he considered truth as an *expression* of life force, individual mental or spiritual life, Dilthey—unlike Heidegger and Gadamer—was not able to grasp truth as an "ontological" issue and thus also failed to overcome "psychologism" and "historicism."[46] For when truth is merely an expression of individual life, then there is no distinction between autobiographical and historical understanding. For Gadamer, on the other hand, a text as the "objective truth" of what is said should not be understood as a mere expression of life but rather be taken seriously in its claim to truth.[47] From an inquiry standpoint of the human sciences, Dilthey's thought seems to encounter serious difficulty: there is a polarization of the human sciences from the natural sciences ("two cultures" of inquiry) on the one hand and that of ontology (being of man) and epistemology (knowledge of man) on the other.

Having said all this about Gadamer's "philosophic" concern and "ontological turn" in relation to Dilthey's "life-philosophy" (*Lebensphilosophie*), however, what is important in our inquiry is the fact that the question of truth has its bearing on the epistemology and methodology of the human sciences. Throughout the text of *Truth and Method*, Gadamer alludes to the question of "inquiry" in relation to his ultimate concern. The methodology of the human sciences is indeed a particular *application* of his philosophical hermeneutics as *universal* reflection. As a matter of fact, the importance of the ontological definition of the aesthetic and hermeneutical enterprise in Gadamer, I think, must be seen against the background of the dominance of both scientific culture and scientific epistemology today. Moreover, it is extremely important to note that the way in which truth itself is disclosed in the cultural sciences ("what truth means in the human sciences") has "a far-reaching consequence" on philosophical hermeneutics. According to Gadamer, "it is in the human sciences as a whole that an answer to the question of truth must be found."[48] The model he uses for philosophical hermeneutics is that of cultural studies (including art as a paradigmatic case) rather than the natural sciences. Emphasis on historical consciousness in his hermeneutics can thus be explained because it is modeled after history or the historical sciences. "It is to the development of historical consciousness," Gadamer declares, "that hermeneutics owes its central function within the human sciences."[49] This is, I think, the true radicality of Gadamer's philosophical hermeneutics. It is the question of how the human cultural sciences contribute to the self-understanding of philosophy itself.

3. HERMENEUTICAL AUTONOMY AS A CRITIQUE OF THE COMPARATIVE STUDY OF POLITICAL CULTURES

Hermeneutics serves as a *critique* of the comparative study of political cultures—especially cross-cultural transformation known as the politics of "modernization" or "political development."[50] Cultural hermeneutics as method is a direct challenge to scientism as an amalgam of conceptual assumptions, formalistic models, and quantitative techniques—which, as a unique product of Western scientific culture, is based on the methodological and epistemological slogan that what is not quantitatively measurable is not knowable. The singular advantage of cultural hermeneutics is the fundamental principle of "hermeneutical autonomy" by focusing on the autopsy of the nature of language which embodies the peculiar character of a culture in which it is used. Hermeneutical autonomy aims at *objectivity* in the social sciences in general and cross-cultural studies in particular. The ultimate aim of cultural hermeneutics is to secure in principle the universal "essences" (in a phenomenological sense) of human culture by discovering the similar in the dissimilar in the "facts" of individual cultures. As the different versions of the life-world as sociocultural world are "subjective-relative" having a variant content, it is ultimately necessary to discover the cross-cultural, invariant nature of human culture itself.

Cultural hermeneutics attempts to correlate the deep archaeology of *subjectivity* and its surface, *objective* counterpart, that is, to analyze the underlying deep structures of culture called "meanings" as they are embodied, expressed, and institutionalized in the actual life of men in their "natural attitude" and to understand them as the people of a particular culture understand them. Thus cultural hermeneutics is an attempt to understand the experiential topography of meanings and values by which people themselves live. This deep sedimentation of cultural meanings and values is the essence of what we have called the life-world. The anthropologists A. L. Kroeber and Clyde Kluckhohn define the essential stuff of culture as meaning and valuation when they write:

> We come now to those properties of culture which seem most distinctive of it and most important: its significance and its values. Perhaps we should have said "significance or values," for the two are difficult to keep separated and perhaps constitute no more than somewhat different aspects of the same thing. First of all, significance does not mean merely ends. It is not teleological in the traditional sense. Significance and values are of the essence of the organization of culture. It is true that human endeavor is directed towards ends; but those ends are shaped by the values of culture; and the values are felt as intrinsic, not as means. And the values are variable and relative, not predetermined and eternal, though certain universals of human biology and of human social life appear to have brought about a few constants or near-constants that cut across cultural differences. Also the values are part of nature, not outside it. They are products of men, of men having bodies and living in societies, and are the structural essence of the culture of these societies of man. Finally, values and significances are "intangibles" which are "subjective" in that they can be internally experienced, but also objective in their expressions, embodiments, or results.[51]

Now, then, culture is the phenomenon which has both deep essences and surface facts. Language as a cultural phenomenon, for example, has both deep and surface structures or subjective and objective dimensions: that dimension of language which is lived by or internalized and that dimension of language which is institutionalized or externalized in rules. As man *is* his language and as language is a cultural phenomenon, the transformation of language in use is the basic grammar of cultural transformation whose flesh is meaning and value. As language crosscuts both deep and surface structures of culture, the grammar of language dictates the transformation rules of culture, that is, the possibilities and limitations of cultural transformation. By the same token, cultural transformation also involves the transformation of language. Any radical or fundamental transformation of culture must involve the complementary transformation of not only its deep structures but of its surface structures as well, that is, both "consciousness" (linguistic, perceptual, affective, and cognitive) and "institution" (linguistic, political, economic, and social). Correlative to the transformation of the deep and surface structures of culture is also a dialectical interchange or complementarity between an indigenous and traditional culture on the one hand and a foreign and new culture on the other.

Hermeneutical autonomy means that to get at the deep structures that underlie surface phenomena in culture, we must come to grips with the structure of intersubjective meanings that are embodied in the common practices and institutions of a particular culture. For culture is a calculus of intersubjective meanings. The fundamental underlying principle of hermeneutical autonomy is the notion that man is a "self-interpreting animal." Charles Taylor declares that "He is necessarily so, for there is no such thing as the structure of meanings for him independently of his interpretation of them; for one is woven into the other. But then the text of our interpretation is not that heterogeneous from what is interpreted; for what is interpreted is itself an interpretation; a self-interpretation which is embedded in a stream of action. It is an interpretation of experiential meaning which contributes to the constitution of this meaning."[52] Unlike natural objects, human beings are *embodied subjects* for whom events and things have meanings by means of interpretation. Intersubjective meanings in a culture are not simply brute facts or data which can fit into preconceived models and the conceptual grid of quantitative analysis. They are not merely subjective meanings alone which constitute the property of one or some individuals. They are not even the converging area of individual beliefs and values but are essentially modes of mutually shared social relationships. The *nexus* of intersubjective meanings is the way of experiencing thought and action (both individual and institutional) which is the very original stuff of practices and institutions in society in a given period of time. To put it differently, cultural "mentality" or "orientation" is *a system of intersubjective meanings* commonly shared by a group of people that has persisted throughout the ages within a given geographical area. "Intersubjective meaning," Taylor writes, "gives a people a common language to talk about social reality and a common understanding of certain norms, but only with common meaning does this common reference contain significant common actions, celebrations, and feelings. These are objects in the world that everybody shares. This is what makes community."[53] The fundamental transformation of culture is the occurrence of change in which the structure of intersubjective meanings penetrate into the layers of the individual's practices and his institutions.

Scientific epistemology both formalistic and "empirical" in search of brute data in cross-cultural studies—especially the study of non-Western political cultures—ignores the concept of man as a self-interpreting animal, that is, the system of intersubjective meanings in a given area as it is understood by its own actors—Chinese, Indians, Africans, etc.—in relating themselves to their surrounding world. Instead of assuring objectivity in cross-cultural studies, scientific methodology carries with it the prejudice of a fundamentally ideological kind. It may very well conceal the cultural bias of the analyst in the garb of the allegedly objective language of his methodology. In warning of the hidden ideological prejudice of a scientific empiricist, Taylor writes:

> the result of ignoring the difference in intersubjective meanings can be disastrous to a science of comparative politics, viz., that we interpret all other societies in the categories of our own. Ironically, this is what seems to have happened to American political science. Having strongly criticized the old institution-focussed comparative politics for its ethnocentricity (or Western bias), it proposed to understand the politics of all society in terms of such functions, for instance, as "interest articulation" and "interest aggregation" whose definition is strongly influenced by the bargaining culture of our civilization, but which is far from being guaranteed appropriateness elsewhere. The not surprising result is a theory of political development which places the Atlantic-type polity at the summit of human political development.[54]

This "empiricist" prejudice is nowhere more clear than in the study of political development or "modernization" in the non-Western

world. The fundamental philosophical underpinning of "modernization" parallels that of the structural-functional approach to political
socialization in scientific methodology. In the functional-structural
analysis of political socialization, emphasis is on *how* socialization is
done rather than *what* socialization is or perhaps what it is for or
ought to be. It seems reasonable to assume that the latter presupposes
the former in that we must first clarify what socialization is before we
can understand how it is done. One important normative implication
of functional-structural analysis is that whatever *functions* is legitimate. Socialization is the mechanism whereby the individual "adjusts"
himself to the already fixed structure of society. Any deviation therefrom is aberration. To use the terminology of modern linguistics, in
the functional-structural analysis of political socialization emphasis is
on "synchrony" rather than "diachrony." The underlying philosophical assumption of this emphasis is twofold. First, whoever is socialized is a passive receptacle who merely absorbs what is given—the
view which is deeply rooted in the long tradition of Anglo-Saxon
empiricism—especially in the epistemology of John Locke. Second,
emphasis on synchrony ends up with minimizing the effect of the
individual who is being socialized on the structure of society. He is a
role-taker rather than a role-maker. The underlying assumption of
functional-structural analysis is that socialization is a kind of initiation
ceremony in the transition of one ontological order (e.g., childhood)
to another (e.g., adulthood) or "immaturity" to "maturity." Thus the
being of man is divided into two separate ontological orders. This
reasoning of ontogenesis is extended to phylogenesis: like the process
of the child's socialization, the process of modernization is the uni-
directional process of reaching "maturity" (or "modernity") from
"immaturity" (or "tradition") in which the standard of what is to be
modernized is set by "developed nations" and scientific methodology
is a sort of passport that insures the passage to the understanding of
modernization. Modernization is the "adjustment" of "developing"
nations to the patterns of "developed" nations. If socialization is an
interchange between the individual and society, it must be dialectical
in that it is a give-and-take process. To put it more abstractly, it must
be a dialectical interchange between the internalization of the external
on the one hand and the externalization of the internal on the other.
In sum: as the conceptualization of *what* socialization is rather than
how socialization is done is in need of a "phenomenology of socialization," [55] so is the conceptualization of political development a "phenomenology of political development."

   This scientific epistemology prevalent in the study of political development is deeply rooted in Hegelianism or Hegel's teleological philosophy of history and culture. For Hegel, the incomparable philosopher of history, the East—China and India—represented the childhood of history. For him, Chinese history, like the rhythm of nature, repeats itself eternally and becomes an unhistorical history—a historical infantilism or paleography in the progression of world history. Chinese history is the static and seamless flow of the eternal yesterday.[56] In the modern European philosophy of history since Hegel, the tendency is to assume explicitly or implicitly the spiritual and moral superiority of Western culture to non-Western culture which is being carried over by and evidenced today in Western specialists and observers on modernization. In the familiar terminology of modernization, the scientific, technological, and industrial civilization of the West is superior to the nonscientific, nontechnological, and nonindustrial culture of the non-Western world. Although it is an ideological phantom, the "third world" is more than a numerical designation: it is indeed a moral ordering.

Against the predestined trajectory of Hegel's rectilinear monism, we shall propose here the view of Merleau-Ponty which assures both hermeneutical autonomy and the possibility of discovering the universal *essences* of human culture beyond relativism. It has its intellectual root in Vico's anti-Hegelianism which envisioned a "mental vocabulary" common to the living and dead deeds (customs, conventions, languages, and the like) of all nations which contains the universal "principles of humanity." Vico was interested in the "adjacency," "parallelisms," and "complementarity" of words, languages, ideas, and cultures, that is, in "the lateral and the dispersed" rather than "the linear and the sequential."[57] We shall call this frame of thinking the *laterality of truth*. Since a "world"—like a "word"—is an organized but ambiguous and multidimensional ensemble of meanings, Merleau-Ponty intended to replace—albeit programmatically—"the notions of concept, idea, mind, representations with the notions of *dimensions*, articulation, level, hinges, pivots, configuration," the plan of which is truly in the Vichian mold.[58] He spoke well of ethnological findings from Marcel Mauss to Claude Lévi-Strauss. Their ethnological methods open up the "lateral universal" which is "no longer the overarching universal of a strictly objective method" but which is acquired "through ethnological experience and its incessant testing of the self through the other person and the other person through the self. It is a question of constructing a general system of reference in which the point of view of the native, the point of view of the civilized man, and the mistaken views each has of the other can all find a place—that is, of constituting a more comprehensive experience which becomes in principle accessible to men of a different time and country."[59] This lateral universality in ethnological findings is arrived at by learning the "diacritical" value of "what is ours as alien and what was alien as our own."[60]

Unlike Hegel who viewed Oriental thought in a cavalier fashion, it is for Merleau-Ponty "immensely interesting," "suggestive," and "instructive." Philosophical truth as absolute and universal knowledge is for Merleau-Ponty not certified by the Occidental seal of approval alone. For him, all thought is part of the life-world as the total meaning horizon of a sociocultural world; all philosophies are anthropological types and none has any special birthright to a monopoly of truth. "If Western thought is what it claims to be," Merleau-Ponty says, "it must prove it by understanding all 'life-worlds'."[61]

For Merleau-Ponty, the arrogant path of Hegel that excludes Oriental thought from absolute and universal knowledge and draws "a geographical frontier between philosophy and non-philosophy" also excludes a good part of the Western past. Philosophy as a perpetual beginning is destined to examine its own idea of truth again and again because truth is "a treasure scattered about in human life prior to all philosophy and not divided among doctrines."[62] Thus the life-world—and its different versions both Occidental and Oriental—is the source from which truth emerges. If so, Western philosophy is destined to re-examine not only its own idea of truth but also related matters and institutions such as science and capitalism. Merleau-Ponty declares:

> From this angle, civilizations lacking our philosophical or economic equipment take on an instructive value. It is not a matter of going in search of truth or salvation in what falls short of science or philosophical awareness, or of dragging chunks of mythology as such into our philosophy, but of acquiring—in the presence of these variants of humanity that we are so far from—a sense of the theoretical and practical problems our institutions are faced with, and of rediscovering the existential field that they were born in and that their long success has led us to forget. The Orient's "childishness" has something to teach us, if it were nothing more than the narrowness of our adult ideas. The relationship between Orient and Occident, like that between child and adult, is not that of ignorance to knowledge or non-philosophy to philosophy; it is much more subtle, making room on the part of the Orient for all anticipations and "pre-

maturations." Simply tallying and subordinating "non-philoso-phy" to true philosophy will not create the unity of the human spirit. It already exists in each culture's lateral relationships to the others, in the echoes one awakes in the other.[63]

In search of truth nothing should be taken for granted or prejudged. It is just here that Merleau-Ponty makes a decisive break with Hegel. As childhood and adulthood are one inseparable ontological order of man, so are Oriental and Occidental cultures one integral order of humanity which together point to philosophical universality. For we learn as much from primitive cultures as from modern cultures re-garding the human condition. Merleau-Ponty declares that "There is not *a* philosophy which contains all philosophies: philosophy as a whole is at certain moments in each philosophy. To take up the cele-brated phrase again philosophy's center is everywhere and its circum-ference nowhere." [64] For Merleau-Ponty, the Orient must also have a place in the museum of philosophies to celebrate its hitherto "secret muted contribution to philosophy." He writes: "Indian and Chinese philosophies have tried not so much to dominate existence as to be the echo or the sounding board of our relationship to being. Western philosophy can learn from them to rediscover the relationship to being and initial option which gave it birth, and to estimate the possi-bilities we have shut ourselves off from in becoming 'Westerners' and perhaps reopen them." [65]

4. SCIENCE AS INTERSUBJECTIVE ACTIVITY

As we have seen above, Husserl's objection to scientism was that it has lost the sight of human subjectivity buried under the sedimen-tation of mathematical ideas and symbols in modern science since Galileo. Thus, for Husserl, the recovery of the life-world is the object of the archaeology of scientific knowledge. This archaeology in order to reveal mathematized or idealized nature as a garb of ideas, that is, its genesis of meaning, is also a historical teleology. Because he was interested in the archaeology of subjectivity in relation to the life-world, Husserl—unlike the positivistic philosophers of science whose primary concern has been the ahistorical "logic of expla-nation"—saw the truth of scientific enterprises and their claims of knowledge in terms of "the communalization of scientists,"[66] that is, a given community of scientists as well as the historical continuity (or discontinuity) of scientific thought. Thus science as human project is a communal or intersubjective enterprise and the truth of scientific knowledge is confirmed or unconfirmed not only by the logic of explanation or the presentation of factual findings alone but also by the entire community of science that evaluates it. To say that science is an intersubjective enterprise is to reject the privatization of scientific meaning (i.e., subjectivism). For "objectivity" is constituted by subjectivity as intersubjectivity, that is, the claim for scientific truth must be universally valid for all scientists as subjects. Scientism which substitutes a method or technique for reality and excludes everything subjective does injustice to the notion of subjectivity in scientific enterprises. To take no account of the scientist as the subject who investigates, excluding subjectivity from the activity of science as does scientism, is to forget the scientist as a human being or the political scientist as a citizen. If phenomenology is a philosophy of subjectivity, then it must focus its attention on science as a human, intersubjective activity. Precisely because scientific abstractions are *human* formulations, they belong to the life-world as a unity. Phenomenologically speaking, therefore, to reveal this fact is the fundamental task of the philosophy of science. In his "Concept and Theory Formation in the Social Sciences" in 1954, Schutz concluded this critical essay on the model of logical positivism by making what I take to be a revolutionary proposal which has so far attracted very little attention by philosophers of science. Schutz proposed:

> It seems to me that the social scientist can agree with the statement that the principal differences between the social and the natural sciences do not have to be looked for in a different logic governing each branch of knowledge. But this does not involve the admission that the social sciences have to abandon the particular devices they use for exploring social reality for the sake of an ideal unit of methods which is founded on the entirely unwarranted assumption that only methods used by the natural sciences, and especially by physics, are scientific ones. So far as I know, no serious attempt has been made by the proponents of the "unity of science" movement to answer or even to ask the question whether the methodological problem of the natural sciences in their present state is not merely a special case of the more general, still unexplored, problem how scientific knowledge is possible at all and what its logical and methodological presuppositions are. It is my personal conviction that phenomenological philosophy has prepared the ground for such an investigation. Its outcome might quite possibly show that the particular methodological devices developed by the social sciences in order to grasp social reality are better suited than those

of the natural sciences to lead to the discovery of the general principles which govern all human knowledge.[67]

Herein lies the revolutionary vision of Schutz's proposal which is the reversal of the positivist insistence that the methodology of the natural sciences, especially physics or mathematized physics (i.e., physicalism), constitutes the absolute paradigm for the general theory of knowledge as well as for the social sciences. Aron Gurwitsch too recognizes the methodological significance of the sociocultural life-world as the basis for a phenomenological theory of the sciences and reaches the following conclusion:

> all of the sciences, including the mathematical sciences of nature, find their place within the cultural world. For that reason, according to Husserl . . . , the cultural or human sciences prove to be all-encompassing, since they also comprise the natural sciences, since nature as conceived of and constructed in modern natural science, i.e., mathematized nature, is itself a mental accomplishment, that is, a cultural phenomenon. The converse, however, is not true. The cultural sciences cannot be given a place among the natural sciences, any more than the cultural world can be reached beginning from mathematized nature or, for that matter, from the thing-world, while, . . . by taking one's departure from the cultural world, one can arrive at the thing-world and the mathematized universe by means of abstraction, idealization, and formalization. In general, then, there is a possible transition from the concrete to the abstract, but not the reverse.[68]

In the context of the modern movement for the unity of knowledge from Bacon, Descartes, Vico, and Kant to logical empiricists,[69] phenomenological philosophy, I think, has now paved the way in which it is possible for us to formulate a unifying philosophy of the sciences both human and natural based on the social-scientific paradigm which is Vichian in origin rather than the natural-scientific paradigm which is Baconian, Cartesian, and positivistic. We shall call particularly Schutz's aforementioned proposal a *social critique of knowledge*. Schutz's social critique of knowledge must not be confused with the sociology of knowledge or the critique of ideology. For his phenomenology of the life-world is as much the social construction of reality as the construction of social reality. Inspired by Husserl's phenomenology of the life-world, Schutz's archaeology of knowledge is no doubt a significant contribution to the sociology of knowledge in elucidating the social derivation of knowledge as "intersubjective mirroring," the presuppositions of knowledge as subjectively experienced and how it is objectified, and how knowledge is transferred and distributed socially in the cultural world. The social critique of knowledge, however, is much more than the sociology of knowledge or the critique of ideology in the Marxian tradition which tends to treat all knowledge simply as the reflection of the social conditions or the dominant class at a given time and place: it tends to treat knowledge as epiphenomenal and relativistic.[70] On the contrary, the social critique of knowledge considers knowledge as social by focusing on the basis of establishing scientific knowledge, both human and natural, in the context of an intersubjective community of investigators (or inquirers) as scientific practitioners or knowing subjects. As such, scientific activity partakes of the *social a priori* of the life-world or the character of the life-world *as social reality*. As Husserl states clearly, "if we cease being immersed in our scientific thinking, we become aware that we scientists are, after all, human beings and as such are among the components of the life-world which always exists for us, ever pregiven; and thus all of science is pulled, along with us, into the—merely 'subjective-relative'—life-world." [71] The life-world is relative in the sense that its "Heraclitean flow" is relative to the perspectives of individuals, societies, and cultures, which constitute a variety of its versions. However, the ultimate task of the phenomenology of the life-world as philosophical anthropology is to discover the invariant patterns out of the variant flux and labyrinth of history and culture, that is, the invariant *essences* of the life-world as a *universal system of meanings* out of its variant *facts*. [72]

As a social critique of knowledge, the phenomenology of the life-world continues the tradition of Vico's *New Science*. Vico's famous formula of *"verum ipsum factum"* is based on the ontological principle that *how to know* (epistemology) presupposes *what to know* (ontology), that is, the truth or true knowledge of history (*verum*) depends on understanding that it is man-made (*factum*). It follows then that all knowledge or conceptualization—historical or mathematical—belongs to the realm of *factum*; it is a human invention. Thus Vico goes so far as to say that "We are able to demonstrate geometrical propositions because we create them; were it possible for us to supply demonstrations of propositions of physics, we would be capable of creating them *ex nihilo* as well."[73] Science itself is a human invention, an institution, or an "academy" which has its own *history*. Vico's anti-Cartesian view of truth rests on the fact that we acquire the apodictic knowledge of history (or culture) because it is made by us or is our own *invention.* Only because history is an order of *factum,* is it *verum* for us. The order of *verum* follows the order of *factum.* Similarly, as we have already seen, Gadamer proposed in *Truth and Method* that hermeneutics as search for historical consciousness owes its central function to the human sciences: it is in the human sciences that an answer to the question of all truth must be found. Historical consciousness as self-making, he insists, is not the abandonment of philosophy's task but is the path granted to us in reaching truth: but for *factum,* there would be no *verum.*

In opposition to the positivist philosophy of science, there emerged today a new breed of philosophers of science in the Anglo-Saxon world: among them are Thomas Kuhn, Michael Polanyi, Norwood R. Hanson, Stephen Toulmin, Hilary Putnam, Mary Hesse, and Paul Feyerabend. Despite their individual differences, they share something fundamental in that they are concerned with the *socio-historical teleology of science as a human institution.* In this sense, they are fundamentally Vichian as opposed to being Cartesian since for Vico "the true philosophy of a science is simply its history." [74] Historical teleology is also a phenomenological vision of science since for Husserl the teleology of science is a philosophical enterprise in seeking to uncover the meaning genesis of scientific activity as a human, communal project in the life-world. The fundamental convergence of these philosophers of science rests on their focus on "doing science" as the basis of the philosophy of science, which is necessarily historical since "doing science" involves knowing what science *has been, is,* and perhaps *will be* which may be in *evolutionary* continuity or *revolutionary* discontinuity. This is why historical consciousness or history especially in the conduct of social-scientific inquiry is important in its emphasis on "doing science" rather than on the logic of scientific explanation. As Abraham Kaplan says, "A study of the history of science, in a variety of disciplines and problematic situations, is likely to be far more rewarding for the actual conduct of inquiry than a preoccupation with an abstract logic of science."[75] Moreover, "doing science" must be understood in terms of the notion of scientific community or the community of scientific practitioners. Thus Polanyi speaks of the "republic of science" and Kuhn regards the "global" sense of "paradigm" as embracing all the shared commitments of a scientific community in which the specific notion of "disciplinary matrix" is only a subset.[76]

Nature and man or the historical order he himself makes are two ontological orders of radically different magnitude. Nonetheless, conceptualization, whether it be of nature or history, mathematical or historical, is always the invented (*factum*) on which truth (*verum*) rests.

The essential but not exclusive fabric of truth in conceptualization as well as mundane social life is *sociality* or *intersubjectivity* which may be the "master key" for a unifying philosophy of the sciences. The verification of all truth or the epistemological unity of the sciences rests on the "social matrix" of communication. Of course, there are differences in the motives of conceptualization and mundane social existence. The direct motive for the latter is "pragmatic," that is, the production of social action, whereas the predominant motive for the former is epistemic or cognitive, that is, the production of knowledge. However, human action as "project"—that meaning structure of action which involves the planning of the course of action in terms of both ends and means—is in part cognitive, just as the production of knowledge in terms of its relevance or application to the world of social action is in part pragmatic. In this sense, Husserl speaks of theorizing—scientific or otherwise—as a special form of *praxis* or social *praxis*. For him, science is fundamentally and foremost a human project and cultural accomplishment; as such, it is a human invention and institution. Both the world of science as a network of interactions among knowing subjects in pursuit of knowledge and social reality as a network of interactions and transactions among acting subjects partake of the same matrix: *sociality*. Epistemic claims for science are grounded in the "academy" of science as the institution of its practitioners which, like the community of a nation, has the structure of authority through which the value of truth is judged and allocated. In this sense, "doing science" or the acquisition of (tacit) knowledge is a kind of pedagogical training: learning and mastering the "trade" of science involves the tradition and authority of science as an institution. For Vico, the sciences are institutions just as are languages—both of which are historical or developmental. Just as with words or languages, the sciences have their histories.

The main themes of Kuhn's *The Structure of Scientific Revolutions*, I think, support the philosophy of the sciences as a social critique of knowledge. For him, science is an institution where scientific research is "a strenuous and devoted attempt to force nature into the conceptual boxes supplied by professional education."[77] Though strictly speaking it is a critique of knowledge only of the natural sciences from a historical perspective, Kuhn's epistemic claims can be easily extended to the human sciences. It focuses on the political sociology of science as the institution of its practitioners. Kuhn's theory of science is a paradigmatic case for Schutz's proposal of the social theory of knowledge in discovering a set of general principles governing all human knowledge. Like Husserl's phenomenology of science and teleology of scientific history based on the "communalization of scientists" and Vico's genetic epistemology, Kuhn's analysis of science is historical and sociological, that is, the structure of scientific knowledge is sought both from the genetic and historical development of science and in the context of an existing community of scientists as practitioners. For Kuhn, therefore, "the explanation [of science] must, in the final analysis, be psychological or sociological. It must, that is, be a description of a value system, an ideology, together with an analysis of the institutions through which that system is transmitted and enforced. Knowing what scientists value, we may hope to understand what problems they will undertake and what choices they will make in particular circumstances of conflict. I doubt that there is another sort of answer to be found."[78]

The process of establishing scientific paradigms in Kuhn is Vichian in that the order of ideas (paradigms) follows the order of institutions: a switch in paradigms occurs within the framework of science as institution. This Vichianism of Kuhn is a result of his focus on science from the historical perspective of "doing science" rather than from the logic of scientific theory formation. For Kuhn, a scientific paradigm on which the puzzle-solving of "normal science" depends requires the total human commitment of a particular scientific community involving "an inextricable mixture" of the descriptive, the explanatory, and the normative—not to mention the aesthetic. The acceptance of a new paradigm rising out of an anomaly or the failure in the puzzle-solving capacity of an old paradigm requires the same total human commitment. A scientific revolution is brought about not merely by the objective evidence it presents but also by the normative judgment of a community of practitioners. It is no accident that for Kuhn a scientific revolution resembles the revolution of political institutions; and a fight for the ruling paradigm is a political fight. He writes that as there can be "no scientifically or empirically neutral system of language or concepts, . . . [s]cientific knowledge, like language, is intrinsically the common property of a group or else nothing at all. To understand it we shall need to know the special characteristics of the groups that create and use it."[79]

Like Kuhn, Polanyi too stresses the idea of the "republic of science" in which the validation of scientific truth is achieved by an admixture of both factual and valuational judgments. Polanyi writes:

> For one thing, there are no mere facts in science. A scientific fact is one that has been accepted as such by scientific opinion, both on the grounds of the evidence in favour of it and because it

appears sufficiently plausible in view of the current scientific conception of the nature of things. Besides, science is not a mere collection of facts, but a system of facts based on their scientific interpretation. It is this system that is endorsed by a scientific authority. And within this system this authority endorses a particular distribution of interest intrinsic to the system; a distribution of interest established by the delicate value-judgments exercised by scientific opinion in sifting and rewarding current contributions to science. Science *is what it is,* in virtue of the way in which scientific authority constantly eliminates, or else recognizes at various levels of merit, contributions offered to science. In accepting the authority of science, we accept the totality of all these value-judgments.[80]

By regarding all knowledge both scientific and otherwise as *personal,* that is, as neither entirely objective nor entirely subjective in the traditional usage of these terms, Polanyi attempts to emancipate the conception of science from the scourge of positivism.[81] He comes to the conclusion that scientific knowledge is personal on the basis of what scientists actually do or how scientific truth is established in the republic of science, that is, of the *logic of tacit knowing* rather than the logic of scientific explanation alone.[82] The logic of scientific explanation such as the formal rules of verification and the fulfillment of predictions alone, according to Polanyi, cannot comprehend the actual experience of doing science or making a new scientific discovery. For "doing science" involves elements of personal judgment (including a moral one), an act of interpretation even in the most elementary stages of scientific cognition, a normative commitment of the fundamental kind, the politics of scientific apprenticeship or learning by doing as the process of socialization which involves the acceptance of communally established rules, the politics of research and publication, etc. They all are embodied in the tradition and institution of science. In claiming a scientific discovery, for example, a scientist "will always meet any opposition of scientific opinion as it *is* by appealing against it to scientific opinion as he thinks it *ought to be.*"[83] To sum up then, the nature of scientific knowledge, according to Polanyi, is ultimately based on the "scientific conscience" of every scientist. By scientific conscience Polanyi means that while the government of science prescribes, albeit tacitly, the rules that individual scientists as players must abide by in determining research, the validation of data and ultimately scientific truth are subject to the interpretation of individual players in it. It is like a game in which "the player has discretion to apply the rules to each run as he thinks fit."[84] Thus the individual scientist "appears acting here as detective, policeman, judge, and jury all rolled into one."[85] It is not merely arbitrary or subjective because it exists within the game of science in which individual scientists participate. In any game, moreover, there are other players with whom a game is being played. In other words, the game of science is not arbitrary or subjective, but it is intersubjective.

All in all, scientific conceptualization is *true* precisely because it is an order of the man-made (*factum*). The rigor of Vico's *verum/factum* principle coupled with the idea of science as institution, I think, paved the radically new way of inventing the "first philosophy" by integrating all the sciences as the spiritual and cultural accomplishments of humanity. To be conceptually rigorous and to be humanly radical are synonymous. For the "origin" of science is man himself: it is made by and for man. Ultimately the end of the "academy," "community," or "republic" of science is the account of humanity for humanity and the end of a new science is the account of humanity for a new humanity.

Chapter 5

A Critique of Political Behavioralism as Scientific Epistemology

The victory of behavioralism in political science has been the victory of the "calculative thinking" of scientism.[1] Inasmuch as "calculative thinking" has been the *Weltanschauung* of modern man and his world, political behavioralism is merely one aspect of its manifestation. In his famous "epitaph for a monument of a successful protest" that accounts for the history and future prospective of political behavioralism as a movement, Robert A. Dahl speculates that political behavioralism will gradually disappear as a distinctive mood and outlook, if it has not already been incorporated into the main body of political science as a discipline, not because it has failed but because it has succeeded, that is, its sectarian and factional outlook will be the first victim of its own triumph.[2] However, Heinz Eulau believes that political behavioralism will continue to remain as a separate and distinct approach in political science unless, of course, there is an unpredictable failure of nerve.[3]

Whether or not political behavioralism is a sectarian epistemology, Eulau once observed that there is fierce resistance to increasing the knowledge of politics through behavioralist analysis and wittingly suggested that the study of *why* it is resisted is assigned to the sociology of knowledge and the study of *how* this resistance might be cured or overcome is relegated to psychoanalysis.[4] In response to Eulau, phenomenology in turn is now able to *show* why scientism has become a thaumaturgy for contemporary political science and how it might be cured. Max Scheler suggests that phenomenology is therapeutic in dealing with ontological "illusion" and epistemological "error" in the way we think and know. According to him, there are two types of psychotherapist: the first is called "the psychic surgeon" who interferes with the psychic experiences of the patient in order to bring about a certain desired result, to bring him back to "normalcy"; the second is a "Socratic" who leads the patient to insight into himself. Scheler writes:

> the Socratic psychotherapist neither can nor will ever criticize the content of his patient's life, morally or in any other way.... His unique goal is to get the patient to see and survey the content of his life as completely as possible. What the patient then does with his life is his own affair (or a matter of ethics), not the doctor's. Psychotherapy cannot change the content or the value of his life. It can change only what and how much the patient takes in and comprehends and the way in which he does so.[5]

In our phenomenological critique of political behavioralism, we hope to adopt the Socratic method of psychotherapy. In discussing behavioralism as a distinct scientific approach in the study of politics, therefore, the aim of this chapter is not so much to show how, as Wittgenstein once described his mission of philosophizing, the fly can get out of its bottle, as to show, hopefully, that it is indeed caught in a bottle.

Insofar as political behavioralism is a revolt against the tradition of institutionalism, not unlike phenomenology it is a return to the concept of behavior as the focal point of its analysis of politics. Most importantly, Eulau in the language similar to Schutz explicitly recognizes the qualitative difference between what is behavioral and what is merely natural. Eulau writes:

> The behavioral persuasion in politics is concerned with what man does politically and the meanings he attaches to his behavior.... The physical scientist seems to have one great advantage over the political scientist; whatever meanings he may give his objects of study, they do not talk back to him. Atoms, neu-

trons, or electrons do not care how they are defined; political actors do mind. This is precisely why a political science that ignores man is necessarily a very incomplete science of politics.[6]

Therefore, Eulau emphasizes the importance of the meaning the actor attaches to his action. The presence of meaning, he insists, makes the study of human behavior different from the study of natural phenomena. Moreover, he maintains that the observation of political behavior must meet the test of an intersubjective agreement between observer and observed. There must be an agreement between the meaning given to behavior by the observer and that given by the actor himself. This, however, means not that the observational language of political science should be the same as the language of the political actor, but rather that their meanings must be compatible with each other. Political behavioralism, as Eulau sees it, raises the basic question of man, beginning with the idea that "the root is man" and ending with the idea that "the goal is man." The behavioral persuasion in politics considers the "analysis of man" and human behavior as its central theme of investigation based on Graham Wallas's theory of "human nature in politics" whose tradition goes as far back as John Locke's, David Hume's, Jeremy Bentham's, and John Stuart Mill's empiricist and utilitarian views of society as analyzable only in terms of "human nature" or individual behavior.[7] Consistent with Mill's "inductive method" of science, political behavioralism shifts the focus of its research toward psychological man dissociating itself from the institutionalist approach, that is, the behavior of a person or a group of persons rather than "events," "structures," "institutions," or "ideologies" has become the center of its attention. The aim of political behavioralism, however, is more radical than Mill's conception of the behavioral sciences as "moral sciences."[8] For, generally speaking, it has nothing to do with a normative philosophy of human nature.

Eulau also rejects the early psychological behaviorism of the "stimulus-response" type as having little in common with modern behavioral inquiry in politics. Whereas early reflexiology exorcised the mental from the social sciences, modern behavioral science

> is eminently concerned not only with the acts of man but also with his cognitive, affective, and evaluative processes. "Behavior" in political behavior, then, refers not simply to directly or indirectly observable political action but also to those perceptual, motivational, and attitudinal components of behavior which make for man's political identifications, demands and expectations, and his systems of political beliefs, values, and goals.

"Behavioral" is, therefore, preferable to "behavioristic," and I shall use it in the dynamic sense.[9]

Insofar as he recognizes the ontological difference between what is behavioral (or human) and what is merely natural, Eulau is not committed to the illusion of physical objectivism. However, insofar as he insists on the "canons of scientific method" as defined in the model of the natural sciences, he is committed to the epistemological error of scientism. What is unresolved or unresolvable in his approach is the paradox between ontological and methodological (or scientific) requirements in the study of political conduct. However, in the end the latter dictates the former. That is to say, in order to keep his scientific method intact, the political behavioralist must identify his notion of behavior with overt (or observable) behavior. Specifically, in order to conserve quantitative measurement, observation, and empirical testability, covert phenomena (such as intentions, beliefs, motives, feelings, and values) must be either translated into the "observable contexts" or inferred from overt behavior or the "behavior event." Thus behavior *is* really overt behavior or only the external indications of action. So-called "private" and motivational phenomena are reduced to overtly "observable" events or the external components of action. Thus "consciousness" is treated often, if not always, as a kind of the philosopher's myth, a fable, or a ghost in a machine. At best, it is treated merely as "sensitivity," "awareness," and "discernment," in contradistinction to "knowledge" or "intelligence."[10]

Correlatively, therefore, political behavioralism—like psychological behaviorism—may know a "physics" of the mind or the body but knows nothing of the human body as an active *subject* of perception, feeling, and cognition. Political behavioralism may understand the body as object (*Körper*), but it is unaware of the body as subject (*Leib*). Without the body as an active mode of his existence, man would be just an "absentee landlord" in the world. By means of his body as an active medium, man relates himself to the world and other people, and he "extends" (Marshall McLuhan's sense) himself to the making of cultural objects. As we have emphasized in chapter 2, it is not only as a rational animal but as a creature of flesh and blood that man distinguishes himself from other animals. Not only his rationality but also his bodily expressions, body language, or the "conversation of gestures" are also uniquely human. The tools or instruments man makes, for example, are referred to as *handi*works or *handi*crafts. In a rudimentary sense the idea of *homo faber* indicates the ability of the human to tame, modify, and change his environment through the movement of his body. Through his body man also mediates between himself and the other. The space defined by his body becomes a precondition for communication between himself and the social world as a whole. Only by recognizing that "I am *here*" am I able to determine that "he is *there*." By means of his spatial position which only the body can mediate, man has direct access to things and people. His body is an indispensable medium not only for the self-interpretation of his own lived experience but also for his perception and understanding of others. In terms of the phenomenological ontology of man as discussed in chapter 2, in short, political behavioralism is inattentive and impervious to (1) the intentional structure of human action as "project" and (2) the body as lived rather than as a merely physical thing—an inert object.

Having noted the inadequacy of the behavioralist conception of human action, the primary question in political inquiry is the nature of political knowledge. Although the center of the controversy between the supporters and the opponents of political behavioralism has been on the nature of value or evaluation, we shall shift the focus of our inquiry to the question of political knowledge. For, broadly speaking, it indeed encompasses the question of value judgments. Questions concerning the nature of political knowledge are not, strictly speaking, scientific: they are questions of philosophy, of which epistemology is only a part. Those political scientists who talk about political science as a discipline, regardless of their persuasions, are in fact turning to philosophy. For political science as a purely empirical discipline cannot deal with these questions. Phenomenology is a metascientific inquiry into political science as an empirical discipline, whereas political behavioralism claims to be a science. Nonetheless, political behavioralism, as "ism" suggests, is also a philosophical approach to the study of politics. To talk about the nature of political behavioralism is not "doing science" but "doing philosophy." Curiously enough, however, political behavioralists in general are rarely willing to admit that they are engaged in philosophical discourse for the reason, I suspect, that they regard philosophy as an exclusively normative discipline. They shun philosophy precisely because they are unaware of philosophy's critical function. To paraphrase Stanley Cavell, philosophy is shunned in political behavioralism not because philosophy zealously guards its own territory but because political behavioralists guard themselves against it.[11]

As a critique of political science, phenomenology is not so much a particular body of knowledge as it is a vigilance or constant reminder not to forget the *human* source of political knowledge. Phenomenologically viewed, the philosopher then is not a possessor of knowledge but rather a perpetual beginner who takes nothing for granted and for whom everything is in principle questionable. On the other hand, there can be no rivalry between scientific knowledge and philosophical questioning. "A science without philosophy," Merleau-Ponty declares, "would literally not know what it was talking about. A philosophy without methodical exploration of phenomena would end up with nothing but formal truths, which is to say, errors."[12] Phenomenology whose battlecry is the return to experiential and factual things is a radical empiricism. In this sense, Merleau-Ponty speaks of "phenomenological positivism"[13] and Don Ihde performs "experimental phenomenology."[14] Following Husserl, Merleau-Ponty insists that the empirical sciences have the "first word," whereas philosophy has the "last word" and as such its autonomy comes *after* rather than before empirical knowledge. There must be a mutual reliance or interdependence rather than a "cold war" or "segregation" between the two. Even from the standpoint of an empirical scientist, therefore, he "philosophizes every time he is required to not only record but comprehend the facts. At the moment of interpretation, he is himself already a philosopher."[15] Phenomenological philosophy, however, is not simply a methodology in the empirical sciences. It insists that what is empirical or factual must not be determined by any prior methodological commitment. When every fact is reduced to method and when science is judged merely on *how* rather than *what* it does, then there is the birth of methodolatry, where the medium becomes the message and what is important is not what but how it is done and said. In scientism as methodolatry, methodological consideration dictates the nature of human reality or the ontology of man: in it, in brief, *ontology presupposes epistemology.*

Rigor as the conceptual *modus operandi* is a declared motto and trademark of political behavioralism as scientific epistemology. In it the garb of scientific ideas has replaced prescientific knowledge in which the nature of man also partakes of the character of physical nature in order to subject it to exact and precise measurement. Human data are being treated like natural or physical phenomena and reduced to the physical or even the artificial. The philosophical justification for the behavioral approach in political science as a *predictive* science with an emphasis on artificial model building is embedded in the spirit and language of logical positivism, naturalism, and operationalism. The methodological isomorphism of the human sciences and the natural sciences has been motivated by the phenomenal success of post-Galilean physics in predicting natural phenomena.

This has been accompanied by technological innovations and break-throughs as well as by mathematical precision and exactitude. Physi-calism attempts to create "a self-consistent system of unified sci-ence capable of being utilized for successful prediction."[16] Sociology (or physicalistic sociology) is for Otto Neurath the way of discovering sociological laws congruent with the laws of physics which can be utilized for prediction. For the positivist doctrine of science, predic-tion is the essence of scientific explanation. In political science, physicalism is the strait–jacket definition of what ought to constitute scientific analysis by casting the abstract methodological net to capture what is concretely political.

On the other hand, however, phenomenology insists that because the human order is radically or qualitatively different from the natural order, it may not be isomorphically amenable to the tech-niques of the natural sciences. The *scientific* character of the human sciences should not be prejudged by the ready-made conceptual and methodological garment of the natural sciences. It must not be judged by how much physics, mathematics, and mechanics are found in it. To be sure, the scientific approach to human behavior is a recent event—in its infancy. The science of politics, however, is as old as the sciences of nature. Certainly, its slow or retarded development toward an exact, measurable, and predictive science, we begin to suspect, is due to something fundamentally endemic to the nature of *human* conduct which, unlike natural phenomena, defies the ideal order of regu-larities and uniformities.[17]

For many practitioners of scientific politics, theorizing or concep-tual analysis is equated with abstract model building. In this respect, T. D. Weldon's *The Vocabulary of Politics*[18] as a critique of the classical notion of political philosophy in terms of the positivist criteria of truth raised some important questions (e.g., the nature of value judgments) for the scientific conception of politics. However, it came under attack recently by the proponents of analytical model building. Brian Barry criticizes Weldon's work as being "an application of unreconstructed logical positivist criteria of meaning to traditional political thought rather than a detailed analysis of concepts" and he defines "analytical politics" as "the attempt to simplify the complex reality of a situation by picking out certain aspects of it and then building a model relating to these aspects."[19] It seems that Barry is critical not so much of Weldon's logical positivism as of the absence in this work of a con-structive, detailed analysis of political concepts themselves. For Barry, J. L. Austin's philosophy is paradigmatic to the model of "analytical politics." However, I believe he is wrong when he identifies the spirit of Austin's philosophy with the abstract analytical models of political science today because, as far as I can determine, analytical model building shares no common elements of the "linguistic phenomenology" (or the concept of language as performative) of which Austin himself speaks. Although it does not attempt merely to criticize traditional political concepts, analytical politics follows closely the positivist and operationalist criteria of meaning in its model building. Precisely because it is obsessed with conceptual model building rather than with the elucidation of the actual uses of political words, analytical politics commits the fallacy of misplaced concreteness.

Anthony Downs's *An Economic Theory of Democracy*,[20] which Barry considers as an *exemplar* of analytical politics, is an exercise in the positivist formulation of politics. For Downs, conceptual rigor is a methodological principle for building theoretical models used ultimately for the sake of prediction or in order to increase the reliability of predictive knowledge. He postulates that, after the model of "economic man," man seeks to maximize his self-interest, and his behavior is "rational" insofar as it is directed primarily toward selfish ends. Thus the model of "positive politics" as both a methodology and a theory of man is constructed from that of "positive economics." In the positivist model, theory is treated as "a body of substantive hypotheses" and is judged by "its predictive power for the class of phenomena which it is intended to 'explain.'"[21] For the exponent of positive economics Milton Friedman, the notion of prediction is limited not just to the forecasting of future events (that is, saying beforehand what will happen on the basis of theory and evidence); it is also extended to the causal explanation of "phenomena that have occurred but . . . on which [observations] have not yet been made or are not known to the person making the prediction."[22] Like the methodology of positive economics, the model of positive politics, too, aims at accurate prediction, which, Downs himself insists, has very little to do with the *real* world or "representation" of political man. Unlike the classical and conventional meaning of *theoria*, theory or model now is "a filing system" (Friedman's phrase) that facilitates prediction. Downs's model building is a methodolatry in the extreme, where conceptual rigor is likened to the rigid formulation of logical axioms and physical and mathematical theories. Analytical politics is eminently nomothetic in seeking political knowledge that is completely impersonal, generalizing, uniform, and lawlike and discredits the factual description of unique and individual events, that is, the ideographic or idiolectic understanding of political things.

For a phenomenological point of view concerning thought and action, the idea of rigor in political behavioralism is exclusively a methodological design, but it ignores another aspect of rigor that clarifies the nature of the theorist or the scientist as a *knowing subject*. The political behavioralist on the sheer weight of "empirical evidence" is able to observe the behavior of the observed, but he is incapable of observing his own behavior as an observer. If phenomenology is self-reflective of the possibility of knowledge, its *therapeutic* aim is to show the role of the scientist as an observing human being in the validation of his epistemic claims. Science is above all, as has already been discussed in the preceding chapter, a human activity which is founded upon the life-world as an ultimate horizon of meaning in everything we do and think; there is no science without scientists as human beings and the scientist cannot ignore his rootedness in the life-world as social reality. Knowing is a participating event or happening, the participation of the knower in the reality of things he observes; the knower is an observing participant in the ambient world. Thus Merleau-Ponty declares that "Because of the fact that the order of knowledge is not the only order, because it is not enclosed in itself, and because it contains at least the gaping chasm of the present, the whole of history is still action and action already history. History is the same whether we contemplate it as a spectacle or assume it as a responsibility."[23] In this light, Weldon's conception of political *philosophy* as a therapy of political words or linguistic confusions is ill-conceived, for it ignores the basic fact that language has no independent existence of its own apart from man who exists in the world. Words themselves do not lie; it is man as the user of words who lies, although he lies always by means of language: a lie without the liar is a scandalous abstraction. Therefore, it seems more correct to say that words do not need therapy; it is the speaking man or the user of language who needs it. To quote Merleau-Ponty again, therefore, "To deal with given languages objectively is not enough. We must study the subject who is actually speaking. To the linguistic of language we must add the linguistic of the word."[24] In the same vein, Peter Winch who follows Wittgenstein's philosophy of language is also critical of Weldon's positivist conception of philosophy as playing "a purely negative role in advancing our understanding of social life."[25] In Weldon, according to Winch, philosophy is crippled by its "underlabor" or "*under*estimation" which assures for itself a life parasitic to the empirical sciences in understanding social life. On the contrary, for Winch philosophy is able to deal with the nature of reality insofar as that reality is intelligible. "We cannot say then, with Weldon," he objects, "that the problems of

philosophy arise out of language *rather than* out of the world, because
in discussing language philosophically we are in fact discussing *what
counts as belonging to the world.* However, philosophy's concern with
language insofar as it *represents* the reality of the world is not an
empirical concern"; rather, philosophical issues are "to be settled by *a
priori* conceptual analysis rather than by empirical research."[26]

In brief, phenomenology as a rigorous philosophy is an archaeology of the knowing subject. Its rigor lies in its search for the presuppositions or sources of theoretical knowledge and activity, scientific or otherwise. It turns to the knowing subject as the locus of
investigation and thus to science as a human project, *praxis,* and
achievement, that is, to man as the thinking subject of the human
sciences. All objective knowledge—especially the objective knowledge
of the human, social sciences—is the abstraction from the straightforward experience of the life-world: "The whole universe of science," as
Merleau-Ponty puts it, "is built upon the world as directly experienced, and if we want to subject science itself to *rigorous scrutiny* and
arrive at a precise assessment of its meaning and scope, we must begin
by reawakening the basic experience of the world of which science is
the second-order expression."[27] The natural scientists, as we have
already pointed out, can abstract nature, discover the ideal order of
regularities and uniformities, control it, and exclude on principle
their personal and cultural concerns from their research. Unlike their
colleagues in the natural sciences, however, the social scientists cannot
exclude what Schutz has called "social reality," the very reality which
they are to investigate and whose subjects they are. In criticizing behaviorism (objectivist psychology) as practicing a "psychological Averroism" in ignoring the infrascientific strata of the life-world, Erwin
Straus comments that "objective psychology cannot exist without a
black market furnished with contraband from the psychology of living experience. For by its observations, descriptions, and communica-
tions it belongs to the human world. The scholar acts and talks, he
is pleased or he suffers, he is a man like all other men."[28] Thus phenomenology is critical of the methodological Averroism in which
the construction of the "artificial puppet" has nothing to do with "real
man." In the name of precision, exactness, and clarity, methodological
Averroists treat the "operational language" of theory as if it were
independent of the "natural prose" of political man, instead of viewing the former as the scientific construct of the prescientific understanding of political man himself. Far more important than this is the
phenomenological insistence that artificial constructionism or for-

malism cannot do away with the ill-structured, ambiguous data of the common-sense understanding of politics in the everyday life-world from which scientific constructs are abstracted.

Take the simple example of so-called "fact." It is like "a sack—it won't stand up till you've put something in it."[29] A fact is not "something out there," independent of an observer, but the result of an interpretation or interpolation, a comprehension of a thing or an event by a conscious, knowing subject. Michael Oakeshott thus declares:

> Fact, whatever else it may be, is experience; without thought there can be no fact. Even a view which separates ideas from things must recognize that facts are ideas. Fact is what has been made or achieved; it is the product of judgment. And if there be an unalterable datum in experience, it certainly cannot consist of fact. Fact, then, is not what is given, it is what is achieved in experience. Facts are never merely observed, remembered or combined; they are always made. We cannot "take" facts, because there are none to take until we have constructed them. And until a fact is established, that is, until it has achieved a place in a coherent world, it is no more than an hypothesis or a fiction.[30]

Facts are no more to be taken as "givens" than are values. A *factum* is a thing done, made, or experienced and as such, it reveals the accomplished performance of one who experiences in relation to an event, i.e., an interpretative participation of the knowing subject. The criterion of relevance always and decisively enters into the determination of a fact. By stressing the interrelatedness of "facts," "observation," and "theory" in scientific discovery, Norwood Hanson regards "facts" as not being "picturable, observable entities."[31] Facts in relation to theory, and in turn theory in relation to facts, are really hermeneutical events. Kuhn also shows that in scientific discovery, which is "a complex event" that "involves recognizing both *that* something is and *what* it is," both theory and fact, both conceptualization and observation are "inseparably linked."[32] For Merleau-Ponty, similarly, Husserl's *Wesensschau* (intuition of essences) is the mental operation which consists of a reading of the essential meaning structure of a multiplicity of facts. In theorizing, the factual and the essential are mutually related.[33] Therefore, there are no facts that are raw and crude (i.e., purely "given"). Needless to say, moreover, the language of statistics without interpolation is a disjointed, meaningless collection of dots, numbers, lines, and graphs. We are inclined to agree with

Sheldon Wolin when he says that "facts are more multifaceted than a rigid conception of empirical theory would allow" and that "nothing . . . is more necessary as a condition for theorizing than that facts not be univocal."[34]

The basic stuff of the life-world is made of approvals and disapprovals, that is, values. As the life-world is the arena of social reality as a network of interactions and transactions, values (and disvalues) embody human action. Political behavioralism maintains, however, the dualism of fact and value in the name of scientific judiciousness.[35] Instead of confusing the two realms, they must be kept apart and considered to be "logically heterogeneous."[36] This hallmark of value neutrality, which juxtaposes fact and value is the most acute manifestation of the behavioralist bifurcation of knowledge, science, methodology, and objectivity on the one hand and action, philosophy, ontology, and subjectivity on the other. The unbridgeable separation between fact and value epitomizes this bifurcation whose leitmotifs are "rigor" and "objectivity." Here political behavioralism is a faithful heir to logical positivism on the following two accounts. In the first place, there is a separation between philosophy and science. Being a philosophy, logical positivism is concerned with the logically and semantically true, relegating what is empirically true to the domain of science, whereas political behavioralism is concerned with the empirically true, regarding philosophy as a normative discipline (not necessarily logical and semantic). In the second place, for both, values are "preferences" which, as the ejaculation of personal emotions and beliefs, are devoid of epistemic content. So the aim of political science behavioralistically viewed is to increase the knowledge of political facts instead of creating political values. The emotive or noncognitivist view of value or ethics maintains that all true statements are descriptive, that is, they report or describe the state of affairs (stating "conditions" rather than professing "preferences"), and that to be true, all scientific statements must be descriptive.

The *logic* of science, political behavioralism argues, entails no moral commitment: science does not and cannot create values. Instead, according to Eulau, political science as "a behavioral science" has not attempted to make "the world a better place to live in. But it has given new hope that it might be a better place if political ignorance can someday yield to political knowledge."[37] The political behavioralist recognizes that values, interests, and even biases do influence a scientist's choice of topics, and may affect his observations and mislead him in reading scientific evidence. Even if "empirical explanation" and "ethical evaluation" are recognized as heterogeneous, the scientific student of political behavior "is not prohibited from asserting propositions of either kind separately or in combination as long as he does not mistake one for the other."[38] Further, the noncognitivist Felix E. Oppenheim distinguishes two kinds of value judgments, intrinsic and extrinsic (or instrumental), although they are not mutually exclusive. Intrinsic value judgments are judgments about what is good in itself, an end in itself, whereas instrumental value judgments are judgments about what is good, not for its own sake, but for the sake of some other goal, i.e., what is instrumental to achieving an intrinsic end. What is important here is Oppenheim's argument that "instrumental value judgments can always be translated without loss of meaning into 'if-then' or 'means-end' statements which contain no value words like 'good' or moral terms like 'ought'. Thus they are purely descriptive and hence ethically neutral; they belong as such to science, not to ethics."[39] In brief, therefore, the use of instrumental value judgments in no way violates the canons of scientific method. Accordingly, political science as a "policy science" (found in, e.g., Machiavelli's The Prince) may be regarded as a value-free scientific enterprise, for it is "an ethically neutral inquiry into the most effective means to reach a certain goal without concern for the question of the intrinsic desirability of the goal itself."[40]

Eulau repeatedly warns that value neutrality must not be confused with value neutralism, at least for the reason that political scientists obviously do participate in the struggle of politics. Whether or not they commit themselves on public issues, they are morally responsible and may be blamed or praised for their commitment or noncommitment. Being an act of morality, however, commitment or noncommitment has no relation to the intrinsic logic of science. It is a dictate of the inner voice of moral conscience, which can never be legislated by philosophy or science. Unlike philosophy, moreover, science knows neither values nor disvalues. Nor can its findings validate or invalidate values. Doing so would violate the norm of scientific judiciousness. What is worse is that, according to Eulau, the scientist has no control over another's use or misuse of his scientific findings. Nonetheless, political behavioralists argue that scientific activity requires social and political conditions conducive to the freedom of inquiry. The scientist must be "a free man," not only to carry on his scientific inquiry but also to make the moral choice of participating in or abstaining from political life; in this respect, science itself dictates a moral choice.

The idea of value neutrality in no way prevents the political behavioralist from investigating values scientifically or factually. For values are scientifically "observable facts." Although scientific inquiry cannot be concerned with what goal is best or what action is just as in moral philosophy, it cannot be prevented from investigating preferences, goals, and policies which are no more inscrutable than other aspects of political behavior. So human values can and should be studied scientifically, that is, according to the strict canons of scientific method. The study of human values is as much the birthright of science as of moral philosophy; ethics does not own a copyright on propositions of value. Eulau suggests, and somewhat arrogantly, I think, that the behavioral scientist, as a moralist but never as a scientist, is in a better position than a moral philosopher to determine the humanity or inhumanity of man, for the behavioral scientist has studied it factually ("I have been there"!) and, having been exposed to the factuality of values, presumably understands the human condition better than a moral philosopher.

In essence, according to the behavioralist doctrine of value neutrality, value judgments that are "categorical" or "intrinsic" are not empirically verifiable in contrast to value judgments that are "instrumental" or "extrinsic" and belong legitimately to the domain of scientific activity. They cannot be validated as "true" or "false," simply because they have no epistemic content, that is, they are emotive. The British philosopher J. L. Austin, however, contends that this emotive theory of value commits what he calls "the descriptive fallacy"; that is, not all statements are necessarily reporting or describing the state of affairs. There are statements which are "performative utterances." Performative utterances are "perfectly straightforward utterances, with ordinary verbs in the first person singular present indicative active, and yet we shall see at once that they couldn't possibly be true or false. Furthermore, if a person makes an utterance of this sort we should say that he is *doing* something rather than merely *saying* something" ("I do," "I apologize," "I promise," etc.).[41] For example, when I say "I promise that... , " I am performing an act; I am *doing* something rather than reporting something, or someone's act of promising, or his saying "I promise." I think political language, the ordinary prose of political man, is largely of a "performative" nature. If Austin's view is right, then the noncognitivist theory of value based on the heterogeneity of value and fact is misleading. For there are indicative statements which are outside its "verifiability" criterion of truth or falsity, validity or invalidity, and the heterogeneous purity of fact and value is no longer the logical question, the logic of the "is" and the "ought," but is the question of an *attitude*. Not only evaluations but perhaps all statements, both descriptive and normative, are expressions of attitudes, and "attitudes are in general but tenuously connected with emotion, since thoughts, words and deeds are much more central manifestations of them."[42] All knowledge is more or less personal or, better, *inter*personal. As political science as a theoretical activity is one of many human life-projects, its language cannot escape the ambiguous character of the prose of political man in the life-world, in which thoughts, words, and deeds are all mixed with "emotion" as well as "reason." Thus Austin's view—at least his treatment of language as "performative utterances"—refuses to accept the watertight containers of fact and value as something separable.

In the final analysis, a political behavioralist's demand for conceptual rigor leads to the insulation of fact from value, scientific objectivity from moral conscience, and the scientist from the moralist. Political behavioralists generally hold that value neutrality is not only desirable but is also the supreme *value* of scientific inquiry, invoking the *logic* of science. In Eulau, there is the apparent paradox of two conflicting claims: "science cannot create value," but "science dictates a moral choice" asserting the inalienable right of the scientist as a free man. At least here is a leakage in the "aseptic container" of values in the sea of detached scientific value neutrality. It appears to be a breakdown in the impeccable logic of science or a failure of scientific nerve in defense of the scientist as a free man. Political behavioralism, its policy science notwithstanding, stands steadfast by the side of scientific knowledge rather than the side of value and action. It has yet to become ambidexterous, that is, equally at home with both fact and value. If man is condemned to meaning, human meaning comes from the inextricable nexus of value and action on the one hand and fact and knowledge on the other. If value neutrality means scientific objectivity, and scientific objectivity means the exclusion of subjectivity or all personal elements, then science itself is unthinkable and scientific knowledge is inconceivable.[43] The logical consequence of value neutrality breeds social and political irresponsibility detrimental altogether to society. Speaking of the social irresponsibility of the behavioral scientist arising from value neutrality, Abraham Kaplan writes that "the policy maker wills ends without scientific assessment of their conditions and consequences, while the scientist exercises power without corresponding responsibility, refusing indeed, 'as a scientist', to assume responsibility."[44] Similarly, there is a kind of incipient nihilism in the logic of value neutrality in political behavioralism, which is not to say that the political behavioralist is a nihilist. When, as Eulau says, political science should be put at the service of "whatever goals men pursue in politics," when the political scientist cannot prevent any misuse of his findings as a scientist, and when he is not able to raise questions concerning whether or not he can act as "a democratic man," "a just man," or "a power seeking man," then the political behavioralist may become an innocent bystander or a fortuitous servant of death, evil, injustice, wrong, and oppression as much as of life, good, justice, right, and freedom. The logical consequence of *advocating* value neutrality as the supreme *value* of scientific inquiry, in addition to being contradictory in itself, is a birth of nihilism when scientific knowledge is exposed equally to good and evil: everything is permitted. Value and fact cannot be neatly divorced from each other in moral living or in scientific activity. For political science is a part of the political world as well as a conception of it. Existence and the conception of it, it is worth emphasizing again, are inseparably linked, for knowing, including scientific knowing, is a way of existing in the world.

To conclude: the phenomenological critique of the epistemology of political behavioralism in this chapter is based on the ideas, first, that the question of the nature of political knowledge cannot ignore the question of political science as a human project, *praxis,* and achievement; and, second, that the methodology of political science must be consonant with the nature of political things, the most basic component of which, the political behavioralist would agree, is the behavioral data of political man. Political behavioralism shows indifference to and intolerance of the living, and often ambiguous, dialectic of the "visible" ("outer") and the "invisible" ("inner") by bifurcating the objective and the subjective, science and the life-world, cognition and affectivity, value and fact, and finally action and thought. Political behavioralism as a scientific technique necessarily reduces the inner to the outer and takes the latter as the only legitimate domain of scientific enterprise. This physicalist view regards human consciousness as an epiphenomenon of the physical and is incapable of understanding the intentional structure of human behavior as a structure of meaning which is neither entirely subjective nor entirely objective in the traditional sense of these terms. Moreover, it ignores the notion of embodiment (*Subjektleib* or *sujet incarné*), the idea that the body is not a mere physical object but essentially is the *subject* of consciousness and behavior. Man may no longer be the physical center of the universe, just as the geocentrism of Ptolemy is replaced by the heliocentrism of Copernicus, but he is still the *meta*-physical center of the world.

The behavioralist methodological ideal of rigor, scientific objectivity, operational exactitude, quantitative measurement, and finally prediction, in order to build the citadel of an exact science after the model of the natural and mathematical sciences, especially mathe-matized physics, points to its indifference to science as a human project and the scientist as a human being living in a community both scientific and ordinary. It ought to be pointed out to the political behavioralist that inexactitude is a hallmark rather than a deficiency of the historical humanistic sciences; it is "only the fulfillment of a demand essential to this type of research."[45] Moreover, it would be a mistake to assume that exactitude translated in the logical language of scientific explanation, quantitative measurement, and mathematical expressions is a fail-safe guarantee for objectivity and its opposite, inexactitude, is an absence of it. Conceptual parsimony, or rather operational stricture, short-circuits the profusion of human experi-ence and is insensitive to the agility, elasticity, and ephemeral quality of human thought, ignoring the direct, experiential knowledge of political things in the everyday life-world as the source of scientific knowledge. The political behavioralist who refuses to recognize him-self as a *knowing subject* in the life-world or who thinks of himself as an *anonymous* epistemological subject may be likened to the philosophical solipsism Wittgenstein once enunciated: (to paraphrase Wittgenstein's passage) the behavioralist self is not the human being, not the human body or the human soul, but rather the scientific subject, the limit of the world—not a part of it.[46] Insofar as it touches on the visible or outer perimeter of man, behavioralist philosophy provides an incom-plete image of man and science. If the incomparable gadfly of ancient civilization, Socrates, is right in professing that the life unexamined is not worth living, then the foremost duty of scientific life is to examine and reflect on itself as a human *praxis*, which is the first order of rigor and magnitude.

Chapter 6

A Critique of the Cybernetic Model of Man in Political Science

The cybernetic model of man as physicalism in the study of politics represents the apex of political behavioralism as scientific epistemology. As such it deserves special attention. The aim of this chapter is to explore the limitations of the cybernetic model of man as both a theory of man and a technique which results in "sociologism" defined as the doctrine that minimizes or denies individual autonomy and initiatives in society and history.

Eulau claims that no segments of political behavior are intrinsically immune to scientific techniques. As scientific creativity knows of no predetermined limitations, all segments of political conduct can in principle, or potentially, be treated "behaviorally," since the future is always contingent, and contingencies are difficult to foresee. Methodology is viewed as potentially a question of technology when Eulau writes:

> I believe this question can be asked only if one assumes, *a priori*, that there *must* be aspects of political behavior intrinsically im-

mune to scientific analysis. But if one assumes the opposite, that political behavior, like all behavior, can be observed by the methods of behavioral science, the limits appear to be technological ones. Scientific technology knows its present limits; it cannot predict its future limits. As technology advances, the range of phenomena amenable to scientific analysis also expands. Therefore, it is really impossible to say that the data of politics are such that they cannot be harnessed by *any* scientific methods and techniques. The presently available technology has made possible the production and processing of political data, or data relevant to political behavior, that was, until recently, unavailable to political science.[1]

What Eulau has in mind is the possible perfection of computer technology and artificial intelligence. At any rate, the cybernetic model of man represents at present the highest stage of technological rationality in the study of politics. Eulau believes that the progress of science, like the "progressive" spirit of liberalism in which he has faith, has no *a priori* or inherent limitations.[2] His scientific faith can be challenged by the phenomenological consideration that man is an *embodied agent,* the idea which seems to point to the absolute limitation of artificial stimulation as applied to the understanding of human conduct. Phenomenology can show Eulau's scientific faith as a *false eschatology of techniques.*[3] The obvious fact that computers are not human or man is not a machine because he is an embodied agent ought to be elaborated. The technological limitations or possible perfection Eulau speaks of here is ultimately the question of whether the computer simulation of human embodied intelligence is limited or possibly perfectible.

The cybernetic model of man is both objectivism and scientism put together in one. To the extent that it incorporates both objectivism and scientism, it is both "illusionary" and "erroneous." It is the ultimate triumph and the paragon of what Heidegger calls "calculative thinking" over "meditative thinking." Thus the cybernetic model of man is the culmination of technological rationality. Heidegger's *The End of Philosophy* and Merleau-Ponty's *Eye and Mind* are by far the severest attack on it.[4]

According to Heidegger, the cybernetic model of man is the *exemplar* of today's Western thinking that is dominated by logistics, calculation, and technology. He envisions a new dawn of human thought with the destruction of technological rationality, the highest development of which is cybernetic thinking. While Husserl was critical of naturalism and scientism since the Galilean mathematization of nature for forgetting its rootedness in the life-world, Heidegger views technology as the forgetting of Being itself, the process of which began not with Galilean physics but with Platonism, the beginning of Western metaphysics. *Through* technology the annihilation of man in the atomic age is already an external possibility; *as* technology the cybernetic model of man is an internal threat to the being of man. As the denaturalization of nature by technology is the death of nature as already evidenced in the ecological crisis, the artificialization of man by cybernetics is the death of man. The artificialization of everything human coincides with what Richard Landers calls the arrival of the "dybosphere" replacing the "biosphere" in the forthcoming era in which everything "natural" will turn into something "artificial": in the new era or new prophesy, "men and machines will converge and become indistinguishable."[5] The artificial age, the age of cybernetics, is a providential fact in which the machine rather than man becomes the guardian of Being or the unmoved mover. In mirroring of man in the machine, the talisman of modern history, the Hegelian dialectic of the master and the slave is reversed or overcome in favor of the machine.[6] Man the machine in cybernetics heightens his "unhappy consciousness." The arrival of this artificial age is a tearless eulogy for the death of man leaving no visible monument behind him—it is tearless because the machine is incapable of sobbing or crying.

Merleau-Ponty is not so sweeping as Heidegger in his critique of cybernetic thinking. The main target of Merleau-Ponty's criticism is directed not so much to science as to the "philosophy of the sciences which reduces thinking to a set of techniques": thinking that reduces science to the functions of "operation" or a set of operations, artificialism imbedded in the ideology of cybernetics, "where human creations are derived from a natural information process, itself conceived on the model of human machines."[7] When man himself becomes the *manipulandum,* according to Merleau-Ponty, "we enter into a cultural regimen where there is neither truth nor falsity concerning man and history, into a sleep or a nightmare, from which there is no awakening."[8] While Stephen in James Joyce's *Ulysses* said that history is a nightmare from which he is trying to awake,[9] there is no awakening from history if it is defined in terms of a cybernetic model. Following Husserl, Merleau-Ponty is urging science which is the "admirably active, ingenious, and bold way of thinking" to restore "the soil of the sensible" as its foundation, to reclaim the body not as an information machine but as a "sentinel standing quietly at the command of my words and my acts"[10] which "operationalism" ignores. Thus for Merleau-Ponty, the notion of *embodiment,* the unity of consciousness and body as a structure of meaning, is the basis of his critique of the cybernetic model of man.

Artificialism or the cybernetic model of man in politics today does not even pretend to be, unlike the medieval, organicist notion of the "body politic," a metaphor or an analogy. For it claims to *be* the whole of man. It is the final outgrowth of the positivist misinterpretation of biology, psychology, epistemology, and ontology. As "to know is to measure" which the physicist Enrico Fermi has reportedly said, mathematics as the universal science (*mathesis universalis*) is the sole standard of measurement and prediction. As physics mathematizes nature, so now cybernetics mathematizes man in politics which inherited the tradition of Descartes's philosophy and Hobbes's philosophical politics as referred to in chapter 4. Hobbes founded the "mathematics of politics." In the theory of politics, he, who in *De Corpore* built the foundation of *De Homine* and *De Cive,* attempted to implement the tradition of both Galileo and Descartes in constructing the political system where the human body (and consequently the body politic) is treated merely as a physical mechanism (i.e., mechanistic psychology). After Galileo and Descartes, Hobbes emulated the ideal of *mathesis universalis.* He claimed mathematics or arithmetic as "a certain infallible art." For him, "reason" is the power of *"reckoning,* that is adding and subtracting, of the consequences of general names agreed upon for the *marking* and *signifying* for our thoughts."[11] In Hobbes's new politics, man is likened to a machine: his heart "a spring"; his nerves "strings"; and his joints "wheels." The Leviathan is an artificial man in which the political *"sovereignty* is an artificial *soul,* as giving life and motion to the whole body."[12] For Hobbes, then, *art* is a device of technology or the craftsmanship of a watchmaker. "The naturalism of a Hobbes," Husserl thus observes, "wants to be physicalism and like all physicalism it follows the model of physical rationality."[13] Since political reality is for Hobbes calculable by means of mathematical and mechanical thinking and its knowledge is the consequence of calculation or "logistics," he is in short the true harbinger of the mathematization of politics and cybernetic politics.[14]

Today in political science two Galileos of the artificial are Karl W. Deutsch and Herbert A. Simon, the authors of *The Nerves of Government* and *The Sciences of the Artificial,* respectively.[15] By reducing "theory" to "model," both claim "rigor" as the motto of any science. As in physics nature is a mathematical manifold, so political man is an artificial manifold. In rigor and theoretical design, both intend to surpass the formalistic logistics of Galileo, Descartes, Hobbes, or Norbert Wiener. For the founder of modern cybernetics, Wiener, the mathematization of man and society "can never furnish us with a quantity of verifiable, significant information which begins to compare with that which we have learned to expect in the natural sciences."[16] Thus he recognized the upper limits of cybernetics as applied to the social sciences because they are in many aspects "narrative," that is unscientific and inexact. Though they disavow the "metaphysical cargo" of Descartes, Deutsch and Simon are inheritors of the "intellectualism" of Descartes, of the Cartesian *Cogito* or the "I think" in formulating only "clear and distinct ideas" and the Cartesian dualism of mind and body. Insofar as Deutsch purports to recognize the ontological *differentia* between the human organism and the machine and the ways they function, Simon is more radical, that is, more artificial than Deutsch in building a model of man, because for Simon cognitive simulation is not just "a tool for achieving a deeper understanding of human behavior" but the proper study of mankind is not man but the science of artificial design and "simulation can tell us things we do not already know."[17]

Deutsch points out the shortcomings of both classical mechanism and organism in that the quantitative approach of the former excludes the qualitative categories of changes, growth, novelty, and purposes and the qualitative approach of the latter lacks details of quantitative measurement. Thus the cybernetic model he proposes is an alternative model to remedy the shortcomings of mechanism and organism in that it is "applicable to problems involving both quantity and quality . . . [by] facilitating the recognition of patterns, together with measurement and verifiable predictions."[18] In seeking a substantial unity between the mental and the physical, Deutsch claims that his model is strikingly different from the Cartesian mode of thought that makes a sharp division between the process of mind and the physical world. Although Deutsch acknowledges the complexity of human information processing, the present technological impossibility of building a complex machine that performs adequately the functions of human thought process and the dynamic quality of the human mind, his cybernetic model nonetheless succumbs to physicalism and scientism. For Deutsch, the human mind is comparable to the information process of artificial intelligence: it is a single-run pattern of information flow in the machine. Information is defined as a patterned relationship between events which is physical, being carried by matter-energy processes; and because it is different from "form" it is analyzable into *discrete units* (or *atomic facts*) that can be quantitatively measured. Subsequently, for Deutsch, in echoing Hobbes's notion of reason, the mind is "any self-sustaining physical process which includes the nine operations of selecting, abstracting, communicating, storing, subdividing, recalling, recombining, critically recognizing and reapplying [discrete] items of information."[19] As a symbol is an order to recall from memory a particular thing or event, meaning is by the same token a physical position in a squence of events. In short: in mapping out his cybernetic geography of man, Deutsch treats consciousness as an analogue to the purely internal processes of any electronic network, though he, not unlike Hobbes who affirms the "romantic doctrine of personality with its assertion of the primacy of will"[20] as the last appetite, criticizes mechanism for leaving no room for consciousness or will.[21] In essence, according to Deutsch, contemporary thought has progressed in such a way as to assert that both the mental and the physical world are accessible to an analysis of science. Although for him there is an important qualitative difference between mind and nature, it is not absolute since the mind itself is not something outside physical nature: it is "one of *nature's* most creative processes." As the mind as well as the body is an extension of nature itself, unlike Descartes, Deutsch is committed to naturalism. When the mind is regarded as the most precious gift of nature itself, there is no incompatibility between intellectualism and naturalism. Insofar as the mind is the "intellect," it is no "ghost in the machine": it is merely of machinelike quality.

For Simon, the science of man *is* the science of the artificial which is here to stay and will be no longer "the target of cheap rhetoric." To "operationalize" human thinking, it must be reduced to the mathematical formulation of artificial intelligence. For the study of artificial intelligence is necessarily mathematical. The model of man in terms of artificial intelligence is then the mathematization of man. As psychology is a science of the artificial, the computer simulation of human thinking is also the mathematization of thinking. To make any concept "operational" is to reduce it to a discrete item or datum. The acquisition of language itself, when operationalized, is the process of artificialization. Simon thus declares that "there is no contradiction, then, between the thesis that a human being possesses, at birth, a competence for acquiring and using language and the thesis that language is the most artificial, hence also the most human of all human constructions."[22]

By "artificial" Simon means "man-made" as opposed to "natural";[23] the synonyms for artificial intelligence are "complex information processing" and the "simulation of cognitive processes." He says that "the world we live in today is much more a man-made, or artificial, world than it is a natural world."[24] And the significant parts of our environment are strings of artifacts called "symbols." For Simon, to explain the behavioral sciences the two most important fields are "cognitive psychology" and "engineering design" (or engineering logistics). Artificiality itself is defined as "perceptual similarity but essential difference, resemblance from without rather than within."[25] In Simon, then, the Cartesian dualism of the inner and the outer disappears when the former is submerged in the latter or when the inner environment becomes simply a function of the outer environment. As simulation is both to understand and to predict the behavior of any system, it is also a technique to understand and predict the organization of the human mind (or the process of thinking) which can be known without knowing the physiological structure of the brain. As physiology or neurophysiology is not necessary to understand the process of thinking, knowledge of the body is not necessary to understand the mind, that is, the inner environment of the "adaptive system" called *"Homo sapiens."* Simon argues for—to use his own term—"the disembodiment of mind." Similarly, when *"only the thinkable is expressible"* and *vice versa*—which Simon considers to be a Kantian formulation, then the inner environment of thinking is determined by the outer environment of symbolic expression, verbal or otherwise (i.e., "behavioral"). To understand and predict it, human behavior must be formalized into "laws" and "rules." Simon then assumes that "in principle at least, human behavior can be represented by a set of independent propositions describing the inputs to the organism, correlated with a set of propositions describing its outputs."[26]

As Hubert L. Dreyfus has recently shown in his *What Computers Can't Do* in the philosophical tradition of Kierkegaard, Husserl, Heidegger, and Merleau-Ponty, the very failure of "cognitive simulation" so far to live up to euphoric predictions for its future achievement indicates that not everything is perfect with the attempt to explain human thinking and acting in terms of cybernetics or artificial intelligence. As long as human thinking is never the function of the disembodied mind, as Simon claims it to be, but of embodiment, of the unity of consciousness and body as a structure of meaning, the sciences of man can never be reduced to the sciences of the artificial. Inasmuch as embodiment is one of the central themes of phenomenology, it is an *antibody* to the cybernetic model of man. By reducing what is human to the "I think" or pure intelligence, Deutsch and Simon are unaware of the body as *subject* (of the "lived body") of everything we do, of thinking, acting, speaking, expressing both verbally and nonverbally, perceiving, feeling, etc. In discussing human thought or knowledge they ignore the tacit dimensions (including that

of the body) that underlie and presuppose it. W: n language is reduced to the artificial strings of symbols and when a word is made
"operational," which means to reduce it to the univocity of meaning as
a discrete item, Deutsch and Simon forget not only the *use* and *performance* of language or language as speech acts but also the fecundity
of human expressions, particularly such bodily expressions as gestures, crying, laughing, frowning, etc. For example, we may say with
Sartre that in societies of men human faces rule; and "the extremity
of the human body"[27] called the human face as an embodiment of
expressions cannot be drawn like a complex object, as Simon suggests,
by inserting first eyes, nose, mouth, ears, hair and then pupils, eyelids,
lashes for the eyes, and so on.[28] We cannot comprehend the "complex
system" of a human expression by "decomposing" it into *discrete* items.
On the contrary, to understand language we must understand it *subjectively* in terms of the way it is used or performed by the subject in a
community of other subjects. Language must be understood as a
"form of life" (Wittgenstein) or Being-in-the-world (Heidegger). The
acquisition of language is the most natural rather than the most artificial of all that is human precisely because it involves

> a kind of *habituation*, a use of language as a tool or instrument.
> The employment of language, which is an effect and also one of
> the most active stimuli of intellectual development, does not
> appear to be founded on the exercise of pure intelligence but
> instead on a more obscure operation—namely, the child's assimi-
> lation of the linguistic system of his environment in a way that is
> comparable to the acquisition of any habit whatever; the learn-
> ing of a structure of conduct.[29]

Also, according to Wittgenstein, the teaching of language to the child
is not "explanation" but is "training."[30] Language in both learning
and teaching is therefore as much natural as human habits. As language is the primal medium of socialization which is the dialectical
interchange of the inner (the subject) and the outer (his environment)
rather than the one-way conditioning of the former by the latter, it
must first be defined in terms of the intentional structure of consciousness as meaning—the product of an interchange of the inner
and the outer. This intentional structure of meaning is called the
"inner form of speech" (*innere Sprachform*) by Humboldt.[31] This is
why language cannot be reduced to a grammar as "the sum of mor-
phological, syntactical, and lexical meanings" alone and also why
speech as an act is prior to language as the established institution of

fixed meanings. Thus, according to Dreyfus, "not all linguistic behavior is rulelike."[32] For Gadamer, too, "language is not a system of signals that we send off with the aid of a telegraphic key when we enter the office or transmission stations."[33] If the performance of language or the speech act is a habituation or is seen as lived, we do not follow strict rules alone: "In general," Wittgenstein says, "we don't *use* language according to strict rules—it hasn't been taught us by means of strict rules either."[34] We should note here that although for Michael Oakshott it is *intrinsically* a language of rules or laws (*lex*), human conduct as the *civil* discourse or transaction of agents cannot be reduced to the naturalistic *regularity* of "behavior." To be sure, rules are authoritative, obligatory, and prescriptive; but they are not a fixed stock of language games. Hence the rule is only an identifiable or specifiable *condition* or *postulate* of human conduct (i.e., the conditionality of rules in the performance of action). Thus in *On Human Conduct*, Oakeshott speaks of

> practices as languages of self-disclosure and self-enactment: the language of diplomacy, of scientific or historical inquiry, the Latin language, or the language of moral utterance and intercourse. For a language is not a fixed stock of possible utterances, but a fund of considerations drawn upon and used in inventing utterances; a fund which may be used only in virtue of having been learned and being understood, which is learned only in being used, and which is continuously reconstituted in use.[35]

Because in communication human linguistic performance does not always follow simply grammato*logical* rules alone, what the speaker is trying to say, even if he makes a grammatical error, is understood by or understandable to the listener: even someone's "broken" speech or language can be understood by others. On the contrary, however, the computer or cognitive simulation "cannot accept ambiguity and the breaking of rules until the rules for dealing with the deviations have been so completely specified that the ambiguity has disappeared. To overcome this disability, AI [artificial intelligence] workers must develop an a-temporal, nonlocal, theory of ongoing human activity."[36]

To identify or equate the "I think" with the "I express" (and *vice versa*), as Simon does, is to ignore the tacit dimensions of thought and expression—the former being far richer than the latter. The identification of thought with expression ignores the active assimilation of meaning (or meanings) that the subject intends or does not intend to express. What is signified (both the "I think" and what is thought) is not identical with what is signifiable (the "I can"). We think more than we can express, for to express is not just to express for others but first to know what we intend. Thus in relation to thought, expression is never total. As for Simon the inner is merely a function or "response" to the outside "stimulus," both thought and expression are ultimately the reactions to the outer environment. If expression is not just for others, then there is a fundamental difference between "saying" and "meaning" on the one hand and between "saying to others" (dialogue) and "saying to myself" (monologue) on the other and it makes sense to say that "we know or mean more than we can express or say." The identification of thought with expression must reject the existence of inner speech, conversation with oneself. If thought is an inner conversation with oneself, then speech is the underlying foundation of thought. As inner speech precedes outer expression, in communicating our thought with others (in expression) the schematization of the signified comes after the act of speech since the former is the result of the latter. "One does not know what one is saying," Merleau-Ponty thus writes, "one knows after one has said it."[37] To do full justice to thought, expression, and ultimately language, we must understand them in terms of their dialectical interchange rather than their one-to-one correspondence (i.e., their causal relationship); we must understand them as capable of a dialectical mediation between the signifying, the signified, and the signifiable.

The cybernetic model of man reduces everything human (including language) to, if not the physical level, the rulelike or lawlike formalization of analyzable, determinate, and unambiguous discrete bits of data or what Wittgenstein calls in the *Tractatus* a set of "atomic facts,"[38] which is the essence of "calculative thinking." "This assumption that the world can be exhaustively analyzed in terms of determinate data or atomic facts," Dreyfus declares, "is the deepest assumption underlying work in AI and the whole philosophical tradition."[39] The cybernetic model of man is an odd combination of both intellectualism and empiricism (particularly logical atomism and physicalism), both of which are unable to understand the intentional structure of human consciousness (including its "intellective" component) and thus *fully* the human. Simon's notion of the disembodiment of mind is crucial to a phenomenological critique of the cybernetic model of man. Insofar as it treats the human mind as a disembodied thing and reduces everything to a "mental" phenomenon, it is in the tradition of Descartes's intellectualism (or idealism); insofar as it further treats everything "mental" as a determinate, unambiguous physical fact or datum for observation and formalization, it inherits the empiricism of Locke and Hume and its tradition. As an odd combination of intellectualism and empiricism, the cybernetic model of man is incapable of describing the peculiar way in which human consciousness (including perceptual consciousness) constitutes its object in the life-world whose experiential events, unlike the atomic facts of physical things, are indeterminate and ambiguously structured. Thus Merleau-Ponty writes:

> Where empiricism was deficient was in any internal connection between the object and the act which it triggers off. What intellectualism lacks is contingency in the occasions of thought. In the first case consciousness is too poor. In the second too rich for any phenomenon to appeal compellingly to it. Empiricism cannot see that we need to know what we are looking for, otherwise we would not be looking for it, and intellectualism fails to see that we need to be ignorant of what we are looking for, or equally again we should not be searching.[40]

The ambiguity and indeterminacy of human consciousness (and thus what is human) can be shown by how its perceptual infrastructure functions. As shown in the famous "Peter-Paul Goblet," perception is a gestalt and of perspectival character. Depending on a focus of attention, on a perspective, one sees in the picture the faces of "Peter and Paul" facing each other or one goblet. As a gestalt or a "field," perception relies on the "figure" and the "background," on the unity of inner and outer horizons (or fringes). Perception as a gestalt is not, as logical atomism claims it to be, divisible into determinate and discrete atomic elements nor, as intellectualism claims it to be, is it just a mental image mirrored in mind. Because the figure and the background are mutually interdependent and also reversible (in perception), they are perceived as two faces at one time and one goblet at another.

The cybernetic model of human thought, as we have said, is unaware of the tacit dimension which underlies conceptualization and symbolization when every word, every meaning, every symbol or sign, and every concept is reduced to an univocity, an unambiguous and discrete item that Descartes calls a "clear and distinct idea." It ignores the tacit dimension which is far richer than conceptual or symbolic thought. However, conceptual or cognitive meaning (*Bedeutung* or *signification*) is the developed refinement of felt and experiential meaning (*Sinn* or *sens*): the latter is the infrastructure of the former. Merleau-Ponty, William James, Gabriel Marcel, and Eugene Gendlin (among others) all express, though in different ways, the same thought. It is in *The Principles of Psychology* (1890) that James made the distinction between "knowledge-about" and "knowledge by acquaintance" and attempted to show the dependency of the former on the latter. As pure (not yet conceptualized) experience is feeling, knowledge by acquaintance is felt knowledge, whereas knowledge-about is thought knowledge: "Through feelings we become acquainted with things [directly], but only by our thoughts do we know about them. Feelings are the germ and starting point of cognition, thoughts the developed tree."[41] One is precognitive, presymbolic, preconceptual, precategorial, preverbal, and felt, whereas the other is cognitive, symbolic, conceptual, categorial, verbal, and thought. Thus there is the mutual relatedness between feeling and symbolization. Insofar as the latter is dependent upon the former, one is "superior" and the other "inferior" in value. According to Gendlin,[42] felt meaning is the presymbolic, ongoing flow of experienc*ing*. It has an important function in what we think, observe, and perceive and in how we behave. Although it is to be articulated fully in symbols, this raw and felt flowing mass of human experience is richer and broader than thought, observation, speech, and action. Unlike symbolic meaning, this felt meaning is "an inward sensing" which is definitely there inside us as "a concrete mass" but it is hard to specify (in thought and expression) just what it is. Precognitive meaning, according to L. S. Vygotsky,[43] is a dim, amorphous, undifferentiated, and composite whole. In his theory of thought and language there is the distinction between "sense" and "meaning." The sense of a word is complex, dynamic, fluid, and protean, whereas the meaning of a word is only "one of the zones of sense." Sense is therefore nascent and latent (i.e., tacit) in relation to meaning; and there is always "a preponderance of the *sense* of a word over its *meaning*." Broadly speaking, then, meaning is not limited to what is symbolically expressive; it is not confined merely to the logical, syntactical, and semantic structures of symbols, i.e., to "analyzable elements or facts." As feeling and symbolization go hand in hand, one is capable of symbolizing his felt meaning or expressing it verbally in words or speech. Our thought is the mediation between felt meaning and symbols, and the latter have a direct and selective reference to the former. To say, as Simon does, that *only the thinkable is expressible* (and *vice versa*) is to ignore the dialectical interchange between thought and expression in human language, the dependency of symbolic meaning on felt meaning, and ultimately the existence of felt meaning altogether. In essence, he argues for *the disembodiment of mind* by means of cognitive simulation. As the computer is capable only of simulating determinate, unambiguous, and completely patterned bits of information, it is incapable of handling ambiguous, indeterminate, and ill-patterned data of the life-world and consequently the sciences of the artificial too are incapable of dealing with the "sloppy data" of the life-world. This is their ultimate limit.

In summary, the basic and radical difference between man and the machine is that man is a fully embodied agent, an agent with the living body necessary for both thinking and acting, whereas the machine is only a thing with an artificial body which, when not out of order, may be faster, more efficient, and more error-free than man. But at best it can be only a replica of man. Not out of human pride, as Simon alleges in the manner of John Stuart Mill,[44] an objection is raised here against the identification of man and the artificial or we insist that the intricacy of human community is radically different from that of an anthill, a beehive, or a society of computers or artificial man.[45] It is indeed feasible to produce servomechanisms that will surpass the human intelligence in speed and accuracy. The objection raised here is based not on the human pride of superiority but on the way in which man in his embodiment thinks and behaves qualitatively *differently* from any other organism or any mechanism whatsoever. In this sense, the machine may be either superhuman or subhuman but never be human. If this insistence is out of human pride, then let it be.

By proposing to reduce human thought to a "program" or "information flow" and the human body to an information container or hardware, Deutsch's cybernetic model and particularly Simon's sciences of artificial intelligence, both of which focus solely on the clear "thinking" or "intellective" component of man, help us to understand him as a "cyborg" but fail to understand him as a natural and embodied being. The computer can be understood as a disembodied brain, but what is human can never be understood by mind or body separately. It must be understood as *embodiment,* as a *psychophysical* unity with no hyphenation. The artificialization of man is a denial of man as embodiment. Herein lies indeed an answer to Eulau's faith that all segments of political behavior are accessible in principle to behavioralist techniques including cybernetics and that the progress of scientific analysis is just a question of technology in due time. The behavioralist philosophy of man and his conduct fails in the end to take into account the dialectic of thought and feeling (or of symbolic and felt meaning) on the one hand, and the body as an active mode of Being-in-the-world on the other. Above all, it suspends or leaves out the theorizer himself as the embodied subject of his own thought and action in the ambiguous everyday life-world as sociohistorical reality. As Socratic ignorance is the beginning of cognition, the tolerance of ambiguity is the beginning of recognition of what is human. In the end, the tolerance of ambiguity is the function of philosophy. Therefore, strictly speaking, there is no "science of science" but only the philosophy of science.

One of the most serious dilemmas that confronts the Cartesian notion of man as a union of mind and body as two *substances* (*res*) and its successor, the cybernetic model, in relation to the *social* sciences, is that they are incapable of rendering a philosophically consistent justification for intersubjectivity or sociality which is also intercorporeal. For, as Sartre has rightly pointed out, once the self and the other are regarded as substances, which is to say two separate substances, solipsism is inescapable.[46] In short, Cartesian substantialism is a denial of man as agent. In echoing the Vichian affirmation of the civil order of *history* as oppsed to the Cartesian *regularity of nature*, Oakeshott proposes that neither "understanding" as the "reflective consciousness" of the agent, which is an "exhibition of intelligence," nor the "civil condition" as a "human invention" (*factum*) is capricious because the understanding of human conduct and the civil condition is ultimately authenticated by the order of "conduct *inter homines*": "The myth of the necessarily egocentric agent is a denial of agency."[47]

Artificial man, man "designed" in the image of the machine or after "artificial intelligence," is neither "laborer," nor "worker," nor "actor." As "pure intelligence," he is no longer a laborer or worker, for to be a laborer or worker he needs "a metabolism with nature" by means of his body or hands to work in order to fabricate durable things. Moreover, artificial man is the "mass man" *par excellence* criticized by Kierkegaard, Marcel, Nicholas Berdyaev, Karl Jaspers, and José Ortega y Gasset. Being unable to have a social metabolism with other men, a collection of artificial men is the formless "crowd." For artificial men are all alike without distinction—without the distinction of being *this* or *that* man as an individual. Thus they are characterized by the undifferentiated sameness. A collection of artificial men is what Sartre calls "seriality" (*series*), a petrified or frozen collectivity rather than a "group" (*groupe en fusion*) in which conscious individuals come together in order to achieve a common project or goal. In short, man may always be more or less artificial but is never artificial. Artificial man is incapable of engaging in social action or interaction with others.

Man is by nature a political animal. This unimpeachable ancient wisdom was echoed recently by Hannah Arendt when she said: "No human life, not even the life of the hermit in nature's wilderness, is possible without a world which directly or indirectly testifies to the presence of other human beings."[48] Alfred Schutz, too, affirms that "as long as man is born of woman, intersubjectivity and the we-relationship will be the foundation for all other categories of human existence."[49] Thus the importance of sociality in man's experience of the world can never be overemphasized in the human, social sciences. In modern philosophy, it was Kant who spoke even of "asocial sociability"; Hegel regarded "recognition" as a matter of life and death and as an essential aspect of the development of self-consciousness; Feuerbach considered human thinking itself as a social process when he said: the true dialectic is "a dialogue between I and thou"; for Buber, all reality is social and nothing is real that is not social; and finally the Scottish philosopher John Macmurray proposes that man as agent in both thought and action is heterocentrically social through and through.[50] For Arendt, the conception of action is indispensable to founding and preserving political bodies; if, as she says, action is the exclusive prerogative of human beings and political action is action *par excellence*, then political action is the exclusive prerogative of human beings. Indeed, the body serves as the *privileged* medium of man's political intercourse.

In political thinking, problems of the body and its correlate, the soul or mind, go as far back as Plato's *Republic*.[51] The myth of Er is a story about the separation of the soul from the body after death, the immortality of the soul pitted against the perishable body. However, it was in medieval political theology that the symbolic and analogical drama of soul and body unfolded itself in politics.[52] The politics of the *sacerdotium* and the *regnum* was the power struggle between the soul and the body. Following Seneca's remarks about Nero—"you are the soul of the *respublica* and the *respublica* is your body"—the Tudor lawyers, for example, enunciated the doctrine that "the king in his body politic is incorporated with his subjects, and they with him." This theory of "the King's Two Bodies" was later denounced by Maitland as "a marvelous display of metaphysical—or we might say metaphysiological—nonsense." Particularly in John of Salisbury's *Policraticus,* the original liturgical idea of the *corpus mysticum* was transformed into the metaphor of polity, the "body politic" (*corpus politicum*)—a simile popularly accepted by many jurists of his time. Sir John Fortescue compared the structural system of polity to the natural body (*corpus naturale*).[53] In recent times, the medieval notion that "the man is the head of the wife, and the wife is the body of the man" has appeared in the revolution of "sexual politics"—a claim for the respect of the politics of the "body" (a female principle) against the politics of the "mind" (a male principle). The restoration of the body in politics has also become a struggle for female dignity as a human being.

While Cartesian metaphysics justifies the solipsistic integrity of the spiritual substance called "soul" encapsulated in the "body," the cybernetic model of man radicalized Cartesianism by eliminating its metaphysical cargo of the "inner man" or regarding the mental or, for that matter, the bodily merely as a filtering mechanism of the external world while retaining the notion of the soul and the body both as substances. The result inevitably is a citadel of sociologism which has two inseparable components: methodological and substantive. The former is a method of investigation, whereas the latter is a theory of man. However, since the question of *what* and *how* to know man cannot be separated in sociologism, they go hand in hand. The gist of our contention here is that Simon's physics of the mind or his sciences of the artificial as well as B. F. Skinner's physics of human behavior and Ralf Dahrendorf's theory of "sociological man" (*homo sociologicus*) ignores a dialectical complicity of the mind and the individual on the one hand and the body and society (or history) on the other. Merleau-Ponty suggests, however, that the phenomenology of speech (or language as speech acts) is best suited to reveal this dialectical complicity which is inaccessible to both individualism and sociologism or, to use his own phrases, "psychologism" and "historicism." Merleau-Ponty writes:

> When I speak or understand, I experience that presence of others in myself or of myself in others which is the stumbling block of the theory of intersubjectivity, I experience that presence of what is represented which is the stumbling-block of the theory of time, and I finally understand what is meant by Husserl's enigmatic statement, "Transcendental subjectivity is intersubjectivity." To the extent that what I say has meaning, I am a different "other" for myself when I am speaking; and to the extent that I understand, I no longer know who is speaking and who is listening.[54]

Skinner's behaviorism is the most radical form of sociologism. It is far more than a philosophy of science because it claims to be a complete philosophy of man and society. The "technology of behavior" is the central theme in Skinner's *Beyond Freedom and Dignity*. Without behavioral technology, technology itself is incomplete. The autonomous man is dispossessed by the reinforced man whose behavioral mediator is the environmental reinforcement with rewards and punishments. Skinner believes that Descartes was the first man who suggested that the environment might play a decisive role in the determination of individual behavior. As he sees it, like biology's natural selection, "the environment not only prods or lashes, it *selects.*"[55] In Skinner's technology of behavior, Cartesian God (the unifier of soul and body) is replaced by the omnipotent forces of environment as the reinforcer of human behavior. It would be a mistake to believe that Skinner rejects "consciousness" or, as he calls it, that small part of the universe which is enclosed within a human skin. Indeed, according to him, scientific analysis rejects only the private, inner man (or the "*homunculus*") who is claimed to be independent of the social environment. For Skinner, consciousness as well as behavior is a mere product of the social environment. Both are nothing but products of society. Thus his behavioral technology is the most thoroughgoing form of sociologism.

The underlying assumptions and theses of Simon's sciences of the artificial have Skinnerian features, although Skinner would consider "behavior," "environment," or "reinforcement" as anything but artificial. Simon argues that "man—or at least the intellective component of man—may be relatively simple; that most of the complexity of his behavior may be drawn from his environment, from his search for good designs."[56] To use a metaphor of the computer, Simon's central concern then is its "software," the "intellective" part, rather than its "hardware."

For Simon, the natural selection is as important to evolutionary biology as it is to psychology—the study of "man's relation to the complex outer environment in which he seeks to survive and achieve."[57] Just as in Skinner's behaviorism, the concept of the environment is a central theme in Simon's sciences of the artificial with a difference: Simon's thesis of the determination of the inner by the outer is not as thoroughgoing as Skinner's since for Simon there are still "a few 'intrinsic' characteristics of the inner environment of thinking man."[58] Nonetheless, their fundamental theory of the conditioning environment is unmistakably similar: as for Skinner "an organism learns to react discriminately to the world around it under certain contingencies of reinforcement,"[59] events within the skin are merely reactions to events without the skin; for Simon, too, the inner environment is knowable by knowing the outer environment. *Homo sapiens* (thinking man) is "an adaptive system." *"A man viewed as a behaving system,"* Simon writes, *"is quite simple. The complexity of his behavior over time is largely a reflection of the complexity of the environment in which he finds himself."*[60] By determining the outer environment of a system, the "rationality" (or goal) of the inner environment is predicted: "The outer environment determines the conditions of goal attainment."[61] Moreover, Simon's argument for the sciences of the artificial is an argument for the causal determination of individual behavior (mainly of thinking) by the social environment. For "insofar as behavior is a function of learned technique . . . our knowledge of behavior must be regarded as sociological in nature rather than psychological—that is, as revealing what human beings in fact learn when they grow up in a particular social environment."[62] Indeed, then, it coincides with Skinner's behaviorism which, as we have examined earlier, regards events within the skin as results of events without the skin, that is, individual behavior is a *social product* or a product of society. In the final analysis, Simon's argument for the sciences of the artificial focused on "cognition" complements Skinner's behaviorism.

Indeed, sociologism is a widespread tendency in the social sciences today—especially functional-structural analysis—to reify "social man" in a conceptual net singlehandedly by constructing models. Each in its own fragmentary way, they jealously guard their own "territorial imperatives"; consequently, there are *homo sociologicus, homo psychologicus, homo politicus, homo economicus,* and so on. These are fragments of man viewed as player of a multitude of roles. It is said that the aim of conceptualizing man as a role-player is to find that conceptual domain in which man and society intersect. Thus Eulau declares that "Role is neither an exclusively individualilstic nor an exclusively collectivistic concept. It is both, and for this reason serves as a 'linkage' term. . . . Role analysis seems to have the virtue of overcoming both the methodological individualism of those who worked primarily with the concepts of clinical psychology and also the methodological holism of those who worked primarily with the concept of global sociology."[63] Similarly, the sociologist Ralf Dahrendorf maintains that it is not the individual as such but rather "sociological man" that constitutes the basic unit of sociological analysis. For Dahrendorf, "at the point where the individual and society intersect stands *homo sociologicus,* man the bearer of socially predetermined roles. To a sociologist the individual *is* his social roles, but these roles, for their part, are the vexatious fact of society."[64]

Socialization, according to Dahrendorf, is the process in which man learns to "internalize" the "prescriptions of society" which entail, like Skinner's positive and negative reinforcement, rewards and punishments. "From the point of view of society and sociology," Dahrendorf writes, "it is by learning role expectations, by being transformed into *homo sociologicus,* that man becomes a part of society and accessible to sociological analysis. Man devoid of roles is a nonentity for society and sociology. To become a part of society and a subject of sociological analysis, man must be socialized, chained to the fact of society and made its creature."[65] Hence "socialization," he continues, "invariably means depersonalization, the yielding of man's absolute individuality and liberty to the constraint and generality of social roles. . . . By learning to play social roles . . . we not only lose ourselves to the alien otherness of a world we never made, but regain ourselves as personalities given shape by the world's vexations."[66] Therefore, Dahrendorf's "sociological man" is one who is *chained* to the prescriptive norms of society which are determined in advance. "Sociological man" is a "role-taker" rather than a "role-maker." Dahrendorf is unaware of a dialectical interchange between the individual and society, between the internalization of the external and the externalization of the internal, or between *homo internus* and *homo externus*. In his "sociological man," "internalization" or *homo internus* is given way to "externalization" or *homo externus*.[67] "Sociological man" is a passive complier and conformist rather than an active agent who can initiate changes and reforms in society.

Since *homo sociologicus* is "the bearer of socially predetermined roles," sociologism is inescapable with Dahrendorf as it is with Skinner's behaviorism. There is one way to conceptualize social roles that commits and one that does not commit the predicaments of sociologism. The former belongs to Dahrendorf's sociology and Skinner's behaviorism and the latter to phenomenology. Dahrendorf's notions of role-playing and societal prescriptions parallel Skinner's "operant behavior" and reinforcement of the environment. Their sociologism is similar with at least this difference: Skinner's "reinforced man" is man in reality whereas Dahrendorf's *homo sociologicus* is claimed to be an abstract image of man. Nonetheless, in Dahrendorf there is conceptual ambiguity between man in society and "sociological man" as a scientific, physicalist construct, that is, whether "sociological man" is a puppet of society or that of the sociologist. On the one hand, Dahrendorf maintains that the "rationality" of *homo sociologicus* is a scientific construct or an analytical tool for sociological analysis and hence is not an attribute of "human nature." On the other hand, according to Dahrendorf, atoms in physics or chemistry and individuals in sociology are indistinguishable.[68] Hence the table of a physicist as "a most unsolid beehive of nuclear particles" tell us something about the table itself, and by the same token the sociologist's *homo sociologicus* or the physics of roles tells something about the social nature of man.

As has been contended from the outset, the phenomenological

critique of sociologism aims to show that sociologism ignores a dialectical complicity between the inner and the outer. As, according to the axial principle of phenomenology, consciousness is intentionality, that is, consciousness is always consciousness *of* something whether it be thinking, perceiving, imagining, or feeling, phenomenology is an *intentional* analysis: it attempts to describe an object, real or ideal, as it appears in consciousness, its meaning (or "phenomenon"). As the subject and the "meant" object are correlates, phenomenology as an intentional analysis is able to avoid both extreme subjectivism and extreme objectivism: "mentalism" and "behaviorism" on the one hand and "individualism" and "sociologism" on the other.[69] There is neither absolute interiority (mind as "subjectivity") nor absolute exteriority (body as "objectivity"). This is the reason why the existential self as an active subject is necessarily social. According to Maurice Natanson, we plunge into social reality because the secret of individual identity may be locked in it.[70] Phenomenology does not object to the characterization of man as the role-player as such; it only objects to the characterization of man simply as "role-taker."Man is both a "role-taker" and a "role-maker" in his active relationship to the surrounding world. Natanson declares that "the genesis of both the alter ego and the ego is seen in a unity of interaction in which structural priority is granted to neither element of the social order. Instead, becoming a self means taking the role of the Other. Concomitantly, awareness of the Other involves the discovery and formation of the self."[71] When the embodied self and the embodied other are seen as coeval or coextensive in the same world, there is no need to dichotomize or polarize individuation and socialization in favor of one for the other resulting in individualism or sociologism: existence *is* coexistence. For Dahrendorf, the role-taking is an absorption of the individual into society rather than their mediation or intersection, and thus he pays only lip service to "internalization," whereas for Skinner the individual is totally lost in the social environment and thus he makes "internalization" or "individuation" nonexistent. Contrary to the sociologism of Skinner, Simon, and Dahrendorf, man is actively social by internalizing the external and externalizing the internal. In this dialectical process of individuation and socialization, *intersubjectivity is necessarily an intercorporeality;* human community is a community of embodied subjects.

Hermeneutical understanding, according to Habermas, permits a dialogue between the individual and society (the "horizontal" level of socialization) or history (the "vertical" level of socialization). Because the individual in relation to society or history is regarded as "productive" of new possibilities by "interpretation" rather than simply "re-productive" of the fixed patterns of social rules, hermeneutical under-standing also compensates for what Habermas calls the "broken-ness of intersubjectivity," that is, it balances the "sacrifice of indi-viduality" and the "isolation of the individualized." As he writes, "lan-guages that are no longer inwardly [as well as outwardly] porous and have hardened into rigid systems remove the breaks in individuals from one another."[72] Thus, from the standpoint of intersubjectivity as the genuine dialectic of the self and the other, the "atomized indi-vidual" and the "mass man" are identical twins, as it were. Dialectically viewed, intersubjectivity avoids being both unsocialized or underso-cialized and oversocialized. It is an affirmation of neither a placid collectivity or "seriality" nor the plurality of isolated monads or sub-jects since it is an active recognition of "being-with" others (*Mitsein*) rather than a total obliteration or a passive toleration of individual differences. In it neither self nor other is sovereign but they are coextensive with each other. Intersubjectivity is the active "synergy" of two or more embodied subjects wherein a genuine reciprocity takes place, that is, the self and the other—or, for that matter, the world—is "reversible." We coexist in "an atmosphere of humanity."

Chapter 7

Ontology and Technology

A Critique of C. B. Macpherson's Theory of Democratic Polity

The inclusion of Crawford Brough Macpherson in a recent anthology of contemporary political theorists in the company of Herbert Marcuse, Leo Strauss, Michael Oakeshott, Karl Popper, Jean-Paul Sartre, Hannah Arendt, John Rawls, and others is indeed a tribute to his intellectual achievement.[1] Although he is not as prolific a writer as are some of the above-mentioned thinkers, Macpherson is no doubt a *systematic thinker*. By systematic thinking and its virtue, we have in mind what Henri Bergson said about the nature of great thinking. According to him, the hallmark of great thinking is to think only one thing or one reality with a single vision. Thus the enemy of systematic thinking is eclecticism. For Macpherson, this single vision is the vision of democratic politics as a humanistic *ontology* accompanied by a critique of liberal ideology as possessive individualism or democracy *for* the market society which is inscribed in the "elegant tombstones" of Thomas Hobbes, John Locke, Jeremy Bentham, John Stuart Mill, Isaiah Berlin, John Rawls, Milton Friedman, Anthony Downs, and others in the time span of four centuries.[2]

This chapter is a critique of this systematic political thought of Macpherson. The main thrust of our argument is twofold. First, Macpherson's "sociologistic" critique in the tradition of Marx's analysis of ideology and Karl Mannheim's sociology of knowledge is a powerful intellectual tool to disclose Hobbes's and Locke's political thought

130

as the "hidden" reflection or superstructure of the market society of their own times and to criticize the contemporary doctrine of value neutrality as an ideology of the *status quo*. However, it alone is inadequate to replace possessive individualism with a new ontology the endeavor of which must necessarily be normative and projective. Second, Macpherson's sociologistic archaeology of possessive individualism fails to see the ontological imports of scientism or scientific epistemology exemplified in Hobbes's philosophy as supportive of the scientific and technological ethos of modern man and his age. It fails to come to grips fully with the nature of technology as the all-inclusive *logos* of everything we think and do and its impact on man's domination over other men as well as nature. By failing to consider systematically the antihumanistic tendencies of technology, that is, technological obstacles in the way of man's "developmental power" which he wishes to promote, his humanistic ontology may in the end turn out to be less humanistic than it purports to be. Indeed, it would benefit from Marcuse's and Jacques Ellul's social critique of technological rationality. The ideology of possessive individualism in which the motive of economic gains becomes an intrinsic rather than an instrumental aim is detrimental to the ecological ethics of conservation on this finite earth as discussed in chapter 3.

Let us begin with what we consider to be three main points in Macpherson's conception of the function of theory or social theory. First, for him epistemological and methodological issues are subordinated to ontological ones as the main function of theory is to clarify substantively the human condition in a social and historical perspective. He is concerned with liberalism as an ontology and the ethics of its possessive individualism. Thus his critique of Friedman's "elegant tombstone" of economics and Downs's economic theory of democracy, for example, lies primarily not in their positivistic methodology—"positive economics" and "positive politics," respectively—but in their ontological assumptions of man and society. Macpherson concentrates on possessive individualism as an ontology which reduces the "essence of man" to the economic relations of a market society.[3]

Second, for Macpherson the issue of value judgment which is most central to the *Methodenstreit* of social theory today is not primarily a methodological one. Rather, the main fault of the battlecry of value neutrality is that it ends up with supporting the *status quo*: whatever works is right. Macpherson writes that "Those who start from the tacit assumption that whatever is, is right, are apt to deny that they are making any value judgment. Those who start from the tacit assumption that whatever is, is wrong, give great weight to their ethical case (while trying to show that it is practicable.)"[4] The clash between possessive individualism and Macpherson's humanistic ontology is an ethical one since for him the essence of ontology is its ethics. His view is "justificatory" in an ethical sense. As such, what is crucial to social theory is the question not of whether something is methodologically or epistemologically "true" or "false" but of which postulate is better suited for the perception of reality and the future fulfillment of the "essence of man." The function of social theory is to understand the human condition at present and to prescribe its improvement for the future in relation to the past. Consequently, the study of the past, that is, the study of the history of political thought, has a didactic function. Macpherson tells us that " . . . the purpose of scholarly reappraisals of political theories is to help us to see the limits and possibilities of a great tradition as applied to our own day. . . . "[5] He thus considers the function of theory as both interpreting the world and transforming it for the better.

Third, what is the most interesting and problematical aspect of Macpherson's conception of the function of theory and thus the relationship between theory and practice is revealed in his critique of liberal ideology as possessive individualism. He does not argue that possessive individualism is intrinsically faulty. Rather, he argues that it is faulty because of its "cultural lag," that is, the postulates of possessive individualism which are the historical product of seventeenth-century bourgeois culture do not match the changed conditions of the twentieth century. "The market assumption," Macpherson writes, "is not now warranted, I think, not because we do not now live in a market society (for we do live in one), but because the rightness or justice of a market society is not now as nearly universally accepted within the society as it was from the seventeenth to the nineteenth centuries."[6] According to him, the liberal version of democracy cannot now be identified with democracy; it cannot claim the monopoly of being democratic because there are two other versions of it: the communist and the third-world variant—the latter being neither liberal nor communist. This, I think, is the Achilles's heel of Macpherson's conception of theory in relation to practice which has its venerable tradition in Marx's critique of capitalism and Karl Mannheim's sociology of knowledge. We shall call Macpherson's view "sociologistic." The function of theory conceived solely as a critique of ideology or the reduction of theory to a sociologistic orientation undermines the normative construction of his own democratic ontology for the purpose of fulfilling the "essence of man" beyond the postulates of possessive individualism both now and in the future. It should be noted that while there are some insights new and unique in his latest work, *The Life and Times of Liberal Democracy*, they do not alter this basic critique of Macpherson's "sociologistic" explanation of political theory. In this work he analyzes four models of liberal democracy in a historical perspective, that is, in a series of "successive models": (1) protective, (2) developmental, (3) equilibrium, and (4) participatory. The first two models belong to the past; the third is presently prevailing; and the fourth is the "prospective" model which is "within the realm of the possible." What is unique in this work of Macpherson is the altered view that liberal democracy in its prospective development is not necessarily bound by the underpinnings of the market economy or capitalism. His advocatory or justificatory framework in discussing the prospective model of participatory democracy which is "in the best tradition of liberal democracy" may constitute the beginning of seeing the function of theory as more than "sociologistic," that is, as a projective endeavor. However, it is yet inconclusive and at best promissory. The thorny problem of untying the double knot of theory as sociologistic on the one hand and as projective on the other yet remains unanswered.

The gist of Macpherson's critique of liberalism as possessive individualism is that in it essence of man is defined in terms of the market system of relations: in it man is viewed as an infinite appropriator, infinite desirer and infinite consumer of utilities. In a market society, men's "extractive power" rules over and stifles their "developmental power" (i.e., nonextractive power). The former is the way men get what they want—both material and nonmaterial things—by controlling others so that a few can increase or maximize their share of satisfactions at the expense of many (i.e., the myth of maximization). The latter is the way in which men are capable of developing their potentiality creatively, freely and fully. According to Macpherson, the assumptions of liberalism as possessive individualism are spelled out most clearly and fully in Hobbes. Macpherson summarizes possessive individualism in the following seven propositions:

(1) What makes a man human is freedom from dependence on the wills of others.

(2) Freedom from dependence on others means freedom from any relations with others except those relations which the individual enters voluntarily with a view to his own interest.

(3) The individual is essentially the proprietor of his own person and capacities, for which he owes nothing to society.

(4) Although the individual cannot alienate the whole of his property in his own person, he may alienate his capacity to labour.

(5) Human society consists of a series of market relations.

(6) Since freedom from the wills of others is what makes a man human, each individual's freedom can rightfully be limited only by such obligations and rules as are necessary to secure the same freedom for others.

(7) Political society is a human contrivance for the protection of the individual's property in his person and goods, and (therefore) for the maintenance of orderly relations of exchange between individuals regarded as proprietors of themselves.[7]

In the background of Macpherson's critique of liberalism as possessive individualism, there looms the influence of Rousseau and Marx,[8] although strictly speaking he belongs to no school of thought. For students of Rousseau and Marx, it is apparent that these seven propositions of liberalism as possessive individualism can be contrasted with the general spirit of Rousseau's political thought and Marx's critique of capitalist political economy—particularly the latter's concepts of "dehumanization," "objectification" (*Vergegenständlichung*), "alienation" (*Entfremdung*), and man as the "species-being" (*Gattungswesen*).[9]

The originality of Macpherson's interpretation of Hobbes's political thought lies in his observation that Hobbes's description of human nature (in the state of nature) as the state of war of everyman against the other is an abstraction from the "anarchy" of the capitalist society of his own time. Macpherson tells us that the moral lesson we learn from Hobbes is that the capitalist or market society needs the strong political sanctions of a Leviathan.[10]

The sociologistic explanation of Macpherson is exemplified in his critique of Hobbes or "Hobbes's bourgeois man." Macpherson not only points to the correlation between Hobbes's mathematical method of politics and the seventeenth-century bourgeois culture of his own time but also stresses, it appears, the fact that the former is subordinated in the order of importance to the latter. For Macpherson, Hobbes's mathematics of politics is primarily a condition of the bourgeois culture of his own time. He writes:

> Hobbes's belief in the certainty of his postulates may be due in part to his mathematical approach, but fundamentally their in-

adequacy is due to the limitations imposed on his vision of man by his observation of a bourgeois society. There is no contradiction here. The predominance of mathematical thinking in the seventeenth century is closely related to the rise of capitalism. Quantitative analysis of the material world, of which mathematics is the purest form, was demanded increasingly from the fifteenth century in the service of capitalist technology and of the nation-state. The bourgeois mind was apt to be a mathematical mind; the mathematical mind was generally a bourgeois mind. The limitations of the one were the limitations of the other. The mathematical method is congruous with the reduction of all men to the equality of the market.... The materialism of the seventeenth century was a mechanical materialism which read into the natural world the kind of relations which the materialist philosophers saw in bourgeois society. The relation of material objects to each other could be stated in laws of mechanical force just as the relations of the individuals could be seen as the relations of units reduced to equality by the market.[11]

However important and penetrating it may be, Macpherson's sociologistic critique of Hobbes is one-sided. The hallmark of modernity embarked on by Hobbes in political theory is Janus-faced. One face is contractual individualism which, according to Macpherson, reflects the bourgeois society of Hobbes's own time; and the other is scientism.[12] What makes Hobbes a paradigm maker in the history of Western political thought, of which he was fully self-conscious, is precisely the wedding or fusing of the two independent motor forces of modernity: the conceptual technique of scientism on the one hand and the individualistic assumptions of man and society on the other.[13] It would, however, be a mistake to assume that there is an inherently logical or formal connection between scientism and bourgeois individualism: the latter does not entail the former. The formal logic of scientism is independent of the morality of the market society for no other reason than that it is the intellectual or conceptual property owned or monopolized not by the bourgeois society alone but the nonbourgeois society as well. Contrary to Macpherson's sociologistic interpretation, we may very well argue that Hobbes's conceptual technique or mathematization of politics was *intended* or *meant* to be a contribution to the scientific *Weltanschauung* of modernity.

Scientism in and by itself is not taken seriously enough in Macpherson's critique of Hobbes when it is treated as a surface structure or superstructure—if not a false consciousness or an epiphenomenon —of the market society. As a result, first, Macpherson fails to come to terms fully with the profound implications of scientism on the ontology of man particularly in his study of Hobbes. Second, Macpherson's critique of Hobbes does not take the self-conscious *intent* of Hobbes as a harbinger of modernity in political thinking seriously enough. There is, however, the alternative way of viewing ideology as the self-conscious effort of such a thinker as Hobbes in which both the intent and the content—or, to use the language of phenomenology, the noetic and the noematic dimension—of his thought are coextensive. Ideology is then the self-conscious way of calculating the view of man's thought and its direction into and consequence on his action in relation to his surrounding world. Hobbes's ideology thus viewed is an integral structure of his self-consciousness concerning man's place in the world rather than merely a superstructure or an epiphenomenon. In short, it is overt, manifest, and explicit rather than latent, hidden, and implicit.[14] Only by focusing on Hobbes's scientism can we account for the coextensive unity of the intent and the content of his thought. Third, the corollary of having not taken Hobbes's scientism *sui generis* or as an independent variable of his thought rather than a surface crust of the deep structures of the market society impairs the construction of Macpherson's own democratic ontology in glossing over the impact on man and nature of advanced technology and its all-inclusive rationality, that is, technology as the *logos* of man's domination of nature as well as man's domination of other men. We call *technocentric rationality* the all-inclusive *logos* of *technē* in everything we *think* and *do* or in every aspect of our thinking and doing today. In our age, Macpherson's ontology of democratic man—or, for that matter, any serious philosophy of man—would be deficient unless it takes into account the ramifications of technocentric rationality for both man and nature. Indeed, the day has now come when technology is an inseparable part of our thinking and doing as "the snail's shell is to its occupant or as the web is to the spider."[15] Here we are contending not that Macpherson is mute on the subject of technology but rather that what he says of it is inadequate in its depth and scope, that is, his view of technology as merely instrumental to the ontology of man is deficient to understand fully the all-inclusive nature of the technocentric rationality of our time. In what follows, the primary aim of our discussion is to show the possibilities and limits of Macpherson's sociologistic thinking in the interpretation of liberal philosophy and further to explore the internal, structural weaknesses of his conceptual framework that is correlated to his treatment of Hobbes's scientism merely as a superstructure of bourgeois individualism on the one hand and to his inability to see fully the impact of technocentric rationality on man's domination of man and nature on the other.

The Galilean and Cartesian mechanistic view of nature, when it is transposed to the view of man, "natural man" as passive and receptive in Hobbes, is mutually supportive of his atomistic individualism. It is true, as Macpherson sees it, that Hobbes's "natural man" is characteristic of the "anarchistic man" of a bourgeois society. However, it is equally true and clear that he is a "naturelike man": external *nature* finds its mechanistic analogue in the internal *nature* of man—that is, in "scientific psychology." The notion of man in Hobbes's scientism as a mechanical substance or artifact in the Galilean and Cartesian model in relation to *social* and *political* philosophy, as revealed in the preceding chapter on "sociologism" as a corollary of the cybernetic model of man, is incapable of rendering a consistent justification for sociality. There is an explicit connection between certain epistemological theories and certain conceptions of man— scientism results in the conception of man as a disembodied, asocial being and becomes structurally consistent with the postulates of atomistic individualism. Let us consider an interesting dimension of how such a philosophical solipsism as Hobbes's scientism is related to the idea of private property. Although one does not emanate from the other, there is nonetheless a structural similarity between the two. Hobbes's scientism in regarding men as mechanical substances or mathematical entities makes fully human sociality impossible. Likewise, private property without being subordinate to the common and general purpose of a political community too presupposes the conception of men as isolated individuals. "Solipsism as a philosophical doctrine," Merleau-Ponty thus notes, "is not the result of a system of private property; nevertheless into economic institutions as into conceptions of the world is projected the same existential prejudice in favour of isolation and mistrust."[16] Indeed, it is informative to observe that the term "memory bank" taken as the fusion of cybernetics and possessive individualism symbolizes the privatization of memory or, more broadly, meaning. In the final analysis, contrary to Macpherson's sociologistic interpretation, Hobbes's scientism is not a direct result of his bourgeois individualism, although there is no denying that they are structurally alike.

Having explored Macpherson's sociologistic critique of liberalism as possessive individualism and an alternative conception of scientism in relation to atomistic individualism, we shall now discuss Macpherson's view concerning the interrelated topic of technology. His view of the role of technology with regard to ontology is clearly stated when, in reference to the technological revolution in the non-Western world, he says: "technology assists ontology."[17] To be sure, he is aware of the fact that technology has well served the development of capitalist society to reach its maturity. What interests him most is the abandonment of the essence of man as an infinite appropriator, infinite desirer, infinite consumer, and infinite antagonist of scarcity toward the development of a new ontology of man. He asserts that with the aid of technology "the rejection of the market concept of man's essence is . . . logically possible as well as now technically possible."[18] "But there is one great difficulty," he continues:

> The technological revolution in Western nations, if left to develop within the present market structure and the present ideology, would have the immediate effect of strengthening the image of man as infinite consumer, by making consumption more attractive. As technology multiplies productivity, profitable production will require the creation of new desires and new amounts of desire. (What will be required may properly be described as *creation* of new desire, in spite of what I said above about advertising not creating new desire, if we reject, as I have argued we should reject, the factual accuracy of the postulate that man as such is naturally infinitely desirous.) Since profits will increasingly depend on creating ever more desire, the tendency will be for the directors of the productive system to do everything in their power to confirm Western man's image of himself as an infinite desirer. Efforts in that direction are evident enough in the mass media now. Thus in the West the immediate effect of the technological revolution will be to impede the change in our ontology which it otherwise makes possible and which I have argued is needed if we are to retain any of the values of liberal-democracy.[19]

Although Macpherson's perceptive observation of the immediate problem of technology that impedes the development of a new ontology of man in the West must not be overlooked, he has not come to grips with some of the most basic issues of technology and its damaging effects on men today. Because Macpherson is preoccupied in the Marxian spirit with the question of the *social relations of men* and with technology solely as the instrument of man's control of nature, the issue of technology as the instrument of man's manipulation of other men is largely excluded from the realm of "extractive power." For him, technology looms by and large as the issue of man's control over nature. So he bemoans the fact that those who study political modernization are neglecting the humanly extractive function of power in favor of the nonhumanly extractive function of control of nature and suggests—rightly so—that remedies can be found if more attention is given to the power of human development, that is, to the nonextractive power of developing men's capabilities and potentialities. However, the point is that the theory of human development is now inseparable from the antihumanistic tendencies of technocentric culture. Moreover, technology is the instrument of the extractive power not of a market society alone but also of a nonmarket society.

In Macpherson's critique of liberalism as possessive individualism and his democratic ontology, the issue of technology is not as prominent and integral as it should be or as it is with such a writer as Marshall McLuhan who considers media technology as a "fourth world." The basic inadequacy of Macpherson's ontology of man is due to his view of technology in modern society: (1) technology is more or less a morally neutral instrument to be used for good or bad; (2) technology is primarily the instrument of control over nature rather than over men; and (3) as such, it is separable from the realm of extractive power—the power of men's control over other men which is primarily the function of economic individualism. As a result, Macpherson fails to explore the utilitarian tendency of "labor" and "work" to exploit nature in strengthening and perpetuating the ethos of technocentric culture as an integral part of Lockean liberalism.[20] Through technology the extractive power of men over nature extends itself to the extractive power of men over other men. More urgently now than ever before, the issue of technology as both a power to exploit nature and a form of extractive power must be resolved in relation to man as an infinite appropriator, desirer, and consumer. To be realistic, the concept of human development or the development of humanity as a whole must come to terms with the basic, unalterable fact that the earth is a finite planet.[21]

In our technocentric culture today, *technology absorbs ontology* rather than, as Macpherson suggests in the spirit of Marx, technology assists ontology. The ideology of Lockean liberalism with its philosophy already laid out by Hobbes promotes the ethos of technological civilization based on the subjugation and negation of nature by labor and industry which builds the society of acquisitive "economic men" who, as Macpherson puts it, are infinite appropriators, desirers, and consumers. To ask how possessive individualism coupled with Judeo-Christian homocentrism or anthropocentrism and the "fetishism" of technology is related to the ecological crisis—the issue to which Macpherson has so far failed to address himself—is to open Pandora's box. William Coleman has recently ventured to put forth the direct

consequences of possessive individualism on the natural environment
and the ecological crisis. While agreeing with Lynn White's famous
thesis of the exploitative potential of Judeo-Christian anthropocentrism on the man-nature relationship,[22] Coleman argues that the consequences of the quest for the economic appropriation of nature for
profit are more direct and critical factors detrimental to the natural
environment than Judeo-Christian anthropocentrism. He contends:

> The Christian tradition has played a significant role in this un-
> happy tale, but that role became truly effective only after Euro-
> pean society had fatefully launched a new and triumphant form
> of economic enterprise. The principal contribution of Christian
> doctrine to our environmental crisis was not, therefore, the sim-
> ple invention of an exploitative ethics, but, instead, the creation
> and willing application of a new apologetic based on that ethic to
> the economic individualism becoming characteristic of Europe
> in the late seventeenth century.[23]

When technology becomes an important aspect of extractive power,
however, its problem transcends the narrow confines of economic
ideology—capitalism versus socialism. The ideology of possessiveness,
too, is not the monopoly of liberalism alone but is cherished as an
almost universally desired goal. In the endless pursuit of economic
gains, possessive collectivism is no better than possessive individualism. Therefore, the acquisitive ethos of "economism" accompanied
by the labor theory of value and the ethics of work to exploit nature
with the aid of science and technology—whether it be individualist
or socialist—must also be a focal issue of humanism.

For Macpherson, technology, scarcity, and property are interrelated
concepts in his democratic ontology in opposition to liberalism as
possessive individualism. Since for him technology assists ontology, it
helps to eliminate scarcity for the development of what is fully human. He argues that the technological revolution of our time makes
"unnecessary" and "unrealistic" the liberal assumption of the essence
of man as an infinite appropriator, desirer, and consumer. Macpherson asserts that if his analysis is right, it would

> demolish the time-bound and now unnecessary and deleterious
> image of man as an infinite consumer and infinite appropriator,
> as a being whose rational purpose in life is to devote himself to
> an endless attempt to overcome scarcity. Scarcity was for mil-
> lenia the general human condition; three centuries ago it be-
> came a contrived but useful goal; now it is dispensable, though

we are in danger of having it riveted on us in a newer and more artificial form.[24]

For a "fully democratic society," therefore, scarcity both genuine and contrived must be overcome, and the heart of democracy is the *belief* that it can be overcome. For Macpherson, scarcity is not primarily—as the Marxist Sartre has it—the negation in man of man by nature which in turn affects the exploitation of man by man.[25] That is to say, it is not "an invariable natural phenomenon" encountered in the pursuit of productivity related to material needs, desires, and demands. Rather, it is viewed as a function of productivity and extractive power in a market society: it is "a culturally determined concept which was needed to get capitalist enterprise into action, but is not needed, and has no warrant, once capitalism has become mature."[26] So scarcity is not an invariable natural phenomenon but is a variable cultural one. As such is the case, scarcity of the means of life too is a socially variable impediment which must be overcome in developing a fully democratic society.

To use the language of Marxism, for Macpherson scarcity is a form of the "reification" of a market society.[27] For reification (scarcity as reified) is the way of defining the social relations of men by the mechanism of producing, buying, selling, and consuming commodities in the market system. In other words, it is a form of the extractive power of men to control other men; with the disappearance of extractive power, it too will disappear. However, although Macpherson is aware of the danger of technology, in contriving wants, needs, and demands for more and more material things and perpetuating a consumer society, to view scarcity as a cultural variable of the market society alone is, again, to take the "banality of evil" in technology too lightly since technology is neither intrinsically capitalist nor intrinsically socialist, that is, it serves both. More importantly, to view scarcity solely as a cultural variable or a social variable of the market society is to fail to see it as an unreified problem of the *economics of the finite earth*. In the end, this will undermine Macpherson's own democratic ontology that aims for the "quality of life." It is no doubt true that scarcity in the modern world is in large part a socio-psychological propensity—the propensity far more visible in industrially advanced, consumption-oriented societies with the highly developed technology of marketing than in industrially developing ones. The nature of man as desirer and appropriator, however, is a psychological quality unforunately shared by both bourgeois and nonbourgeois man, although the former's desires and needs are more artifically induced and reinforced by his social conditions (i.e., more "contrived") than the latter's. In the context of the economics of a finite planet, the quality of life is the question that requires a definition and resolution of *what* human basic needs are, *how* they can be fulfilled, and what is a just or fair allocation of scarce resources between the rich and the poor within a nation or among nations. The root of our problem, as we have above stressed, is "economism" viewed by the utilitarian philosophy of *homo faber* as the end of life which sets no limits to economic gain and growth. This is the rationale shared basically by both Locke and Marx—with, of course, a difference in appropriating the way in which productive processes affect the governance of man's relations with other men—because they saw nonhuman external nature simply as a means to satisfy human needs, desires, and ends.

The essence of liberalism as possessive individualism is the concept of private property whose *value* is determined by labor as a productive capacity and a commodity of exchange. Thus, in possessive individualism labor is defined in terms of its exchange value rather than its use value which Macpherson's democratic ontology aims to overcome. For him, the concept of labor (or laborer) as an exchange value is a victim of extractive power in a market society. To make labor human, it must be defined as "enjoyment" and "exertion." Rather than being an instrument for the sake of production or the accumulation of wealth, labor has an intrinsic meaning. Nor is labor as exertion done for the sake of gaining free time or leisure.[28] *Homo faber* and *homo ludens* are not dichotomous but are companions. As labor is a form of exertion, so is property not something just marketable. For Macpherson, therefore, labor and property are defined in terms of Marx's distinction between "exchange-value" and "use-value." The meaning of labor and property is derived from their "use-value" rather than their "exchange-value" as it is in a market society. Unlike Marx, however, Macpherson is not attempting to eliminate the institution of property or private property. On the contrary, his originality lies, I think, in modifying and expanding both liberal and Marxist notions. For Macpherson, the essence of property is not ownership and possession but is the *right* of participation and exertion. As such, the concept of property is extended as a share in political power to live a full life in the absence of extractive power. In essence, property is a right to the means of attaining a fully human life.

In conclusion: the originality of Macpherson's thought lies in its tenacious and systematic critique of liberalism as possessive individualism in which the essence of man is reduced to an economic entity with marketable values and in sketching out the synoptic view of a democratic ontology by eliminating extractive power and by nurturing developmental power in social relations among men. Although his critique of possessive individualism has a cutting effect, his democratic ontology still requires structural articulation and elaboration. For it is defined in terms of what it *is not* rather than what it *is*. In other words, his primary achievement rests on the *negative* criticism of bourgeois individualism rather than the *positive* construction of a democratic ontology.[29] This is by no means to belittle his intellectual accomplishment but is only to suggest that further work has to be done.

The essence of Macpherson's theory is the affirmation that democracy is neither solely a system of government nor solely a system of economics: it *is* an ontology—the way of man's total existence in the world. It is this "ontological turn" beyond methodological and epistemological issues that deserves our most serious attention in his political theory, although he is oblivious to the implications of epistemology (i.e., scientism) on the ontology of democratic man. Insofar as his democratic ontology is a claim for making man and society fully and freely human, it is a humanism which finds its sympathizers and allies both within and without the Marxist camp. However, Macpherson's theoretical undertaking is weakened by two essential considerations.

First, his sociologistic orientation undermines his vision of democratic ontology as a theory, although in the tradition of Marx's critique of ideology it serves as a powerful instrument with which to criticize liberalism as possessive individualism. For the normative function of theory beyond its interpretative one becomes paralyzed if it is merely viewed as a reflection of or abstraction from existing social reality. In this case, theory is impotent to prescribe remedies for the transformation of existing social relations which means for Macpherson the transformation of liberalism into a new conception of man and society. In an attempt to prescribe a new ontology of democratic man as an alternative to bourgeois individualism, the logic of Macpherson's sociologistic orientation encounters an impasse or paradox which is surely unintentional on his part. For if theorizing is merely a reflection of the existing social conditions of one who theorizes, Macpherson must by necessity deny the truly *creative* function of theory in the *transformation* of society or the world. In order to change the world, we must first change the very thought of the world: the demand to transform the world by doing involves first the transformation of it by thinking. By virtue of this transformative character of thinking, man alone can be said to have a world rather than an environment. Man is human precisely because he is capable of transforming or transcending a given social condition seen as undesirable; he is the only creature who knows that he is making and changing history, that is, he is capable of thinking an alternative future and achieving it at the same time. This is what Heidegger meant by "understanding" as "project." With him we should see that thinking is not a passive activity to reach a predestined goal but is likened to the *clearing* or opening up actively of the untrodden paths of woods which is venturesome but never reckless. Macpherson wishes to affirm this transformative character of theorizing in order to replace liberalism with a new ontology of democratic man. However, the logic of his own sociologistic thinking denies him that very possibility. The achievement of Macpherson's sociologistic thinking as a critique of liberalism is also its very limitation: in brief, it is a mixed blessing. We are likely to become impressed far more with the power of his negative critique than with that of his positive thinking, although no doubt the former is a precondition for the latter.

Second, Macpherson's democratic ontology or the ethics of human development is preoccupied—albeit self-consciously—with the relation of men to men, with their social relations. In so doing, it ignores the relation of men to nature and its limits which has dire consequences on men's social relations. As a result, the issues of scientism, technocentric rationality, the economics of the earth as a finite planet, and scarcity as the dialectics of socio-psychological propensities and the limits to natural and productive resources are not attended to as integrally as they should be. Because Macpherson separates these two types of relations—relations of men to men and relations of men to nature—and because he views technology as a morally but not ideologically neutral instrument, he fails to come to grips with the destructive, antihumanistic tendencies of technology as the *logos* of everything we think and do today. "Men," Sigmund Freud observed, "have gained control over the forces of nature to such an extent that with their help they would have no difficulty in exterminating one another to the last man."[30] If so, the ethics of human development or the development of a *fully* democratic society must include in it the effects of the alienating, objectifying, repressive, and destructive tendencies of the technocentric culture which is ours. Humanism that ignores the antihumanistic tendencies of technocentric rationality cannot be fully humanistic. It is no accident that Macpherson subordinates the importance of scientism to that of sociologistic explanation in interpreting Hobbes. However, the relationships of subject and object, theory and practice, and the individual and society are three related versions of the same odyssey of man and humanity. Their dignity implies one another; by weakening one, we weaken the rest.

Chapter 8

The Life-World, Historicity, and Truth

Leo Strauss's Encounter with Heidegger and Husserl

L eo Strauss commands the respect and admiration of even his critics and his intellectual carpentry is sharp, cutting, and often rebuking whether its cutting edge be Machiavelli, Max Weber, historicism, positivism, or political behavioralism.[1] In retrospect, Strauss—along with Eric Voegelin—was no doubt a forerunner of what has today become known as the "post-behavioral revolution" in political science. This post-behavioral revolution has now gathered momentum with the inspiration of such diversified sources as the philosophy of Thomas Kuhn, Michael Polanyi, Sheldon Wolin, phenomenology, and the critical theory of the Frankfurt school. The common target of its frontal attack is political behavioralism as epistemology. Strauss has in mind political behavioralism, particularly its value neutrality, when he says: "Only a great fool would call the new political science diabolic: it has no attributes peculiar to fallen angels. It is not even Machiavellian, for Machiavelli's teaching was graceful, subtle, and colorful. Nor is it Neronian. Nevertheless, one may say of it that it fiddles while Rome burns. It is excused by two facts: it does not know that it fiddles, and it does not know that Rome burns."[2]

For Strauss who faithfully interprets the classical tradition particularly of Plato and Aristotle (i.e., "premodern philosophy"), the aim of political philosophy is to seek timeless truth about political things. He is opposed to what he considers to be the two main streams of contemporary philosophy: positivism and historicism.[3] For him, both make political philosophy impossible because they are incapable of seeking timeless truth about political things, that is, because one avows value neutrality and the other value relativity. For Strauss, political philosophy is radically "unscientific" and "unhistorical." It is quite evident that in opposing positivism and historicism he is tempered by absolute moralism, although according to him political philosophy is, strictly speaking, transpolitical, transreligious, and transmoral. It is the moral nihilism of contemporary civilization which Strauss deplores and by which he judges the danger of humanity and the decay of political philosophy itself. He turned to classical thought for guidance. So he writes:

> The meaning of political philosophy and its meaningful character is as evident today as it always has been since the time when political philosophy came to light in Athens. All political action aims at either preservation or change. When desiring to preserve, we wish to bring about something better. All political action is then guided by some thought of better or worse. But thought of better or worse implies thought of the good. The awareness of the good which guides all our actions has the character of opinion: it is no longer questioned but, on reflection, it proves to be questionable. The very fact that we can question it directs us towards such a thought which is no longer opinion but knowledge. All political action has then in itself a directedness towards knowledge of the good: of the good life, or the good society. For the good society is the completest political good.[4]

In defining the concept of political philosophy, however, Strauss always desired to preserve the tradition rather than to change it.

In his two essays published shortly before his death,[5] Strauss revealed his personal acquaintance and academic contact with Husserl and Heidegger and recounted his philosophical encounter with them at Freiburg. In the following pages we shall critically examine Strauss's account of Heidegger's existential ontology and Husserl's phenomenology in relation to his own conception of political philosophy. First, Strauss encounters Heidegger and Husserl on account of historicism or its absence. Second, phenomenology in its transcendental, existential, or hermeneutical version shares with Strauss its critique of scientism. Strauss's focal critique of scientism is on its

value neutrality whereas phenomenology attempts to show the fundamental constitutional or ontological difference between what is human
and what is merely natural or physical and rejects their symmetry.
Because of this difference in focus or attention, phenomenological
thinkers such as Jaspers, Merleau-Ponty, Ricoeur, Schutz, and Maurice
Natanson are far more sympathetic than Strauss toward the "interpretive sociology" of Weber. As has been already intimated, it is
the social phenomenology of Schutz that attempts to reconcile the
"intepretive sociology" of Weber with Husserl's phenomenology and
to go beyond it. Strauss is in sympathy with Husserl's conception
of phenomenology as a "rigorous science" whose rationality goes
back to the Greek notion of *theoria* and the common-sense rationality of political man as the basis of conceptualization in political
science which for Strauss is characteristic of Aristotle's conception
of political science and for the ignorance of which political behavioralism is criticized. Third, according to Strauss, historicism is *the
spirit of our time*. Positivism is necessarily transformed into historicism when the understanding of the latter becomes the necessary basis
of an empirical science of society. From his point of view, to treat
political philosophy as a historical phenomenon is to *relativize* it. By
affirming the essentially historical character of society and of human
thought, historicism is in Strauss's view incapable of raising questions
concerning *the* good society, the completest political good. For him,
then, historicism is a metaphysical position that rejects or is incapable
of justifying the meaning of truth as timeless or transhistorical.[6] It
ends up with denying the idea that "to be" is "always to be." Philosophy is transhistorical in that it transcends the structure of any particular historical period and of the existential *situation* of an individual
thinker. In Strauss's view, this historicist doctrine is embodied, since
Hegel, in the thought of Nietzsche, R. G. Collingwood, and above all
Heidegger.[7] In contrast to existential ontology or "existentialism," we
call this formulation of Strauss "essentialism" or ontological objectivism since it asserts that to know *that* man is (thatness or existence)
must presuppose *what* man is (whatness or essence). To be sure, they
both are concerned with the ontology of man. However, the crucial
difference between them is that the former is an ontological determinism and the latter an ontological indeterminism. One is the version of "human nature" which is predetermined, unchanging, and
universal, whereas the other considers man as "project" or a task to be
achieved which is changing, open, and indeterminate. Strauss contends that the distinction between right and wrong cannot be made if
the nature of man is viewed as historically changing, situated, or con-

ditioned. His focus is on the epistemological issue of *objective* and *universal* knowledge of the good based on the Greek notion of *physis* —the epistemology which avowedly is free of value neutrality (in scientism) and value relativism (in existential ontology or historicism). What is assumed here is that the unchanging structure of *physis* assures the certainty of objective and universal knowledge or intelligibility of the good.[8] Here it is worth emphasizing again as we have in chapter 2 that temporally speaking, phenomenological ontology is an affirmation of the open future in the passage of time, whereas essentialism is a fidelity to the past. *Man is a historical being.* History is real history only if there is man who is its subject; and man is the subject of history insofar as he is historically situated. In other words, there is an indelible dialectic between consciousness and history: not only is history a product of consciousness but consciousness is also a product of history. Man is never unconditioned freedom or total absence of freedom caught in the universal world of *conceived* relationships in the manner of Hegel's or Strauss's intellectualist objectivism. On the one hand, therefore, concretely lived history as the embodiment of interconnected situations is not inscribed in the abstract books of philosophy; rather, when concretely viewed, history is an "open notebook" in which acts and events are yet to be written, that is, the future is a contingency in which the advent or invention of meaning occurs.[9] On the other hand, freedom is a dialectical mediation between man's subjectivity and his situatedness in history: his freedom is the result of both constituting and constituted history. To be *effective,* freedom is neither completely constituted facticity nor unlimited transcendence but is the concrete *choice* of one alternative among others on occasions of meaning and action.[10] Consequently, history as the arena of freedom and action, that is, as *responsibility,* is neither capricious nor necessitarian. The phenomenological thought we are propounding here for our purpose traverses a midpoint between the Scylla of human nature as immutable and the Charybdis of its Heraclitean flux.[11] It is the dialectical way in which the absolute "freedom" and the absolute "nature" of man are disarmed.[12] In the end, the two opposing conceptions of man between phenomenological ontology and Strauss's essentialism will lead to two equally opposing conceptions of hermeneutics as the art of interpretation—in the very language Strauss uses, the irreconcilable quarrel between the "ancients" and the "moderns." If we were to call a stand-off between these two conceptions of man and hermeneutics and to refuse to acknowledge the superiority of ours over his, we would be historical relativists, and that would make our present argument superfluous.

For Strauss, Heidegger—along with Husserl, Bergson, and White-head—ranks as one of the great philosophers of our century. The target of Strauss's criticism of Heidegger is not that Heidegger along with the others has neglected political philosophy but that his philosophy lying at a "hard center" rather than a "flabby periphery" of existentialism has reached the peak of historicism which renders impossible the very conception of philosophy (and thus political philosophy) as Strauss defines it.[13] For him, there is no room for political philosophy in Heidegger's thought. Despite his critique of the alleged historicism of Heidegger, Strauss respects him as a revisionary thinker and scholar.[14] In comparing the "new thinking" of Franz Rosenzweig with that of Heidegger, Strauss tells us that the latter had a keener sense than the former of what is demanded in order to overcome or surpass the traditional philosophy which rests on the Greek foundations although admittedly "Heidegger's new thinking led far away from any charity as well as from any humanity."[15] Whereas Rosenzweig regarded most Platonic dialogues as "boring," Heidegger in contrast took Greek philosophy seriously. To be sure, Heidegger himself thought that along with German, Greek is the most spiritual of all languages. Although according to Strauss it was the direct influence of his friend Jacob Klein who led him to the discovery of the importance of Greek philosophy, perhaps one cannot minimize the influence of Heidegger (except for his revisionary intentions) on both Klein and Strauss in pointing *the way* to Greek philosophy. Strauss is certainly right in pointing out that Heidegger turned to Greek philosophy (and the history of philosophy) for the purpose of uprooting it. Heidegger's intention was obviously to revise and surpass the tradition whereas Strauss tries to preserve and conserve it. It is mistake to think, however, that Heidegger's deconstruction or call for the end of (Western) philosophy or metaphysics is an invitation to irrationalism or to end human reason. On the contrary, he declares that with the end of philosophy thinking does not come to an end but comes to another beginning.[16]

Therefore, Heidegger's existential ontology or "fundamental ontology" in *Being and Time* must be understood in relation to his later thought after his celebrated enunciation of "reversal" or "turn" (*Kehre*) in *Letter on Humanism* in 1947. In the foreword to William J. Richardson's study on his thought, Heidegger wrote: "The thinking of the reversal *is* a change in my thought. But this change is not a consequence of altering the standpoint, much less of abandoning the fundamental issue, of *Being and Time*."[17] All along Heidegger's thought has been centered around the question of Being in which the being of man or human reality as "Being-in-the-world" has only an ontological privilege among other beings.[18] Although Strauss is aware of Heidegger's later thought, he consistently identifies the spirit of Heidegger's thought with existentialism (as historicism)—that thought which claims the priority of human *being* or historical existence over Being. Contrary to Strauss's interpretation, even in *Being and Time*—let alone in the train of his thought—Heidegger not only *absolutizes* rather than relativizes historicity but also elevates the ordinary language of common existence to the level of philosophical terminology, the feat of which Strauss so much admires in the philosophy of Aristotle as opposed to the technical jargon of political behavioralism. It is certainly true that Heidegger has a *sense of history* and faces up to it rather than ignores it. For this very reason, as we have already noted, Heidegger exalts the Marxist view of history over all the others. Historical consciousness, however, is not identical with historicism as Strauss defines it. It is precisely from the sense of history, that is, the sense of relevance of premodernity to modernity that Strauss himself turns or returns to the classical or premodern tradition of philosophy. Otherwise, premodernity would be only a historical relic without relevance to modernity.

In Strauss's view, Heidegger betrays the philosophical spirit of his teacher Husserl. For Husserl's philosophy is contrary to Heidegger's historicism. Thus Strauss in turn uses Husserl's notion of philosophy as rigorous science to attack Heidegger's historicism. Although in *Being and Time* Heidegger radicalized Husserl's phenomenology of internal time-consciousness, he never disavowed the validity of phenomenology itself. Rather, he proposes a revision of phenomenology of which Husserl himself never approved. Nonetheless, it is perfectly in the spirit of Husserl's philosophical endeavor which always sought to open up a new avenue or beginning of phenomenology. He emphasized *doing* phenomenology rather than edifying it as an unchanging set of doctrines. Even in *Being and Time*, Heidegger defines the aim of phenomenology as the *disclosure* (disclosure) of what it *is* as it *is* without prior conceptual prejudice or reification. This is Heidegger's interpretation of *physis* as *aletheia* which opposes the reduction of it to "Nature."

Although according to Strauss, Heidegger's historicism has no room for political philosophy, he is not alien to politics. Strauss points to Heidegger's brief involvement with Nazism in the early 1930's and cites Heidegger's mention in 1953 of German National Socialism for its inner truth and greatness.[19] There are personal dimensions as well as different conceptions of philosophy in conflict. In his student days

Strauss was interested in theology and politics and became a political
Zionist at the age of seventeen. Justifiably Klein comes to the conclusion that though Heidegger is an intellectual giant of our time, his
moral qualities are unfortunately no match for his intellectual ones.[20]
By his own confession, Strauss could not "stomach" the moral teaching of Heidegger or the absence of it. He seems to think that there is
an inner logic between Heidegger's commitment to Nazism and his
doctrine of "resoluteness" (*Entschlossenheit*) in *Being and Time*.[21] What
Strauss could not stomach was the absence or lack of direction to
which Heidegger's notion of resoluteness leads. Is there really an
ineluctable logic between a philosopher's own *theoria* and his social
and political *praxis*? In judging Heidegger, Strauss seems to think that
there is.[22] Although there is a world of difference between the politics
of Hitler and that of Nixon, Strauss publicly supported Nixon in the
presidential campaign of 1971. If he were still alive today with the
knowledge of Nixon's politics of deceits and lies in the Watergate
affair including his anti-Semitic remarks, I wonder what Strauss
would now say.[23] Does the fallibility or infallibility of Strauss's political
commitment necessarily emanate from the intrinsic makeup of his
philosophy? I think not. If it does, then his political philosophy must
be judged in the same way he judges Heidegger's philosophy. Perhaps
the validity of one's philosophy should not be judged as lodging in the
failure or success of his political nerves; one's political commitment
alone will not suffice to judge the validity of his philosophy. The
lacuna of political commitment and philosophical reflection is in a way
the persisting twilight zone of *theoria* and *praxis*. As for me I endorse
neither Strauss's nor Heidegger's political commitment even if I ap-
prove of their common critique of scientism as the spirit of modern
times. The most important issue involved here is not, I think, a matter
of recounting and forgiving or forgetting the past political errors of
Heidegger but how to interpret and apply creatively his philosophical
insights concerning the nature of thinking and human reality for
political understanding. Herein lies the real potential of Heidegger's
thought for political theorizing which is yet fully to be explored.[24]

As he is opposed to historicism and the ambiguity of moral fortitude
in Heidegger, Strauss takes Husserl's view of philosophy as rigorous
science as forsaking the temptation of historicism.

It was the emergence and increasing influence of Husserl's phenomenology, according to Strauss's assessment, that brought about
the downfall of the Marburg school of neo-Kantianism founded
by Hermann Cohen. Although Strauss attended Husserl's lectures
regularly at Freiburg in 1922 after finishing his doctorate at Ham-

burg, he says that he did not derive any great benefit from them; he attributes this lack of benefit from Husserl to his intellectual immaturity. The more likely reason, however, seems to be the fact that at that time Strauss was interested in theology while Husserl was engaged in developing a new philosophy called phenomenology as a descriptive science. When Strauss once asked Husserl about theology, Husserl replied: "If there is a datum 'God' we shall describe it."[25] What impressed Strauss most about phenomenology seems to be Husserl's own comment that it begins with "the foundation" whereas the Marburg school begins with "the roof."[26] Indeed, in "Philosophy as Rigorous Science" (*Philosophie als strenge Wissenschaft*)[27] Husserl speaks of phenomenology as a "philosophy from the ground up" (*Philosophie von unten*)[28]—the philosophy that brings back to light the "things themselves," the experiential data of conscious life.

Two pieces of Husserl's work that particularly attracted Strauss's attention are "Philosophy as Rigorous Science" in an issue of *Logos* (1910-11) and a lecture Husserl delivered before the Vienna Cultural Society (*Wiener Kulturbund*) on May 8 and 10, 1935 which was received enthusiastically by the audience. The original title of this lecture, commonly known as "The Vienna Lecture," was "Philosophy in the Crisis of European Humanity" (*Philosophie in der Krisis der europäischen Menschheit*).[29]

In "Philosophy as Rigorous Science," Husserl is critical of two major schools in contemporary thought: naturalism and historicism. On the one hand, he carefully distinguishes phenomenological psychology based on the intentional structure of psychic life from naturalism or physicalistic psychology which reduces all forms of conscious activity to merely physical phenomena. As the naturalization of consciousness is the death of consciousness, it makes the psychology of consciousness and thus the science of man impossible. On the other hand, Husserl is also critical of historicism—not history or historiography but the doctrine that interprets truth as relative to the historical development of consciousness. By historicism Husserl had in mind the *Weltanschauungsphilosophie* or *Lebensphilosophie* of Dilthey whose legitimate heir Strauss thinks is Heidegger. Since philosophy as a *Weltanschauung* is an expression of a given period of history varying from one period to another, the *Weltanschauungsphilosophie* of Dilthey denies philosophy as standing for absolute, timeless values. As Husserl puts it, "For the sake of time we must not sacrifice eternity."[30] Philosophy as rigorous science is "supratemporal," not limited by relatedness to the spirit of one period of time or another. Husserl offers phenomenology as alternative epistemology to historicism thus defined. It is phenomenology as a theory of essence (*Wesen*) which is capable of extending itself from individual facts to general essences or ideal entities concerning the entire spectrum of human culture (*Geist*) whether it be religious, aesthetic, ethical, political, legal, or technological. Thus for Husserl, phenomenology as rigorous science alone is capable of providing the foundation for a philosophy of human culture. There is a structural similarity between Husserl's critique of naturalism and historicism and Strauss's critique of positivism and historicism, since political philosophy is for Strauss radically "unscientific" and "unhistorical." While Husserl is concerned with a critique of Dilthey in particular, Strauss focuses on a critique of the historicism of Heidegger's thought.

The Vienna Lecture of Husserl was written at the wake of Nazism in Germany, a political nihilism and the beginning of a holocaust for European Jewry. It reflects the plight of the time, and so Husserl speaks of the sickness of Europe and the existential plight of European humanity. The role of philosophy is passionately defended by Husserl as the guide not only for European man but also for the whole of humanity. For him, philosophy as Greek *theoria* exercises its function as "one which is archontic for European civilization as a whole"[31] and as such constitutes the root and springboard for the whole of humanity. So the philosopher is the "civil servant" of humanity. As the crisis of philosophy is also the crisis of human existence, the sense of history depends on the sense of philosophy.

Husserl's Vienna Lecture opposes the spectrum of *objectivism* which forgets the subjectivity of *theoria* and *praxis* and the rootedness of theoretical consciousness or attitude in the intersubjective life-world as its "meaning-fundament." It is no longer the historicism of Dilthey that is under attack. Husserl calls him "one of the greatest humanists" who devoted his whole life to a clarification of the relation between the human and the natural, although Husserl believes that it is a mistake for the humanistic disciplines to compete with the naturalistic disciplines for equal status.[32] Instead, the humanists—the philosopher in particular—must focus on the "forgotten" dimension of subjectivity as the fountainhead of all achievements in the history of European philosophy and science independently of the naturalists. The autonomy of philosophy from the yoke of positivism is for Husserl tantamount to the establishment of a new theoretical attitude. For positivism decapitates philosophy.

For Strauss, however, the essence of the Husserlian philosophical spirit that comes closest to the contribution of political philosophy lies in the notion of philosophy as rigorous science and thus the Vienna

Lecture of 1935 is a continuation of this single thought. Strauss approvingly cites a passage from Husserl's Vienna Lecture: "Those conservatives who are satisified with the tradition and the philosophical men will fight each other, and the struggle will surely occur in the sphere of political power. The persecution begins at the very beginnings of philosophy. Men who live for these ideas become objects of contempt. And yet, ideas are stronger than any empirical powers."[33] Husserl's description of philosophy's predicament and exaltation may be likened to those of Socrates who confronted the dilemma of reconciling the *telos* of philosophy with the morality of the city. For Strauss this passage of Husserl suggests that in order to understand philosophy as rigorous science one must look at the essential character of the political conflict between the two antagonists. Thus the aim of philosophy to replace opinion (the element of the city) by knowledge not only is subversive in intention but also manifests itself ultimately as a political conflict.

In contrast to his conception of political philosophy derived from the study of premodern philosophy, Strauss contends that modern philosophy has a radically different character in that it attempts to bridge the lacuna between philosophy and the polis by two innovations: (1) the identification of the aim of philosophy with that of the city and (2) the diffusion of philosophical results among the men of the city which is highlighted by Kant's teaching of the primacy of practical and moral reason over theoretical reason. Even if phenomenology is a *modern* philosophy, Strauss is sympathetic to it *only* as rigorous science which is a continuation of the premodern spirit of philosophy. As he sees it, then, phenomenology as rigorous science is "unscientific" and "unhistorical."

By the same token, for Strauss, Hobbes did *not* make a radical break with earlier political philosophy as he once had thought. Instead, Machiavelli deserves the honor of being the originator of modern political philosophy. For Hobbes's imitation of Galilean new physics, however important it may be, is secondary to the founding of modern science by Galileo and Descartes.[34] Hobbes's philosophy of politics (or civil philosophy) in its vital substance, that is, in its political and moral content, is independent of his scientific view of man and the world. On the contrary, for Husserl the crisis of modern philosophy culminating in naturalism began with Galileo's mathematization of nature. Naturalism or naturalistic psychology continues from Hobbes and Locke to Wilhelm Wundt.[35] For the Husserlian point of view, therefore, as modernity begins with Galileo and his mathematization of nature, it is Hobbes who deserves the honor of being the originator of modern political philosophy by creating consciously in his *magnum opus Leviathan* the "mathematics of politics" comparable to the Galilean mathematization of nature.

Although Strauss refers to Husserl's *Crisis*, especially the Vienna Lecture of 1935, he evaluates it in terms of its continuity with Husserl's earlier view of philosophy as rigorous science. Strauss recognizes many changes which have taken place in Husserl's thought after "Philosophy as Rigorous Science." He fails to see, however, a radical change of focus if no break occurred in the Vienna Lecture and the Prague Lectures which were incorporated into the *Crisis* manuscript.[36] Thus our critical note on Strauss is based as much on what he has *not* said as on what he has said. In the *Crisis*, Husserl's preoccupation is no longer with historicism but with naturalism or positivism which denigrates philosophy. Here he attempts to develop the phenomenology of the life-world. Philosophical *rigor* changes its accent by focusing on the archaeology of the knowing subject rooted in the everyday life-world as the ultimate and most comprehensive horizon of meaning that constitutes the *foundation* of *theoria*. Like Heidegger in *Being and Time*, Husserl comes forthrightly to terms with history and the historicity of theoretical consciousness by way of transcendental subjectivity as intersubjectivity. In view of Heidegger's *Being and Time* and Husserl's *Crisis*, we can conclude that while positivism takes for granted the everyday life-world or prescientific world and, for this very reason, may be charged with negligence, Strauss's conception of political philosophy is guilty of self-contradiction.

Strauss's conception of philosophy, his essentialism based on the premodern tradition is self-contradictory because it fails to reconcile itself with the intersubjective life-world as the "meaning-fundament" of theoretical consciousness and neglects to explore and show the way in which the "theoretical attitude" is dependent upon the "natural attitude." In the *Crisis* and also *Experience and Judgment*, in getting at the foundation first rather than the roof, Husserl attempts to show and justify the everyday life-world as the ultimate horizon of meaning which is presupposed in all theoretical activity both philosophical and scientific. The life-world is the universal founding soil upon which all *praxis* is based—not only the *praxis* of everyday life but also the *praxis* of cognition and judgment. The primary task of phenomenology is to discover and show the genesis of meaning in the life-world as it is related to the "natural attitude," the experiential infrastructure of *theoria*. The being of the world in totality is for Husserl the presupposition of all judgment. It is the self-examination of philosophy as human activity and achievement rooted in the life-world that is absent in Strauss's conception of political philosophy.

Strauss, however, understands Husserl's endeavor as the way of getting at the foundation rather than the roof—this foundation being the prescientific world as the theoretical understanding of the world starts from "our common understanding of the world, from our understanding of the world as sensibly perceived prior to theorizing."[37] In *Natural Right and History*, Strauss himself speaks of the "prescientific" or "natural" world, "the world in which we live and act," which is not "the object or the product of a theoretical attitude." It is the world of "things" or "affairs" which we handle rather than the world of mere objects at which we detachedly look. Strauss is critical of Weber for the error of not having attempted "a coherent analysis of the social world as it is known to 'common sense,' or of social reality as it is known in social life or in action."[38] Based on his interpretation of Aristotelian political science, Strauss equally deplores political behavioralism which is deeply embedded in the tradition of the *modern* conceptualization of science primarily because it takes for granted the common-sense language of political man which the technical language of political science presupposes. This same argument, as we have already noted, is used by Schutz in his phenomenological critique of the positivist methodology of the social sciences. Although for Strauss the ultimate aim of science in the sense of Greek *epistēmē* is to free itself from the bondage of prescientific opinion (*doxa*) and thus the ultimate aim of political science is to replace political opinion with political knowledge, he recognizes the dependence or rootedness of scientific understanding on the prescientific or common-sense understanding (or "natural cognition") of political things. Jacob Klein observes that "In Greek science, concepts are formed in continual dependence on 'natural,' prescientific experience, from which the scientific concept is 'abstracted.' The meaning of this 'abstraction,' through which the conceptual character of any concept is determined, is *the* pressing ontological problem of antiquity. . . ."[39]

If, however, Strauss's notion of the prescientific world was influenced in any way by Husserl's phenomenology of the life-world, he misunderstood it in a significant way because he interprets it as a historic concept. For Strauss, we cannot identify the prescientific world with the world in which we *now* live because the latter "is already a product of science. To say nothing of technology, the world in which we live is free from ghosts, witches, and so on, with which, but for the existence of science, it would abound"; therefore, "to grasp the natural world as a world that is radically prescientific or pre-philosophic, one has to go back beyond the first emergence of science or philosophy. It is not necessary for this purpose to engage in extensive and necessarily hypothetical anthropological studies."[40] On the contrary, for Husserl the everyday life-world is primarily an analytic rather than a historic concept. As such, to discover the structure of the life-world it is not necessary for us to go back to the "primitive" or "prehistoric" conditions of man or to engage in what Strauss calls "hypothetical anthropological studies"—although in search of "natural man" and the "primitive" they may help us to uncover the garb of our "second nature" dressed up in the name of "civilization" or "history." For the world of science or scientific knowledge "flows" into the everyday life-world in which we *now* live, and accordingly the common-sense world of ordinary men in the street progressively absorbs it. For the very reason that scientific knowledge flows into or permeates the everyday life-world, it makes sense to characterize modern culture as a scientific one.

No doubt there is ambiguity in Husserl's formulation of the life-world and its structures. In his recent study of Husserl's phenomenology and the problem of history, David Carr points out that there are two distinguishable if not incompatible meanings in Husserl's notion of the life-world: the "cultural world" on the one hand and the "perceptual world" on the other. Carr further suggests that these two meanings may be reconciled by subsuming the latter under the former.[41] It is Merleau-Ponty who takes up the theme of Husserl's life-world and develops it fully into a phenomenology of perception. For Merleau-Ponty, as we have noted, the perceived world (the "prelinguistic" and "precultural" world) is the presupposed foundation of all cultural rationality—the rationality of everyday *praxis* as well as that of *theoria*.

While he approves of Husserl's treatment of philosophy as rigorous science extending to the *Crisis* and poses it against the historicism of Heidegger, Strauss is curiously silent on the problem of historicity or the historicity of subjectivity (or transcendental subjectivity) which for the first time in the *Crisis* Husserl takes seriously. Recent studies on Husserl point increasingly to the predicament or paradox of Husserl's ideal of transcendental phenomenology as apodictic and universal science on the one hand and historicism on the other. They have come to the conclusion that in Husserl the ideal of philosophy as universal science is split with the historicism of the *Crisis* and their ontological rift is beyond repair. Is Husserl's dream of phenomenology as universal science over? Is Husserl's reduction condemned to incompletion? Although according to Carr the attainment of phe-

nomenology as nonrelative and transhistorical truth is essential to
Husserl's conception of philosophy, his earlier ideal of transcendental
phenomenology must be radically altered. Paraphrasing Merleau-
Ponty's celebrated remarks on phenomenological reduction, Carr
states that "the most important lesson which the *historical* reduction teaches us is the impossibility of a complete reduction."[42] The
term "historical reduction" was coined by Carr who forthrightly captures Husserl's spirit of rigorous scrutiny in grappling with the problem of historicity even at the risk of "dismantling" his earlier posture
or forsaking his absolute epistemological stance on philosophy as a
transhistorical enterprise. Carr comes to the conclusion that Husserl's
"absolute standpoint" or idea of nonrelative and transhistorical truth,
though essential to Husserl's conception of philosophy, nonetheless
plays "the role of an unfulfilled *telos,* a project which gives philosophy its senses."[43] To be sure, historical reduction is Husserl's way
of arriving at the invariant general structure that underlies all relativities or variant versions of the life-world as the cultural world.
As he himself says, the life-world is "historically changing in its particular styles but [is] invariant in its invariant structure of generality."[44]

What we learn from Husserl's historical reduction but not from
Strauss's conception of philosophy is the *radical* and *critical* rigor of
philosophizing. One might say in the end that while Strauss begins
with the roof and never reaches the foundation, Husserl begins with
the foundation and reaches the roof by way of historical reduction. In
other words, Husserl goes to the *root* of the matter by finding,
whenever possible, problems previously overlooked and unexplored,
asking new questions, and revising and transcending what has immediately preceded. Even his last, not completely finished manuscript
Crisis has the subtitle "an *introduction* to phenomenological philosophy." As we have already emphasized in chapter 1, it is in this critical
spirit in search of the fundamental and elemental that Husserl
opened up new avenues for answering philosophical questions—a
truly Socratic method. As a critical enterprise, philosophy is a constant
reminder not to forget the *existential,* human source of all knowledge.
Only in this sense must Husserl's phenomenology be understood as
an archaeology of subjectivity as the source of both *theoria* and *praxis.*
This is the only way in which Husserl's phenomenology as a movement can be *under*stood.

Whether or not Husserl succeeds in grappling with historical reduction or resolving historicism, what is most important is the fact that he
has attempted to come to terms with historicity whereas Strauss sim-

ply bypasses it. As long as there is history, the historicity of philosophy will not simply disappear beyond the dark clouds of temporality by declaring philosophy's disavowal to it or allegiance to the presence of eternity or eternal truth. As Carr puts it, "instead of being historically naive, he [Husserl] proceeds, through historical reduction, with the explicit consciousness of the historical context within which he operates."[45] Strauss's own return to premodern philosophy is predicated on the idea that in presupposing its superiority over modern philosophy, it is historically *relevant* to modernity, i.e., the need of the past for the present, which in itself is a historical act. Premodern philosophy definitely has a *message* for modernity. To say that for the ancients philosophy was not just peculiar to their own time and place is to *interpret*. Only by way of interpretation is the past transformed into a living present for us—the *presence* of eternity. If philosophy is freedom from prejudices (i.e., from pre-judgments), nothing must be taken for granted. It is concerning the nature of hermeneutics as the art of interpretation that Strauss and Gadamer confront each other. They command each other's respect. Gadamer regards Strauss as "a radical critic of the political thought of the contemporary world." Strauss, in turn, regards Gadamer's *Truth and Method* as "the most important work written by a Heideggerian."[46] For Gadamer, the famous *querelle des anciens et des modernes*, which began near the end of the seventeenth century with the French literary circle, ceases to be a real alternative. He considers it resolved in his hermeneutical ontology, whereas for Strauss this quarrel still constitutes the "fundamental difference" between his stand for antiquity and Gadamer's hermeneutics.

For Strauss, the most basic exegetical principle is that the exegete must understand an author as he understood himself in opposition to the "historicist" claim that the thought of the past can be understood better than it understood itself—it was Dilthey who viewed the final goal of hermeneutics to be "to understand the author better than he understood himself."[47] On the one hand, Strauss views the role of interpretation as a fidelity to authorial meaning, as "ministerial" or canonical to the original text, or as essentially "reproductive," and thus belongs admittedly to the tradition of "prehistoricist" hermeneutics. On the other hand, Gadamer views the existential act of interpretation as "productive," that is, as the dialectical appropriation of transmission and renewal without violating authorial meaning based on his important notions of "historically operative consciousness" and a "fusion of horizons" which, as we have already discussed in chapter 4, bear the assimilated imprints of Heidegger's ontology and Husserl's phenomenology. In essence, hermeneutics as the art of interpretation is never merely reproductive duplication or replication.

Three essential points must be made to answer Strauss's allegation of "historicism" or, more precisely, historical relativism in Heidegger and Gadamer. Strauss must show or account for rather than assume or assert the "unhistorical" character of philosophical thought. Although Strauss's works make a significant contribution to hermeneutical theory as his careful exegesis of classical thought abounds, Gadamer is correct in observing that Strauss (in his exegesis of classical thought) shows only that the classical philosophers thought "unhistorically"—that is, "differently from the moderns"—but says nothing about the possibility of thinking "unhistorically" today since, unlike the ancient originators, the moderns have their *tradition* of thought before them.[48] Correlatively, moreover, Strauss underestimates the difficulties involved in exegesis—such a question as whether the author understood what he said in only one way, that is, "clearly." Does the author always mean what he says? Does he really know so exactly what he means in every word or sentence? Does Strauss himself not say that the daylight of what is said even clearly must be seen in the light of the night of what is unsaid? Gadamer's contention that Strauss does not show how the "moderns"—equally with the "ancients"—can think "unhistorically," I think, pinpoints Strauss's failure to come to grips with the hermeneutical problematique of historicity or historical consciousness and falls into historical naïveté. This naïveté is a prejudice against the prejudice of historicity (i.e., the prejudice of intellectual essentialism). The problem of historicity is *universal* insofar as man remembers the past and projects himself into the future. Accordingly, the hermeneutical problem of historical consciousness is universal in every kind of inquiry. Not only is Heidegger's ontology not a form of "historicism" as defined by Strauss, but also the impasses of historicism, according to Gadamer, were overcome by and led to a new development in Heidegger: "For the hermeneutic importance of temporal distance could be understood only as a result of the ontological direction that Heidegger gave to understanding as an 'existential' [project] and of his temporal interpretation of the mode of being of there-being [*Da-sein*]."[49] In short, either the effectiveness of historical consciousness must be demonstrated as in Gadamer's hermeneutical phenomenology or the "unhistoricity" of philosophical truth must be proved which Strauss fails to do. The naïveté of Strauss lies in not suspecting or examining his own prejudice, that is, truth as "unhistorical." For Gadamer, on the contrary,

"True historical thinking must take account of its own historicality [sic]."[50]

Second, the hermeneutical thought of Heidegger and Gadamer does not assume the superior perspective of the present over the past. In the case of Gadamer, he specifically disavows the "historicist" claim of Dilthey that the aim of interpretation is to understand an author better than he understood himself. Gadamer insists that hermeneutical vigilance through "historically operative consciousness" aims to see the past in its own terms rather than in terms of our contemporary criteria and prejudices. He continues:

> Historical thinking has its dignity and its value as truth in the acknowledgement that there is no such thing as "the present", but rather constantly changing horizons of future and past. It is by no means settled (and can never be settled) that any particular perspective in which transmitted thoughts present themselves is the right one. The "historical" understanding, whether today's or tomorrow's, has no special privilege. It is itself embraced by the changing horizons and moved with them.[51]

As the meaning of a text not occasionally but always goes beyond its author, understanding or interpretation has not merely a "reproductive" but always a "productive" orientation as well, which is not to say that this productive element is some sort of superior understanding.

Third and last, Strauss is forgetful of that form of historicism which is the genuine alternative to scientism—that view in which because of the radical ontological difference between what is merely natural and what is genuinely human, the social and historical sciences must *accordingly* adopt a methodology radically different from that of the natural sciences. This forgetfulness of Strauss is due simply to the fact that he is preoccupied with the question of knowledge of the good in his critique of modernity. Historicity is nothing but man's self-consciousness of what he makes in a unified fusion of temporal horizons. Insofar as time itself is ineradicable, the question of what is "transhistorical" must be sought and resolved indeed within rather than without the concept of history. Because of the finitude of man and thus of his thought, in the final analysis, philosophical reflection can only glimpse eternity in time or the ephemeral *presence* of eternity here and now. This glimpse, as the life and thought of Strauss so eloquently testify and exemplify, is both its possibility and limitation. This, I think, is the highest tribute we can accord to a philosopher living or dead.

PART FOUR——Conclusion

The end of a philosophy is the account of its beginning.

—*Maurice Merleau-Ponty*

Chapter 9

The Triumph of Subjectivity in the Conduct of Political Inquiry

If, as Merleau-Ponty says, "the end of a philosophy is the account of its beginning,"[1] it is only befitting for us to recount what we have said in the beginning of this study concerning the nature of phenomenological thinking in relation to political inquiry. We have described phenomenology as a new way of thinking about man as both knower and actor. Like Kuhn, the economist and philosopher Kenneth E. Boulding some years ago characterized revolution or a new way in thinking as requiring the *conversion* of knowledge in which the messages of the outside world are being filtered through the conscious working of an individual that causes a radical transformation in his conduct—both conceptual and behavioral.[2] In our discussion on phenomenology as a new way of thinking, however, we have focused on *conceptual* transformation in political inquiry, that is, the nature of thinking about political things. Reflective autonomy demands a distanciation from the world of practical interests and concerns. However, in demanding autonomy, the former does not relinquish the latter; rather, they are in a dialectical mediation not only because the world is a totality of both the given

165

and the constructed but also because, in order to change the world, we must first change our way of thinking about it. As Alan F. Blum puts it:

> Theorizing consists of the methods for producing a possible society. A possible society is the theorist's method for re-forming his knowing of society. Since the theorist is engaged in re-forming *his knowledge* of society, he can be seen as re-forming his knowledge. One who is re-forming his knowledge is re-forming his self: theorizing is then best described not as a sense-transforming operation but as a self-transforming operation, where what one operates upon is one's knowledge of the society as part of one's history, biography, and form of life.[3]

Only in this sense is thinking a special way of existing in the world, and in it there is an intimate nexus between *meaning* and *existence*. Existence without thought is *meaningless* and thought without existence is *aimless*. Therefore, for Arendt as for Merleau-Ponty, "To think and to be fully alive are the same. . . . [Thinking] is an activity that accompanies living and is concerned with such concepts as justice, happiness, virtue, offered us by language itself as expressing the meaning of whatever happens in life and occurs to us while we are alive."[4]

What is radical and rigorous in phenomenological thinking in relation to political inquiry is twofold: (1) the recovery of ontology as the basis of epistemology and (2) the self-examination of thinking consciousness itself as human project. The aim of political thinking is to think about politics. However, all political knowing, even the most simple and crude, implies an idea of man. Like phenomenological thinkers, Leo Strauss and C. B. Macpherson dwell on the nature or essence of man which defines the aim of their political thought. However, their ontological concern is flawed—each in a different way. While his "sociologistic" thinking in the tradition of Marx's critique of ideology and the modern sociology of knowledge is a useful intellectual tool to uncover the limitations of liberalism as possessive individualism, Macpherson's conception of theorizing is flawed because it is in conflict with the "projective" or "prospective" character of theorizing which he wishes to promote in constructing a humanistic ontology of democratic polity as an alternative to possessive individualism. On the other hand, Strauss defines the nature of man as ahistorical and immutable. Thus the fundamental difference between his intellectualist objectivism and the phenomenological view of man is an ontological one rather than the mere conception of philosophy alone, that is to say, it is a conflict in the very philosophy of man. For the former, "human nature" is a fixed, determinate, and finished essence subject to no historical vicissitudes and vectors whose eternity alone certifies knowledge or "truth," whereas for the latter, man is a task to be accomplished in which his "ontological privilege" is not like "painting endless murals on the walls of time in order to find out what his nature has always been."[5]

It is in political behavioralism and particularly the cybernetic thinking of man as scientism or scientific epistemology, however, that ontological issues are ignored or the ontology of man is defined in terms of the epistemological model of the physical sciences. It is ignorant of man as *embodied project*. If the aim of political thinking is to think about the nature of political things *as they are*, behavioralist epistemology takes for granted the fundamental ontological *differentia* between what is uniquely human and what is merely natural, organic, or artificial. Schutz's phenomenological plea for "subjective interpretation" in the social sciences is merely an extension of the recognition of this ontological issue: unlike the natural sciences, the social sciences cannot take for granted the meaning structures of the life-world as "social reality" precisely because it is their very observational field. Thus "subjective interpretation" alone is the prerequisite condition in assuring *objectivity* in the social sciences and "hermeneutical autonomy" in cross-cultural studies. Moreover, political behavioralism inevitably results in a false eschatology of techniques for the same reason that it is ignorant of the primacy of ontology over epistemology.

The existentiality or historicity of man affirms both that he *stands out from* nature and that as an individual he *stands out from* other individuals in which their individual differences thicken the density of intersubjectivity. It should be emphasized that to recognize the ontological *differentia* between man and nature, that is, the *privileged* position of man from the rest of nature is not to fall into homocentrism or anthropocentrism. It is not the negation by man of nature in the manner of Hegel and his followers. The *social principle* of man and nature is the idea of harmony as infused unity of *differences* or a multiplicity of different living beings and nonliving things. It is technocentric thinking that is homocentric and thus destroys the social principle of man and nature.

Social phenomenology also views the nature of man as a dialectical mediation between absolute "freedom" and absolute "nature," between constituted facticity and unlimited transcendence, or between the Heraclitean flux of "history" and the immutable patterns of "nature." Merleau-Ponty thus declares that "Human existence will force us to revise our usual notion of necessity and contingency, because it is the transformation of contingency into necessity by the act of carrying forward. All that we are, we are on the basis of a *de facto* situation which we appropriate to ourselves and which we ceaselessly transform by a sort of *escape* which is never an unconditioned freedom."[6] Concerned with the "human condition," Arendt too argues that uniqueness or distinction and plurality or equality are not mutually opposed categories. "Plurality," she writes, "is the condition of human action because we are all the same, that is, human, in such a way that nobody is ever the same as anyone else who ever lived, lives, or will live."[7] Man lives as a distinct and unique being among human equals. Thus human plurality has the twofold character of equality and distinction in both deed and speech. On the one hand, if men are not equal, that is, not human, they cannot understand other men—predecessors, consociates, contemporaries, and successors or those groups of individuals who lived, live, and will live. On the other hand, if men are not distinguished from other men, they would be in no need to make themselves understood to or communicate with others.[8] Moreover, Arendt argues forcefully for the human situation conditioned by the external world of matter when she writes:

> Men are conditioned beings because everything they come in contact with turns immediately into a condition of their existence. The world in which *vita activa* spends itself consists of things produced by human activities; but the things that owe their existence exclusively to men nevertheless constantly condition their human makers. In addition to the conditions under which life is given to man on earth, and partly out of them, men constantly create their own, self-made conditions, which, their human origin and their variability notwithstanding, possess the same conditioning power as natural things. Whatever touches or enters into a sustained relationship with human life immediately assumes the character of a condition of human existence. This is why men, no matter what they do, are always conditioned beings. Whatever enters the human world of its own accord or is drawn into it by human effort becomes part of the human condition. The impact of the world's reality upon human existence is felt and received as a conditioned force. The objectivity of the world—its object- or thing-character—and the human condition supplement each other; because human existence is conditioned existence, it would be impossible without things, and things would be a heap of unrelated articles, a non-world, if they were not the conditioners of human existence.[9]

So man is conditioned by things both living and nonliving or man-made as well as the existence of other men. Accordingly, we must redefine our notion of "nature" and "history" (or "culture") in such a way that they will not become dichotomous or one-sided. Merleau-Ponty indeed envisioned an intertwinement of the "visible" nature and the "invisible" mind by means of the body as their natural, living bond. This is why it is so important for him to look into the body as "flesh" in a new way that may unlock the mystery of the visible and the invisible. Most importantly, however, man's existence is conditioned by "coexistence" or "plurality," by the existence of other men. To designate more vividly the intertwined web of conditioning and being conditioned in human relationships, we need a new term: *interexistence* which is in need of cohabitation with nature on this earth. As there are no two separate worlds of *men* and *things* both natural and cultural, this planetary cohabitation may be called, following Merleau-Ponty, the "interworld" (*entremonde*).

What is most radical and rigorous in phenomenology is the self-questioning of thinking itself as human activity. This Socratic attitude is nothing but the requirement of thinking about what we are doing when we think. Philosophy as *interrogation* as defined by Merleau-Ponty is a set of questions wherein he who questions is himself implicated by the question. In this attitude of interrogation, nothing must be taken for granted or presupposed. With Husserl we can say: "If he [the philosopher] is to be one who thinks for himself [*Selbstdenker*], an autonomous philosopher with the will to liberate himself from all prejudices, he must have the insight that all the things he takes for granted *are* prejudices, that all prejudices are obscurities arising out of sedimentation of tradition—not merely judgments whose truth is as yet undecided [*Vor-Urteile*]—and that this is true even of the great task and idea which is called 'philosophy.'"[10] In order for philosophy to be unprejudiced, initial questioning is only the beginning of a new questioning: philosophy as interrogation is indeed a perpetual beginning. To be rigorous and radical, the true thinker does not forget the "origin" of his thinking, that is, the original rootedness of his conceptual thinking in the primordial, preconceptual life-world. Science itself is an idealizing abstraction from the life-world. In scientism, however, what was once a method and the result of that method came to be taken or mistaken for "true being" or reality. With this birth of methodolatry in which it is idolized for its method or technique, science can not know literally what it is doing: it loses the sight of its *human meaning*. Gadamer contends that "The method of modern science is characterized from the start by a refusal: namely, to exclude all that which actually eludes its own methodology and procedures."[11]

We have also proposed a new paradigm for the philosophy of the sciences on the basis of science as human project and cultural achievement. Because all science is a human, communal project, it is more fruitful to argue for the absolute paradigm for all knowledge on the basis of how social-scientific rather than natural-scientific knowedge is acquired. This unitary philosophy of the sciences is a direct result of the "ontological turn" in phenomenological philosophy which proposes not only the primacy of ontology over epistemology but also the vision of man as a totalizing process. Insofar as the sciences of nature themselves are the historical and cultural accomplishments of man, they are integral parts of the cultural sciences. Viewed in this way, there is the unity of the human and the natural sciences: there can be no separation of "two cultures." Max Scheler was indeed prophetic when he said in *Man's Place in Nature (Die Stellung des Menschen im Kosmos)* in 1928 that in our age man has become more problematic to himself than in any other age in recorded history and he bemoaned the dismal state in which the study of man finds itself.[12] Today, the fragmented image of man in the human sciences into *homo politicus, homo economicus, homo sociologicus, homo psychologicus, homo religiosus, homo symbolicus,* etc., mirrors the fragmentation of man himself. The specialized division of academic labor or what Gadamer calls the "egoism of the specialist,"[13] is more a curse than a blessing in understanding man fully. No unified idea of man is in sight despite—or, better, *because of*—a proliferation of special sciences or disciplines. Nor has the knowledge industry and information exponentiality in both speed and volume (i.e., quantity) been able to guarantee a unified idea of man for the improvement of the "quality" of human life on earth. On the contrary, it conceals more than it reveals the nature of man. It is in our intellectual narcissism that we carve out and jealously safeguard our academic "territorial imperatives." When the study of man becomes fragmented, the unified vision of man necessarily suffers and is likely to fall into oblivion. What we need urgently, therefore, is *philosophical anthropology* which can provide us with a unified vision of man in nature and society in a time of crisis.

Anchored in this new vision of man, the immediate aim of phenomenological reflection in relation to political inquiry is to rescue science from the scourge of methodolatry by recovering subjectivity in science, that is, the human meaning of science. For *man* is subjectivity—the original source of a cornucopia of meanings. Emphasis on subjectivity must not be construed as a denial of objectivity or rationality; rather, it secures an anchorage for both. Unfortunately, however, subjectivity has been a perjorative term and anathema in the prevailing current of political inquiry due largely to the pervasive influence of positivism. Both objectivism (as ontology) and scientism (as epistemology) ignore man as subjectivity. They weaken objectivity by refusing to consider the necessary conditions of subjectivity underlying science as a human activity. The crisis of political understanding is the crisis of objectivity without subjectivity: it is due to the "incestuous fixation" of subjectivity in objectivism and scientism in political inquiry. "Crisis" in Chinese is composed of two ideograms, "danger" and "opportunity." Having sensed the danger of objectivism and scientism, phenomenology now opens an opportunity for a new angle of vision or a new "paradigm" (in the Kuhnian sense) to overcome their limits. The present study aims to show how the crisis of political understanding can be overcome by restoring and reclaiming the natural landscape of subjectivity lost in the scientific algorithms of political inquiry.

Ernest Nagel proposes too narrow a view of epistemology when he says: "The recommendation to use scientific method is the recommendation of a way for deciding issues of factual *validity* and *adequacy*; it is not the recommendation of an exclusive way in which the universe may be *confronted* and *experienced*."[14] For epistemology presupposes explicitly or implicitly an ontology and an axiology of man. When it is confined to the narrow question of *how* rather than *what* to know, that is, epistemology without ontology and axiology, epistemology degenerates into a method or technique, into methodolatry. As "to say that metaphysics is nonsense *is* nonsense,"[15] "logic without metaphysics" or science without ontology is a technique without human meaning. Even Wittgenstein who in the *Tractatus* confined himself to "the lucid, ordered crystal palace of mathematics, logic, science, a world secured against all ambiguity,"[16] closed his remarks by concluding polemically that "what we cannot speak about we must consign to silence." This should be interpreted not as a concession to the antimetaphysical stance of the Vienna Circle but as an affirmation of the "unsayable" world *beyond* the scientific view of the world as "the totality of facts" or as "pictured" in the totality of propositions in logical space. In order to see the world aright, according to Wittgenstein, one must transcend propositions of natural science or eventually recognize them as "nonsensical": "He must, so to speak, throw away the ladder after he has climbed up it."[17] Thus to consign to silence or the unsayable is not to concede to the antimetaphysical value of factual propositions in science as held in logical positivism and political behavioralism but to affirm the world of silence as having a higher quality of value than what is sayable in the world of science, logic, and mathematics. "Wittgenstein's silence in the face of the 'un-utterable'," Allan Janik and Stephen Toulmin declare, "was not a mocking silence like that of the positivists, but rather a respectful one. Having decided that 'value-neutral' facts alone can be expressed in regular propositional form, he exhorted his readers to turn their eyes away from factual propositions to the things of true value—which cannot be *gesagt* but only *gezeigt*."[18] Viewed in this way, the Wittgen-stein of *Philosophical Investigations* is a severe critic of the Wittgenstein of the *Tractatus*,[19] for the former says what is unsayable in the latter. Behavioral pragmatics or the interrogation of how ordinary language is *used* or *lived* as "a form of life" is of higher value than technical language as pictured in the logical and factual space of propositions.[20]

If for Wittgenstein "*the unsayable alone has genuine value*,"[21] then the aim of philosophy is to say what is unsayable in science, logic, and mathematics or merely in propositional form. Insofar as it goes be-yond the sayable world of science, logic, and mathematics, philosophy is a critique of knowledge as it defines the possibilities and limits of knowledge in terms of human existence. For Kierkegaard, philosophy is a possibility of thinking defined in terms of subjectivity as existing. Unlike the Cartesian *Cogito* or Hegel's objective thought (or thought without a thinker), existence is that which gives the thinker his thought, time, and place (i.e., his temporal and spatial placement in the world). Kierkegaard thus declares that "concepts, like individuals, have their histories and are just as incapable of withstanding the rav-ages of time as are individuals."[22] Concepts, scientific or otherwise, are as temporal and localized as individuals who are finite and perish-able. The subjective thinker or the inquirer as an existing subject is never an acosmic and eternal spirit but is a temporal and localized being; and thinking itself is an *event* or an existential act. In *Concluding Unscientific Postscript*, Kierkegaard contends that to catch existence or the subjective thinker by abstract thought is like trying to catch time by the tail. Such an effort is a "phantom" or a "glittering illusion." For the existing subject is neither solely the subject of cognition nor the object of scientific knowledge: to infer existence from abstract thought is a contradiction. Existence as subjectivity alone is both truth and reality. Thus the "absent-mindedness" of science, objectivity without subjectivity, is the target of criticism in Kierkegaard's existential philosophy as in Husserl's phenomenology. For, as Kierkegaard says, "science organizes the moments of subjectivity within a knowledge of them, and this knowledge is assumed to be the highest stage, and all knowledge is an abstraction which annuls existence, a taking of the objects of knowledge out of existence."[23] As for Wittgenstein the world of silence or the unsayable is beyond the world of facts and propositions, for Kierkegaard "the subjective thinker is not a man of science, but an artist. Existing is an art. The subjective thinker is aesthetic enough to give his life aesthetic content, ethical enough to regulate it, and dialectical enough to interpenetrate it with thought."[24] The limit of science and also of political behavioralism is that of the sayable. However, philosophy must say what is unsayable in science, logic, and mathematics; it must speak of subjectivity in flesh and bones. As a philosophy, phenomenology is a critique of knowledge and action in one; it is an attempt to define the possibilities and limits of knowledge and action in terms of subjectivity in the life-world. In phenomenology which is a revolution in man's understanding of himself as both knower and actor in the life-world, the rationality of philosophy coincides with that of humanity: philosophy becomes the guardian or servant of humanity, its homeland. In the end, philosophy's call for the life-world is a call for the quiet celebration of its homecoming.

The aim of Husserl's *archaeology of subjectivity* is to deconstruct or dismantle primarily the sedimented tradition of objectivism, particularly of scientism which may be overcome by "a heroism of reason"— the rational sense of life which in rescuing despair from the crisis of European humanity will rise up "the phoenix of a new life-inwardness and spiritualization as the pledge of a great and distant future for man."[25] Moreover, if we read Husserl's ontology of the life-world rightly, we will also find a critique of that persistent tradition of thought which forgets its indebtedness to and rootedness in the life-world as its founding soil. For the ontology of the life-world is directed against concentration on how to *think* about the world to the neglect of how to *experience* and *live* in the world. "Indeed," David Carr writes, "the world as thought about is surreptitiously substituted for the world as experienced, so that the latter is not simply neglected but described in a distorted way."[26] In order to avoid this "fallacy of misplaced concreteness," the life-world must be described in its own terms without conceptual prejudices. By casting an acosmic conceptual net to catch a fixed, determinate, and finished entity, the theorizing *spectator* ends up misplacing the concreteness of the life-worldly existence. The fundamental merit of the ontology of the life-world lies in integrating thought with life and in viewing thinking itself as a form of life or as the *act* of participation in the full expanse of life.

Thus the aim of Husserl's ontology of the life-world to dismantle scientism is fundamentally similar to Heidegger's call for ending or deconstructing the sedimented tradition of logocentrism from Platonism to cyberneticism. The end of philosophy or traditional philosophy then signals a new beginning or rebirth of thinking without conceptual reification. In this respect, Heidegger's and Husserl's thought cannot be juxtaposed as there can be no juxtaposition between existence (or Being) and cognition.

To repeat for the last time what has been stressed from the very beginning of this study: phenomenologically speaking, the philosophy of political science *is* at the same time the philosophy of the political world. Theoretical activity, scientific or philosophical, is a special way of existing in the world, and political knowledge is a part of the political world as well as a conception of it, for the world is an active synthesis of what is given and what is constructed. Like action, thought itself is an active mode of participation in the world. Theory thus conceived is no longer a formalistic enterprise—for example, a logical, linguistic, and mathematical analysis. A phenomenology of politics or, better, the hermeneutics of politics suggests a new perspective or "paradigm" in political theory that is capable of synthesizing philosophy and science, fact and value, and knowledge and action. In other words, phenomenology claims to be *a complete philosophy of man and of social reality*. It is capable of synthesizing *theoria* and *praxis*, the tension of which has been the twilight zone of Western political theorizing since its inception in ancient Greece. If the end of political theorizing is man, it cannot merely be an epistemological and methodological credo: it is ultimately an ethical one.[27] For the human sciences are the sciences *for* as well as *of* man and humanity. It is most instructive to take notice of Vico's complaint in his *On the Study of Methods of Our Time* (1709) against the prevailing pedagogic methods of scientific epistemology in his own time which is very contemporary in its message and thus relevant to that moral education of public conduct which he boldly called the "science of politics." He wrote:

> . . . the greatest drawback of our educational methods is that we pay an excessive amount of attention to the natural sciences and not enough to ethics. Our chief fault is that we disregard that part of ethics which treats of human character, of its dispositions, its passions, and of the manner of adjusting these factors to public life and eloquence. We neglect that discipline which deals with the differential features of virtues and vices, with good and bad behavior-patterns, with the typical characteristics of the various ages of man, of the two sexes, of social and eco-

nomic class, race and nation, and with the art of seemly conduct in life, the most difficult of all arts. As a consequence of this neglect, a noble and important branch of studies, i.e., the science of politics, lies almost abandoned and untended.[28]

What is central to this humanistic defense of Vico for the art and science of politics is ethical in nature. In this Vichian mold, we can say with Husserl that the theorizer, the scientist as well as the philosopher, is the servant of humanity, and it is this phrase that defines his true *vocation*. He can no longer remain as an ethical amnesiac or agnostic.

In conclusion, thinking or philosophizing with *care* and *vision* is inevitably a hermeneutical act that encounters the dialectic of the knower and the known, the signifier and the signified, and the interpreter and the interpreted, that is, the irreducible nexus between "life as the bearer of meaning and the mind as capable of linking meanings into a coherent series."[29] Philosophical reflection does not in the end desert the mundane world of everyday existence but indeed supports and sustains it. In it there is an intertwining link between meaning and existence and, particularly in our context, between the philosophy of political science and the philosophy of political reality. A "hermeneutics of the I *am*" contains a "hermeneutics of the I *think*"—to borrow the phrases of Ricoeur—and the *logos* of the latter sustains the *telos* of the former. Only in their mediation or mutual support can we say that *we are because we think and we think because we are*: "Knowledge and action," Merleau-Ponty asserts, "are two poles of a single existence."[30] The present study is a pathfinding effort in a small measure to impress this message on the conduct of political inquiry, which must be continued in any future comprehensive work on the *phenomenological critique of politics*.

Notes

CHAPTER 1. THE NATURE OF PHENOMENOLOGICAL THINKING

1. Josiah Royce, *The Philosophy of Loyalty*, pp. 16–17.
2. Thomas S. Kuhn, *The Structure of Scientific Revolutions*. Hereafter cited as "SSR."
3. The crisis situation of contemporary political science is apparent in the obvious themes of the "post-behavioral revolution" in recent writings. For example, see David Easton, "The New Revolution in Political Science." He speaks of "post-behavioralism" that stands for the most recent contribution to our heritage and the "post-behavioral revolution" that represents an opportunity for necessary change in political science.
4. See Maurice Merleau-Ponty, *Adventures of the Dialectic*, pp. 9–29. Hereafter cited as "AD."
5. Martin Heidegger, *The End of Philosophy*. Hereafter cited as "EP."
6. Edmund Husserl, *The Crisis of European Sciences and Transcendental Phenomenology: An Introduction to Phenomenological Philosophy*. Hereafter cited as "CES." Particularly in reference to Husserl's notion of the life-world, we agree with Don Ihde when he says that "phenomenology is a revolution in man's understanding of himself and his world." Don Ihde, *Sense and Significance*, p. 162. Hereafter cited as "SS." Husserl's frequent use of the term "introduction" to his work, as Aron Gurwitsch points out, should be understood neither as an elementary exposition for beginners nor as presenting phenomenology for the first time, but means "opening up a *new* avenue of approach to an already existing body of phenomenological thought." Aron Gurwitsch, "Comment on the Paper by H. Marcuse," p. 292. Hereafter cited as "CPM."
7. See Paul Ricoeur, *Husserl: An Analysis of His Phenomenology*, p. 162. In an attempt to graft phenomenology with Marxism, Enzo Paci maintains that "what Husserl did not know is that the crisis of the sciences, as the occluded use of the sciences that negate the subject, is the crisis of the capitalist use of the sciences, and, therefore, the crisis of human existence in capitalist society." Enzo Paci, *The Function of the Sciences and the Meaning of Man*, p. 323. Hereafter cited as "FS." The first treatise that relates phenomenology to Marxism is Tran-Duc-Thao, *Phénoménologie et Matérialisme Dialectique*. For an excellent argument for the complementarity between phenomenology and Marxism, see Fred R. Dallmayr, "Phenomenology and Marxism: A Salute to Enzo Paci."

8. Husserl, CES, pp. 6, 9.

9. *Ibid.*, p. 7.

10. A classical example of the dispute as to whether or not existential philosophy and phenomenology are compatible is found in *The Journal of Philosophy*, 57 (January 21, 1960): 45–84 that contains John Wild, "Existentialism as a Philosophy"; Herbert Spiegelberg, "Husserl's Phenomenology and Existentialism"; and William Earle, "Phenomenology and Existentialism."

11. The most comprehensive treatment of the history of phenomenology indicates this: see Herbert Spiegelberg, *The Phenomenological Movement: A Historical Introduction*.

12. Martin Heidegger, *On Time and Being*, p. 82. See also Martin Heidegger, *Being and Time*, p. 60. Hereafter cited as "BT." Werner Marx writes that "A memorial to Martin Heidegger . . . must draw attention to the great turmoil occasioned in thought by his work and point out a few stages, 'milestones,' that characterize this thinking, which has always understood itself as being 'on the way.' Heidegger has requested that we attend only to the path of his thinking—a thinking which for him was never the preoccupation of an academic discipline, but came forth with a claim to a transforming, history-grounding power, and for which it was a matter of helping bring it to pass that mankind one day would find its way to an other, 'creative' domicile in this world." Werner Marx, "In Remembrance of Martin Heidegger," p. 3.

13. Martin Heidegger, *What Is Called Thinking?*, p. 4. Hereafter cited as "WCT."

14. Hannah Arendt, *The Life of the Mind*, 1:4. Volumes 1 and 2 are entitled *Thinking* and *Willing*, respectively. The projected work on *Judging* was not completed before her death in 1975. Hereafter cited as "LM."

15. The importance of this idea in Heidegger is suggested by the recent collection of his essays: Martin Heidegger, *The Piety of Thinking*.

16. Heidegger, WCT, p. 159.

17. Arendt writes that *"The need of reason is not inspired by the quest for truth but by the quest for meaning. And truth and meaning are not the same.* The basic fallacy, taking precedence over all specific metaphysical fallacies, is to interpret meaning on the model of truth. The latest and in some respects most striking instance of this occurs in Heidegger's *Being and Time,* which starts out by raising 'anew the question of the meaning of Being.' Heidegger himself, in a later interpretation of his own initial question, says explicitly: '"meaning of Being" and "Truth of Being" say the same. (LM, 1: 15). This reproach of Arendt must be tempered by the following statement of Walter Biemel: "We have arrived at the point where *aletheia* shows itself as that primordial reality which we always overlook and leave out of consideration in favor of that which has arisen from it. *Aletheia* can no longer be equated with truth, for it is that which grants truth first of all—truth in the sense of correspondence or of the absolute certainty of knowledge. In this connection, Heidegger criticizes the attempt in *Being and Time,* from which we started out, in so far as it was based on translating *aletheia* as truth. And he also criticizes his own phrase 'truth of Being' (as in 'On the Essence of Truth' and the 'Letter on "Hu-

manism"')." Walter Biemel, *Martin Heidegger: An Illustrated Study*, p. 176. According to Heidegger, the original meaning of *aletheia* as disclosure or unconcealedness was transformed by Plato into the "correctness" of knowledge.

18. See particularly Martin Heidegger, *Discourse on Thinking*.

19. Paul Ricoeur, *The Conflict of Interpretations: Essays in Hermeneutics*, p. 246. Hereafter cited as "CI."

20. Eric Voegelin uses the term "scientism" in both an ontological and an epistemological sense (a combination of what we call "objectivism" and "scientism") when he defines it as having three principal dogmas: "(1) the assumption that the mathematized science of natural phenomena is a model to which all other sciences ought to conform; (2) that all realms of being are accessible to the methods of the sciences of phenomena; and (3) that all reality which is not accessible to the sciences of phenomena is either irrelevant or, in the more radical form of the dogma, illusionary." Eric Voegelin, "The Origins of Scientism," p. 462. Voegelin's definition of scientism, unlike ours, encounters difficulties in answering the contention that positivism is only an epistemology. As far as I know, Hans J. Morgenthau's *Scientific Man vs. Power Politics* is the first systematic attack on the dogmatic faith of scientism or scientific rationalism in the study of politics. "Politics," he writes, "must be understood through reason, yet it is not in reason that it finds its model. The principles of scientific reason are always simple, consistent, and abstract; the social world is always complicated, incongruous, and concrete. To apply the former to the latter is either futile, in that the social reality remains impervious to the attack of that 'one-eyed reason, deficient in its vision of depth'; or it is fatal, in that it will bring about results destructive of the intended purpose. Politics is an art and not a science, and what is required for its mastery is not the rationality of the engineer but the wisdom and the moral strength of the statesman" (*ibid.*, p. 10). Hereafter cited as "SM."

21. Max Scheler uses the terms "illusion" and "error" solely in determining two types of falsehood in cognition: "illusion always has its proper sphere in immediate cognition; error, in indirect or mediated cognition, especially in inferences." See Max Scheler, *Selected Philosophical Essays*, p. 12. Hereafter cited as "SPE."

22. Maurice Merleau-Ponty, *The Visible and the Invisible*, p. 27. Hereafter cited as "VI." For Merleau-Ponty's discussion on philosophy as interrogation, see particularly *ibid.*, pp. 3-40 and *Themes from Lectures at the Collège de France 1952-1960*, pp. 99-112. Hereafter cited as "TL." This radicality of philosophy as a perpetual beginning is persistently underscored by Merleau-Ponty whose phenomenology is a search for the "origin" of every rationality and mediation. For a critical analysis of Merleau-Ponty's thought in this respect, see John Sallis, *Phenomenology and the Return to the Beginnings*.

23. Maurice Natanson, *Edmund Husserl: Philosopher of Infinite Tasks*, p. 159. Hereafter cited as "EH."

24. Merleau-Ponty, VI, p. 28. In this regard, Kurt H. Wolff's notions of "catch" and "surrender" in their dialectical ebb and flow are both intriguing

and captivating from the standpoint of social inquiry. See Kurt H. Wolff, *Surrender and Catch: Experience and Inquiry Today.*

25. This is why we oppose Gerard Radnitzky who makes the sharp distinction between the philosophy of science and metascience in his excellent work: Gerard Radnizky, *Contemporary Schools of Metascience,* pp. 4-7.

26. Jürgen Habermas, *Knowledge and Human Interests,* pp. 316-17. A sympathetic, though critical, account of the achievements of Husserl's epistemology is found in Leszek Kolakowski, *Husserl and the Search for Certitude.* Habermas also states elsewhere that "confronted with the dogmatic heritage of the philosophy of history, critical sociology must guard against overburdening the concepts of the philosophy of reflection [German Idealism]. From the conceptual strategy of transcendental philosophy there results (already in the followers of Kant, and today also among those who wish to develop a Marxist theory of society in conjunction with Husserl's analyses of the 'life-world') a peculiar compulsion to conceive the social world as a continuum in the same way as the world of the objects of possible experience." See Jürgen Habermas, *Theory and Practice,* p. 13. Hereafter cited as "TP." Habermas's *Knowledge and Human Interests* generated a considerable number of commentaries. See Fred R. Dallmayr (ed.), *Materialien zu Habermas' "Erkenntnis und Interesse."* For a critical analysis of the Frankfurt School on the nexus of theory and practice, see Phil Slater, *Origin and Significance of the Frankfurt School: A Marxist Perspective,* especially pp. 54-93. Sympathetic accounts of critical theory are found in Martin Jay, *The Dialectical Imagination: A History of the Frankfurt School and the Institute of Social Research, 1923-1950* and Susan Buck-Morss, *The Origin of Negative Dialectics: Theodor W. Adorno, Walter Benjamin, and the Frankfurt Institute.*

27. Concerning Habermas's theory of "knowledge" and "interests," Paul Ricoeur observes that "in principle the anthropology underlying the theory of interests expresses the same subordination of theory and knowledge to the profound movement of human existence as that which is expressed in the Heideggerian theory of care. I willingly admit that the primacy accorded by Habermas to the concept of interest proceeds from a happy contamination between the Marxist concept of *praxis* and the Heideggerian concept of care much more than from any kinship with the concept of utility in the tradition of English utilitarianism or with the concepts of American pragmatism. Yet the most important aspect of the theory of interest is not its rootedness in an anthropology whose basic terms remain undetermined, but its recourse to a hierarchical principle. The distinction between an instrumental interest, a practical interest, and an interest in emancipation outlines a system of preferences which, in turn, appeals to a discernment of the rank of values which can hardly be conceived of as a creation, but which may be conceived of as the recognition of an order, which in its final sense is less distant from Max Scheler than it might appear to be. In brief, I do not see how anyone can construct a theory of interest and interests without the help of an anthropology and an axiology," Paul Ricoeur, "Ethics and Culture: Habermas and Gadamer in Dialogue," p. 161. Of course, there is nothing revolutionary about treating the concept of interest as the motivating force and normative con-

cept of human action. In the intellectual tradition of Germany in this century, it was Max Weber who observed that "Interests (material and ideal), not ideas, dominate directly the action of men. Yet the 'image of the world' created by these ideas have very often served as switches determining the tracks on which the dynamism of interests kept actions moving." Cited in Hans J. Morgenthau, *Politics among Nations: The Struggle for Power and Peace*, p. 9. It is worth mentioning that the concept of interest defined as power is the underlying foundation of Morgenthau's realism in the theory of international relations. For his influential theory of international relations based on the idea of the *national interest*, see Hans J. Morgenthau, *In Defense of the National Interest: A Critical Examination of American Foreign Policy*.

28. Edmund Husserl, *Experience and Judgment*, p. 29. Hereafter cited as "EJ." Cf. Natanson, EH, p. 157. By noting the self-contradiction of the notion of a "disinterested observer," Stephan Strasser comments that "one who carefully observes something is, by that very fact, interested in it. Interest is, in fact, characteristic of an observer as an observer. One can refer here to a hunter who watches an approaching deer, a mother who keeps an eye on the behavior of her child, or to a spectator who watches a game in the World Series. The scientific observer, too, looks with intense attention at something that raises his professional interest. Generally speaking, we do not even notice things that do not interest us at all." Stephan Strasser, *The Idea of Dialogal Phenomenology*, pp. 9-10. Richard M. Zaner speaks of the methodological demand of "disengagement" as radical: "To dissociate is at once to ignore certain affairs and to focus attention on others, those which are specifically relevant to the task at hand . . ." and we disengage from ourselves in order to engage ourselves in ourselves critically. In this sense, disengagement and criticism both as radical go hand in hand. See Richard M. Zaner, *The Way of Phenomenology*, pp. 187-88.

29. Maurice Merleau-Ponty, *In Praise of Philosophy*. Hereafter cited as "IPP." Arendt too warns of "an inevitable flaw" in all critiques of the human faculty called "Will"—the basis of "doing" or "acting"—simply because "every *philosophy* of the Will is conceived and articulated not by men of action but by philosophers, Kant's 'professional thinkers,' who in one way or another are committed to the *bios theōrētikos* and therefore by nature more inclined to 'interpret the world' than to 'change it'" (LM, 2: 195). So what matters in the flight of political philosophy is to maintain the *optimal altitude* which is neither too high nor too low to be able to survey effectively the landscape of political action whereby its own critical attitude serves as an altimeter. Therefore, political philosophy must not be exclusively "utopian" or exclusively "ideological" in the sense of Karl Mannheim's distinction of these two terms. See Karl Mannheim, *Ideology and Utopia: An Introduction to the Sociology of Knowledge*.

30. Natanson, EH, p. 125 (italics added).

31. Paul Ricoeur, *History and Truth*, p. 218. Hereafter cited as "HT." Ricoeur uses the same argument in his critique of Ludwig Wittgenstein's treatment of language as a "form of life" (*Lebensform*) when Ricoeur insists that the constitution of the sign as sign presupposes the break with life, activity, and

nature which, according to him, Husserl symbolized in the *epochē*. Ricoeur insists that language as a system of signs originates in the distance between thought and life and that it is not enough to "look" but has to be thought. Thus the true function of hermeneutics is to *think* language as a system of signs which requires a distanciation of thought from the reality of life activities. See Paul Ricoeur, "Husserl and Wittgenstein on Language."

32. Karl Marx, *Writings of the Young Marx on Philosophy and Society*, p. 402. When Natanson comments that Marx's eleventh thesis on Feuerbach is "the most profoundly antiphilosophical sentence ever written by a philosopher," he is overstating his case although he is right in saying that "the splitting apart of interpretation and reality is itself the result of interpretative analysis" (EH, p. 203). For a mixture of the influence and criticism of Heidegger's and Husserl's thought in an attempt to construct a Marxian praxiology, see Karel Kosík, *Dialectics of the Concrete: A Study on Problems of Man and World*.

33. Mihailo Marković, *From Affluence to Praxis*, p. 6. Hereafter cited as "FAP." For a notable effort to construct the foundation for a "dialectical theory" of the political based on the Marxian tradition which attempts to avoid the "conflation" of theory and practice, see Dick Howard, *The Marxian Legacy*, particularly pp. 3-18.

34. Marković, FAP, p. 6. (italic added).

35. Cf. Paul Ricoeur who writes: "*La prise de conscience qui soutient l'oeuvre de réflexion développe des implications éthiques propres: par ceci que la réflexion est l'acte immédiatement responsable de soi*. Cette nuance éthique que l'expression *aus letzter Selbstverantwortung* [Husserl's term] semble introduire dans la thématique fondationelle n'est pas le complément pratique d'une entreprise qui, en tant que telle, serait purement épistémologique: l'inversion par laquelle la réflexion s'arrache à l'attitude naturelle est en même temps—du même souffle, si l'on peut dire—épistémologique et éthique. La conversion philosophique est l'acte suprêmement autonome. Ce que nous appelions la nuance éthique est donc immédiatement impliquée dans l'acte fondationnel, dans la mesure où celui-ci ne peut être qu'autopositionnel. C'est en ce sens qu'il est ultimement responsable de soi." Paul Ricoeur, "Phénoménologie et Herméneutique," pp. 226-27.

36. Hannah Arendt, *The Human Condition*, p. 5. Hereafter cited as "HC."

37. Arendt, LM, 1: 8. "The everywhere of thought," Arendt continues, "is indeed a region of nowhere. But we are not only in space, we are also in time, remembering, collecting and recollecting what no longer is present out of 'the belly of memory' (Augustine), anticipating and planning in the mode of willing what is not yet. Perhaps our question—Where are we when we think?—was wrong because by asking for the *topos* of this activity, we were exclusively spatially oriented . . . " (*ibid.*, p. 201).

38. *Ibid.*, pp. 7-8.

39. Edmund Husserl, *Cartesian Meditations: An Introduction to Phenomenology*, p. 197.

40. See Herbert Marcuse, "Heidegger's Politics: An Interview with Herbert Marcuse by Frederick Olafson" which will be cited hereafter as "HPI" and Theodor W. Adorno, *Tlhe Jargon of Authenticity*.

CHAPTER 2. THE PHENOMENOLOGICAL ONTOLOGY OF MAN

1. In his Zaharoff Lecture at Oxford University in 1963, Jean Hyppolite stated: "La philosophie de Merleau-Ponty est une méditation sur cette connexion intime de l'existence et du sens. Notre existence ne s'enracine dans le monde et dans l'histoire que parce qu'elle y découvre ou y invente un sens. Ce sens n'est pas écrit dans la nature de choses, ou dans un esprit éternel, il est l'oeuvre précaire et toujours menacée de l'existence que nous sommes nous-même." Jean Hyppolite, *Sens et Existence dans la Philosophie de Maurice Merleau-Ponty*, p. 3. Hyppolite further noted that "existence" refers to "the world and its inhabitants" rather than the subject and object of a theory of knowledge and that "sense" or "meaning" is that which is in question in relation to existence.
2. John Wild, "Foreword" to Hwa Yol Jung (ed.), *Existential Phenomenology and Political Theory: A Reader*, p. ix.
3. John Wild, *Existence and the World of Freedom*, p. 41. Hereafter cited as "EWF."
4. Werner Heisenberg, *The Physicist's Conception of Nature*, p. 29. Hereafter cited as "PCN."
5. So far the most comprehensive treatment of phenomenology and the social sciences mentioned here is found in Maurice Natanson (ed.), *Phenomenology and the Social Sciences.*
6. Maurice Merleau-Ponty, *Sense and Non-Sense*, p. 152. Hereafter cited as "SNS."
7. Heidegger, BT, p. 73.
8. According to Heidegger, "projecting has nothing to do with comporting oneself towards a plan that has been thought out, and in accordance with which Dasein arranges its Being" (*ibid.*, p. 185).
9. See Alfred Schutz, *The Phenomenology of the Social World* and *Collected Papers*, vol. 1: *The Problem of Social Reality*, pp. 67–96. Hereafter cited as "PSW" and "CP," respectively. Schutz says that "the projection of an action is in principle carried out independently of all real action. Every projection of action is rather a phantasying of action, that is, a phantasying of spontaneous activity, but not the activity itself. It is an intuitive advance picturing which may or may not include belief, and, if it does, can believe positively or negatively or with any degree of certainty" (PSW, p. 59).
10. Compare Schutz's notion of the project with John Dewey's definition of "deliberation" as "a dramatic rehearsal (in imagination) of various competing possible lines of action. It starts from the blocking of efficient overt action, due to that conflict of prior habit and newly released impulse to which reference has been made. Then each habit, each impulse, involved in the temporary suspense of overt action takes its turn in being tried out. Deliberation is an experiment in finding out what the various lines of possible action are really like. It is an experiment in making various combinations of selected elements of habits and impulses, to see what the resultant action would be like if it were entered upon. But the experiment is carried on by tentative rehearsals in

thought which do not affect physical facts outside the body. Thought runs ahead and foresees outcomes, and thereby avoids having to await the instruction of actual failure and disaster. An act overtly tried out is irrevocable, its consequences cannot be blotted out. An act tried out in imagination is not final or fatal. It is retrievable." See John Dewey, *Human Nature and Conduct*, p. 179. It should be noted here that Dewey's emphasis is on the instrumental rather than the intrinsic value of deliberation, on how to act rather than on what to act.

11. Ricoeur, CI, pp. 246-47.

12. Max Scheler, *The Nature of Sympathy*, p. 227.

13. Raymond Polin, *La Création des Valeurs*, p. 3.

14. Simone de Beauvoir, *The Ethics of Ambiguity*, p. 129. Hereafter cited as "EA."

15. John Wild, "Foreword" to Maurice Merleau-Ponty, *The Structure of Behavior*, pp. xiv-xv.

16. Schutz, PSW, p. 63. "Confronted with the objectivism of strictly behavioral sciences," Habermas writes, "critical sociology guards itself against a reduction of intentional action to behavior" (TP, p. 10).

17. Max Scheler, *Man's Place in Nature*, p. 29. Hereafter cited as "MP." The same point is made by Erich Fromm in his polemology and his analysis of necrophilia. See Erich Fromm, *The Anatomy of Human Destructiveness*, especially pp. 1-85. Hannah Arendt writes that "while I find much of the work of the zoologists fascinating, I fail to see how it can possibly apply to our [human] problem. In order to know that people will fight for their homeland we hardly had to discover instincts of 'group territorialism' in ants, fish, and apes; and in order to learn that overcrowding results in irritation and aggressiveness, we hardly needed to experiment with rats. One day spent in the slums of any big city should have sufficed. I am surprised and often delighted to see that some animals behave like men; I cannot see how this could either justify or condemn human behavior. I fail to understand why we are asked 'to recognize that man behaves very much like a group territorial species,' rather than the other way round—that certain animal species behave very much like man. (Following Adolf Portmann, these new insights into animal behavior do not close the gap between man and animal; they only demonstrate that 'much more of what we know of ourselves than we thought also occurs in animals.') Why should we, after having 'eliminated' all anthropomorphisms from animal psychology (whether we actually succeeded is another matter), now try to discover 'how theriomorph man is'? Is it not obvious that anthropomorphism and theriomorphism in the behavioral sciences are but two sides of the same 'error'? Moreover, if we define man as belonging to the animal kingdom, why should we ask him to take his standards of behavior from another animal species? The answer, I am afraid, is simple: It is easier to experiment with animals, and this not only for humanitarian reasons—that it is not nice to put us into cages; the trouble is men can cheat." Hannah Arendt, *On Violence*, pp. 59-60.

18. Schutz, PSW, p. 61.

19. Erwin W. Straus, *Phenomenological Psychology*, p. 198. Hereafter cited as "PPS."

20. Arendt, HC, p. 237. Cf. Scheler who quotes Nietzsche: "Man is an animal that can make promises" (MP, p. 41). Hannah Arendt, *Crises of the Republic*, pp. 92-93: "Promises are a uniquely human way of ordering the future, making it predictable and reliable to the extent that this is humanly possible. And since the predictability of the future can never be absolute, promises are qualified by two essential limitations. We are bound to keep our promises provided that no unexpected circumstances arise, and provided that the mutuality inherent in all promises is not broken"; and Stuart Hampshire, *Thought and Action*, p. 71: "The future is that which is in principle alterable by action, the past that which is in principle unalterable by action." Hereafter cited as "TA."

21. Arendt, HC, p. 237.

22. Schutz, PSW, p. 61.

23. Rollo May, *Psychology and the Human Dilemma*, p. 220. Hereafter cited as "PHD."

24. *Ibid.*, p. 212.

25. Beauvoir, EA, p. 76.

26. Herbert Marcuse, *One-Dimensional Man: Studies in the Ideology of Advanced Industrial Society*, p. 219. Hereafter cited as "ODM."

27. May also declares that "*human values are never a simple one-way street, but always involve a 'no' as well as a 'yes'*—what I shall call here a *polarity of will*" (PHD, p. 215).

28. Beauvoir, EA, p. 92.

29. Cited in Carl J. Friedrich, "Phenomenology and Political Science," p. 195.

30. Schutz, PSW, pp. 139-214.

31. Arendt, HC, p. 177.

32. Hans Jonas emphasizes the importance of Arendt's notion of natality when he says: "With 'natality' Hannah Arendt not only coined a new word but introduced a new category into the philosophical doctrine of man." Hans Jonas, "Acting, Knowing, Thinking: Gleanings from Hannah Arendt's Philosophical Work," p. 30.

33. Henri Bergson, *Matter and Memory*, p. 23.

34. Eugène Minkowski, *Lived Time: Phenomenological and Psychopathological Studies*, p. 83.

35. Simone de Beauvoir, *The Coming of Age*, p. 361.

36. Maurice Merleau-Ponty, *Phenomenology of Perception*, p. 382. Hereafter cited as "PP." John O'Neill is right when he says that "social action is not an unlimited projection of possibilities: it starts from an understanding of the human situation which is simultaneously a structure of limits and possibilities." John O'Neill, "Scientism, Historicism and the Problem of Rationality," p. 24.

37. Beauvoir, EA, pp. 24, 14-15.

38. Joseph J. Kockelmans (ed.), *Contemporary European Ethics: Selected Readings*, p. 184.

39. An increasing number of neo-Marxists have come to view freedom as the

central issue in their social theory. In this regard, Gajo Petrović is the best example of the neo-Marxist movement. For him, freedom is central to the philosophy of human action. The essence of freedom as transcendence lies not in subjection of the given or facticity but in the creation of something new. In rejecting the compatibility of freedom and necessity, he says that "[a] basic defect in necessity theories of freedom is that they are in essence conservative. If everything occurs of necessity, it is then natural to accept what is and not attempt to change it." In short, for Petrović as for existentialists, human existence *is* freedom: "*Unfreedom is not merely the death danger for man, unfreedom is man's death.* Through becoming unfree, man ceases to be man." Gajo Petrović, *Marx in the Mid-Twentieth Century*, pp. 115-34.

40. Jean-Paul Sartre, *Being and Nothingness*, p. 556. Hereafter cited as "BN."

41. Jean-Paul Sartre, *Critique de la Raison Dialectique*, vol. 1: *Théorie des Ensembles Pratiques* (Paris: Gallimard, 1960) has been translated into two parts: *Search for a Method* and *Critique of Dialectical Reason*. Cited hereafter as "SM" and "CDR," respectively.

42. Sartre, SM, p. 93. Martin Heidegger comments that "Because Marx by experiencing estrangement attains an essential dimension of history, the Marxist view of history is superior to that of other historical accounts. But since neither Husserl nor—so far as I have seen till now—Sartre recognizes the essential importance of the historical in Being, neither phenomenology nor existentialism enters that dimension within which a productive dialogue with Marxism first becomes possible." Martin Heidegger, *Basic Writings,* pp. 219-20. Hereafter cited as "BW." In all fairness, however, Heidegger's comments must be revised by the following observations: first, Husserl had a sense of history in relation to philosophy; second, Heidegger refers to the Sartre of *Being and Nothingness* rather than to the Sartre of *Critique de la Raison Dialectique;* and third and most importantly, Heidegger is unaware of Merleau-Ponty's phenomenology of history. In Merleau-Ponty's thought from PP to VI, there has been a persistent dialogue between phenomenology and Marxism.

43. Sartre, SM, p. 96.

44. Merleau-Ponty, AD, p. 39.

45. *Ibid.*, p. 40.

46. Merleau-Ponty, IPP, pp. 52-53.

47. See Straus, PPS, pp. 137-65. Speaking of the mind and the body, Straus writes that "Both kingdoms are of equal sovereignty: the mind does not determine the body's behavior, nor does the body determine the mind. Yet there is, it seems, an unavoidable distinction to be made, a difference which gives a privileged status to the body. The body of an organism is related to other bodies; it is a part of the physical universe. The mind, however, is related to one body only; it is not directly related to the world, nor to other bodies, nor to other minds" (*ibid.*, p. 211).

48. Gabriel Marcel, *The Mystery of Being*, p. 124.

49. Eugene O'Neill, *A Moon for the Misbegotten*, p. 103 (italics added).

50. Maurice Merleau-Ponty, "Husserl et la Notion de Nature (Notes Prises au Cours de Maurice Merleau-Ponty)," p. 259. Hereafter cited as "HNN."

51. Giambattista Vico, *The New Science*, par. 237. Hereafter cited as "NS."

Allusions to the Vichian connection in phenomenology throughout this book have been treated systematically in my paper, "Vico, Hermeneutical Phenomenology, and the Human Sciences: Toward a New Paradigm for the Philosophy of the Sciences."

52. Vico, NS, par. 405.
53. Merleau-Ponty, HNN, p. 261.
54. Maurice Merleau-Ponty, *The Prose of the World*, p. 137. Hereafter cited as "PW."
55. Merleau-Ponty, VI, p. 139.
56. *Ibid.*, p. 146.
57. *Ibid.*, pp. 11–12.
58. Maurice Merleau-Ponty, *The Primacy of Perception*, p. 13. Hereafter cited as "PPE."
59. Merleau-Ponty, VI, p. 212.
60. Merleau-Ponty, HNN, p. 260.
61. Paci, FS, p. 231.
62. See Erwin W. Straus, *The Primary World of Senses* which will be cited hereafter as "PWS"; Helmuth Plessner, *Laughing and Crying* which will be cited hereafter as "LC"; F. J. J. Buytendijk, *Pain: Its Modes and Functions;* and Stephan Strasser, *Das Gemüt: Grundgedanken zu einer phänomenologischen Philosophie und Theorie des menschlichen Gefühlslebens.*
63. Plessner, LC, p. 45.
64. *Ibid.*
65. *Ibid.*, p. 43.
66. *Ibid.*, p. 50. For a discussion of the body's expressive acts, see Jonathan Benthall and Ted Polhemus (eds.), *The Body as a Medium of Expression.*
67. Maurice Merleau-Ponty, *Humanism and Terror*, pp. 109–10 (italics added).
68. Merleau-Ponty, AD, p. 90.
69. See Ricoeur, HT, pp. 223–46.
70. The phrase "the language animal" is used by George Steiner in the title of a chapter in his work: George Steiner, *Extraterritorial: Papers on Literature and the Language Revolution*, pp. 58–101. Hereafter cited as "EX."
71. Paci, FS, p. 208.
72. Vico, NS, par. 234.
73. Humboldt views language as man's *intrinsic* humanity and spirituality and as the dialectical interchange of the inner and the outer or of human subjectivities and objective expressions. "Man," he writes, "is man only through language; to invent language, he would have to be man already. As soon as one imagines that it happened gradually . . . , that by means of a bit more invented language, man became more human, and being more human, thus was enabled to invent a little more language, one fails to recognize the indivisibility of human consciousness and human speech, and the nature of the intellectual act which is necessary to comprehend but a single word, but which then suffices to comprehend all of language." See Wilhelm von Humboldt, *Humanist without Portfolio: An Anthology of the Writings of Wilhelm von Humboldt*, p. 240.
74. Heidegger, BW, p. 193. Marjorie Grene makes an interesting comment

with this passage in mind: "Heidegger calls language 'the house of Being.' One could *almost* say, contrariwise, that Being is the house of language. For language comes to be, wherever it erupts out of silence, as *one* expression (not *the* expression) of *Logos.*" Marjorie Grene, "Merleau-Ponty and the Renewal of Ontology," p. 621. For Heidegger's thought on language, see further Martin Heidegger, *On the Way to Language* and *Poetry, Language, Thought.*

75. Maurice Merleau-Ponty, *Signs,* pp. 84-97. Hereafter cited as "SI."

76. Maurice Merleau-Ponty, *Consciousness and the Acquisition of Language,* p. 75. Hereafter cited as "CAL."

77. Plessner, LC, p. 45.

78. Merleau-Ponty, CAL, p. 81. For extensive discussions on the prelinguistic acts of expression, see Don Ihde, SS and *Listening and Voice: A Phenomenology of Sound.*

79. Merleau-Ponty, PP, p. 189.

80. *Ibid.*, pp. 177-78.

81. Merleau-Ponty, VI, p. 144. Merleau-Ponty attributes this idea to Paul Valéry.

82. See Marcel Mauss, "Les Techniques du Corps." For a comprehensive treatment of the self and society in terms of the constraints of the "body social" on the "body natural," see Mary Douglas, *Natural Symbols: Explorations in Cosmology.* Today, Marxism as well as psychoanalysis has an element of the upsurge of the "body natural" against the "body social." See Herbert Marcuse, *Eros and Civilization* and Norman O. Brown, *Life against Death* and *Love's Body.*

83. Terrence Des Pres, *The Survivor: An Anatomy of Life in the ,Death Camps,* p. 69. For a personal account of survival in the Nazi concentration camp as the point of reference for a "search for meaning" and for the development of the psychotherapeutic theory called "logotherapy," see Viktor E. Frankl, *Man's Search for Meaning: An Introduction to Logotherapy.*

84. It is no accident that the logocentric philosophy of language whose battlecry is "clarity" cohabits with the technocentric culture which is obsessed with "cleanliness" by deodorizing the body natural. Here I have modified an idea in John O'Neill, *Making Sense Together: An Introduction to Wild Sociology,* pp. 28-29.

85. Merleau-Ponty, CAL, p. 75.

86. Merleau-Ponty, PP, p. 185. Cf. Paci, FS, p. 211.

87. Ludwig Wittgenstein, *Philosophical Investigations,* p. 226e. Hereafter cited as "PI."

88. See J. L. Austin, *Philosophical Papers,* pp. 220-39 which will be cited hereafter as "PPA"; *How to Do Things with Words;* and "Performative-Constantive." See also John R. Searle, *Speech Acts: An Essay in the Philosophy of Language* in which Searle maintains that as all linguistic communication involves linguistic acts, speaking a language is performing speech acts and that an adequate study of *parole* (speech acts or language as rule-governed intentional behavior) is a study of *langue (ibid.,* pp. 16-17).

89. See Jacques Derrida, *Speech and Phenomena and Other Essays on Husserl's Theory of Signs.* Hereafter cited as "SP."

90. See Murray Edelman, *Politics as Symbolic Action; The Symbolic Uses of Politics;* and *Political Language: Words That Succeed and Policies That Fail.*

91. Hans-Georg Gadamer, *Truth and Method,* p. 498 (italics added). Hereafter cited as "TM." For a comprehensive treatment of metaphor as the most creative, generative, and novel dimension of language, see Paul Ricoeur, *The Rule of Metaphor: Multi-Disciplinary Studies of the Creation of Meaning in Language.*

92. Garth Gillan, "In the Folds of the Flesh: Philosophy and Language," p. 39.

93. *Ibid.*

94. Karl Marx and Frederick Engels, *The German Ideology,* p. 19. Cf. Hampshire, TA, p. 89: "My assurance of my own position in the world, and my knowledge of other things, develops in this communication and could not conceivably develop except in this social context. To learn to speak and understand a language, as a child, is to enter into a set of social relationships in which my own intentions are continually understood and fulfilled by others and in which I encounter their corresponding intentions. I learn to describe and to think about things, and to think about my own actions, only because of this interchange and through the social conventions that constitute the use of a language." V. N. Vološinov proposes a Marxist theory of language which in many ways intersects the phenomenological philosophy of language presented here. V. N. Vološinov, *Marxism and the Philosophy of Language* and also cf. Raymond Williams, *Marxism and Literature,* particularly pp. 21–44.

CHAPTER 3. TOWARD A NEW HUMANISM: THE SOCIAL PRINCIPLE OF MAN AND NATURE AS THE POLITICS OF CIVILITY

1. This chapter is a shortened and revised version of my article coauthored with Petee Jung, "Toward a New Humanism: The Politics of Civility in a 'No-Growth' Society."

2. Arendt, HC, p. 2.

3. G. W. F. Hegel, *Hegel's Philosophy of Right,* p. 13.

4. Albert William Levi, *Humanism and Politics,* p. 15.

5. For discussions on this subject, see particularly Hwa Yol Jung and Petee Jung, "To Save the Earth"; Michael E. Zimmerman, "Heidegger on Nihilism and Technique"; J. Glenn Gray, "Heidegger's Course: From Human Existence to Nature"; *On Understanding Violence Philosophically and Other Essays,* pp. 45–67; and "Heidegger on Remembering and Remembering Heidegger" which will be cited hereafter as "HR."

6. Daniel Bell, *The Coming of Post-Industrial Society: A Venture in Social Forecasting.*

7. *Ibid.,* pp. 488–89.

8. Ludwig Feuerbach, *Principles of the Philosophy of the Future,* p. 72.

9. See Martin Buber, *I and Thou* and *The Knowledge of Man.*

10. Heidegger, BT, p. 242.

11. Henry Bugbee, Jr., *The Inward Morning,* p. 159. For a discussion of the nexus of man, woman, and nature, see Simone de Beauvoir, *The Second Sex.*

12. R. D. Laing, *Knots,* p. 82. By characterizing the "first law of ecology" as everything being connected to everything else, no one argues more forcefully than Barry Commoner that the fragmentation of science, technology, and

society both within each category and from each other is the origin of our present ecological crisis when he writes: "we can trace the origin of the environmental crisis through the following sequence. Environmental degradation largely results from the introduction of new industrial and agricultural production technologies. These technologies are ecologically faulty because they are designed to solve singular, separate problems and fail to take into account the inevitable 'side-effects' that arise because, in nature, no part is isolated from the whole ecological fabric. In turn, the fragmented design of technology reflects its scientific foundation, for science is divided into disciplines that are largely governed by the notion that complex systems can be understood only if they are first broken into their separate component parts. This reductionist bias has also tended to shield basic science from a concern for real-life problems, such as environmental degradation." Barry Commoner, *The Closing Circle: Nature, Man and Technology*, p. 193.

13. Gray describes the proper translation of the German *"versammeln"* in Heidegger's work into "to gather" which is derived from the Greek *"to agathon,"* the good (HR, p. 62).

14. Heidegger, BT, p. 76. Cf. Mikel Dufreune, "La Mentalité Primitive et Heidegger," in *Jalons*, pp. 127-49.

15. See Stanley Diamond, *In Search of the Primitive: A Critique of Civilization* and "The Search of the Primitive" which will be cited hereafter as "SPR."

16. Diamond, SPR, p. 227.

17. Mircea Eliade, *The Myth of the Eternal Return*.

18. Johann Gottlieb Fichte, *The Vocation of Man*, p. 29.

19. Speaking of Western theology, Conrad Bonifazi declares that it has concerned itself with "man as a spiritual being to the exclusion of interest in his roots in the earth; its absorption with 'history' has permitted it to assume the theological irrelevance of nature." Conrad Bonifazi, *A Theology of Things*, p. 17.

20. Merleau-Ponty, TL, p. 80.

21. Loren Eiseley, *The Invisible Pyramid*.

22. Husserl, CES, p. 271.

23. Heidegger, EP, p. 109.

24. Marcuse, ODM, p. 158. See also Jacques Ellul, *The Technological Society*, especially pp. 319-427. Jürgen Habermas is also concerned with the problems of production, finite resources, population, and pollution in relation to advanced capitalism. "Capitalist societies," he writes, "cannot follow imperatives of growth limitation without abandoning their principle of organization; a shift from unplanned, nature-like capitalist growth to qualitative growth would require that production be planned in terms of *use values*. The development of productive forces cannot, however, be uncoupled from the production of *exchange values* without violating the logic of the system." Jürgen Habermas, *Legitimation Crisis*, pp. 42-43. In contrast to Habermas who, I think, fails to go beyond the position of the "mature Marx," Paci comes to the conclusion that "phenomenology is closely connected to the foundation and meaning of political economy, which essentially encompasses the prob-

lem of the function of the sciences and of the meaning of man in an intentional horizon which gives him back his integrity, his inorganic body, the planet Earth, and the authentic function of philosophy" (FS, p. 447).

25. William Leiss, *The Domination of Nature,* p. 175.

26. See Jürgen Habermas, *Toward a Rational Society,* especially pp. 81-122.

27. The Frankfurt Institute for Social Research, *Aspects of Sociology,* p. 94. For a classical discussion on the subject, see Max Horkheimer, *Eclipse of Reason.*

28. Alfred Schmidt, *The Concept of Nature in Marx,* p. 27. Hereafter cited as "CNM."

29. Karl Marx, *Karl Marx: Selected Writings in Sociology and Philosophy,* p. 246.

30. Schmidt, CNM, p. 155. According to Kostas Axelos, "He [Marx] firmly believed that an *exploitation of nature by men,* based on a technique freed from private ownership, would entail no *exploitation of men by men.*" Kostas Axelos, *Alienation, Praxis, and Technē in the Thought of Karl Marx,* p. 305. Schmidt also writes that "Whenever Marx writes of the 'slumbering potentialities' of nature, he is always referring to the objective possibility, inherent in nature, of its transfer into definite human use-values" (CNM, p. 162).

31. Marcuse, ODM, pp. 236-37. Marcuse also notes that "Hegel's concept of freedom presupposes consciousness throughout (in Hegel's terminology: self-consciousness). Consequently, the 'realization' of Nature is not, and never can be Nature's own work. But inasmuch as Nature is in itself negative (i.e., wanting in its own existence), the historical transformation of Nature by Man is, as the overcoming of this negativity, the liberation of Nature. Or, in Hegel's words, Nature is in its essence non-natural—'Geist'" (*ibid.,* p. 236, n.7).

32. Herbert Marcuse, *Counterrevolution and Revolt,* p. 69.

33. For a discussion of this shift, see Leo Strauss, *Natural Right and History,* pp. 51 ff. Hereafter cited as "NRH."

34. Thomas Hobbes, *Leviathan,* p. 82. Hereafter cited as "LE."

35. Jean-Jacques Rousseau, *The Political Writings of Jean Jacques Rousseau,* 1: 285.

36. Sheldon S. Wolin, *Politics and Vision: Continuity and Innovation in Western Political Thought,* p. 302. Hereafter cited as "PV."

37. See Robert Paul Wolff, *The Poverty of Liberalism.*

38. Victor C. Ferkiss, *The Future of Technological Civilization.* Hereafter cited as "FTC."

39. John Locke, *Two Treatises of Government,* pp. 315-16.

40. Ferkiss, FTC, p. 286.

41. John Stuart Mill, *Principles of Political Economy,* p. 748. Robert Denoon Cumming maintains that although he aspired to apply the methods of Physical Science "duly extended and generalised" to the "Moral Sciences" (or the sciences of human behavior) to remedy the latter's "backward states," Mill rejected in his political economy the individualistic assumptions and conclusions of Hobbes and Locke. See Robert Denoon Cumming, *Human Nature and History,* 2: 151-87. Of course, we must keep in mind that Mill's defense of individual autonomy, particularly in *On Liberty* (1859), should also be seen in terms of its opposition to the anonymity of mass society, conformism, the

"tyranny of the majority," and "collective mediocrity," the tendency of which was discovered already by Alexis de Tocqueville in nineteenth-century American democracy.

42. R. H. Tawney, *The Acquisitive Society,* p. 184.

43. Karl Marx, *Critique of the Gotha Programme,* p. 8. To this William Leiss adds: "Actually, the damage goes much deeper. To pursue Marx's analogy, we might say that the societal offspring is akin to the heroin addict's baby, who becomes hooked on its mother's habit in the womb and whose postnatal agonies duplicate the withdrawal symptoms of the deprived junkie." William Leiss, "Critical Theory and Its Future," pp. 345-46.

44. Karl R. Popper, *Objective Knowledge,* p. 32.

45. Charles Taylor, "The Agony of Economic Man," pp. 233-34.

46. Arendt, HC, p. 154.

47. *Ibid.,* p. 157. Cf. Paul Valéry who says of the utilitarian view of knowledge: "Knowledge, which was a consumer value, became an exchange value. The utility of knowledge made knowledge a *commodity,* no longer desired by a few distinguished amateurs but by Everybody." Paul Valéry, *History and Politics,* p. 34. Hereafter cited as "HP."

48. Although he was unable to transcend the notion of man as *homo faber* and technologist, Marx pinpointed the dehumanizing effects of modern industrial civilization in alienating men and women from each other. With him, Heidegger sees clearly that "The 'world wars' and their character of 'totality' are already a consequence of the abandonment of Being. They press toward a guarantee of the stability of a constant form of using things up. Man, who no longer conceals his character of being the most important raw material, is also drawn into this process. Man is the 'most important raw material' because he remains the subject of all consumption. He does this in such a way that he lets his will be unconditionally equated with the process, and thus at the same time becomes the 'object' of the abandonment of Being" (EP, pp. 103-4).

CHAPTER 4. THE LIFE-WORLD, LANGUAGE, AND POLITICAL KNOWLEDGE: TOWARD A NEW PARADIGM IN THE PHILOSOPHY OF THE SCIENCES

1. Alvin W. Gouldner, *For Sociology: Renewal and Critique in Sociology Today,* pp. 105, 106 and *The Coming Crisis of Western Sociology,* p. 13.

2. John Wild programmatically sets forth the role of phenomenology in investigating the various areas of the life-world when he says: "Four different kinds of phenomena are found in the *Lebenswelt,* each of which is now the object of a distinct mode of scientific investigation: man himself, the realm of nature, other men and the realm of human culture, and, finally, the transcendent. In each of these regions, however, foundational questions arise which involve first philosophy and the *Lebenswelt* as a whole and which cannot be settled by science alone. In the case of man himself, it has been shown that there are vast regions of lived experience hitherto dismissed by objective reason as 'subjective' which are absolutely essential to man and which can be

described and understood by a disciplined phenomenology. Hence, in addition to psychology and what is now called anthropology, a philosophical anthropology which studies the total existence of man in his *Lebenswelt* is required. Some real light has been shed on these matters, and the further development and refinement of this discipline is of the first importance." See John Wild, "Interrogation of John Wild," p. 177. The social and political implications of Wild's conception of the life-world are sketched out in his works: John Wild, EWF and *Human Freedom and Social Order: An Essay in Christian Philosophy.* The most extensive discussion on the life-world is found in Gerd Brandt, *Die Lebenswelt: Eine Philosophie des konkreten A Priori.*

3. Schutz, CP, p. 53. Aron Gurwitsch rightly points out that "one of Schutz's original contributions consists in his contention that the social character belongs to the life-world *essentially* and *intrinsically*. That world is a social and intersubjective world from the outset and throughout; it does not become so subsequently, as was maintained in a certain sense by Husserl." Aron Gurwitsch, *Phenomenology and the Theory of Science*, p. 124 (italics added). Hereafter cited as "PTS." In addition to the writings of Schutz and Merleau-Ponty, we should add particularly the following works directly relevant to our discussion on the phenomenology of the social world: Mikel Dufrenne, *The Notion of the A Priori* and Emmanual Levinas, *Totality and Infinity* and *Autrement qu'Être ou au-delà de l'Essence.* According to Alfred Schutz and Thomas Luckmann, in the everyday life-world intersubjectivity itself is taken for granted in the following ways: "(a) the corporeal existence of other men; (b) that these bodies are endowed with consciousness essentially similar to my own; (c) that the things in the outer world included in my environs and that of my fellow-men are the same for us and have fundamentally the same meaning; (d) that I can enter into interrelations and reciprocal actions with my fellow–men; (e) that I can make myself understood to them (which follows from the preceding assumptions); (f) that a stratified social and cultural world is historically pre-given as a frame of reference for me and my fellow-men, indeed in a manner as taken for granted as the 'natural world'; (g) that therefore the situation in which I find myself at any moment is only to a small extent purely created by men." Alfred Schutz and Thomas Luckmann, *The Structures of the Life-World*, p. 5.

4. Maurice Natanson, *Phenomenology, Role, and Reason: Essays on the Coherence and Deformation of Social Reality.*

5. Cf. Mary Hesse who writes: "A study of the logical structure of science is not intended in the first place as an aid to scientific research, much less as a descriptive manual of experimental method. . . . Science has been remarkably successful in pursuing its own aims independently of philosophical disputes. But that is not to say that the philosophical critique of the foundations of science itself can ultimately be ignored, for that critique is concerned both with the understanding and justification of the aims of science itself, and with the existence and character of modes of knowledge other than the scientific." Mary Hesse, *The Structure of Scientific Inference*, p. 7. Hereafter cited as "SSI."

6. Paci, FS, p. 55.

7. Martin Heidegger, *The Question Concerning Technology and Other Essays*, p. 176. Hereafter cited as "QT."

8. Husserl, EJ, p. 30.

9. Merleau-Ponty, PP, p. ix.

10. Alfred North Whitehead, *Process and Reality*, p. 27. Whitehead writes elsewhere that " . . . modern philosophy has been ruined. It has oscillated in a complex manner between three extremes. There are the dualists, who accept matter and mind as on an equal basis, and the two varieties of monists, those who put mind inside matter, and those who put matter inside mind. But this juggling with abstractions can never overcome the inherent confusion introduced by the ascription of *misplaced concreteness* to the scientific scheme of the seventeenth century." Alfred North Whitehead, *Science and the Modern World*, p. 56. In this context, allusions of Whitehead's thought to phenomenology are made in Calvin O. Schrag, *Experience and Being: Prolegomena to a Future Ontology*. Schrag writes: "It is also my contention that insufficient attention has been given to the role of experience in the thought of the Anglo-American philosopher, Alfred North Whitehead. It is unfortunate (and for this misfortune Whitehead is himself partly responsible) that the metaphysical scaffolding of his speculative cosmology has virtually eclipsed his seminal insights into the dynamics and texture of experience. What is sorely needed in Whitehead scholarship today is a reexamination of his philosophy in light of his theory of experience" (*ibid.*, p. xii).

11. Gurwitsch, CMP, pp. 300-1. "Galileo," Gurwitsch writes elsewhere, "inherited not only geometry as a body of technical knowledge but also the Platonic interpretation of geometry as embodying the ideal of true knowledge. Following Cassirer, Koyré, and Crombie, I consider Galileo as a 'Platonist' and, going even further, I maintain that the whole of modern physics—the 'physics of Galilean style'—is of Platonic inspiration" (PTS, pp. 50-51).

12. Gurwitsch, PTS, p. 47.

13. For an excellent discussion on this issue in Descartes, see James Collins, *Descartes' Philosophy of Nature*.

14. Ernst Cassirer, *The Myth of the State*, p. 165. For an extensive discussion on the implications of Hobbes's mechanism on the study of politics, see Thomas A. Spragens, Jr., *The Politics of Motion: The World of Thomas Hobbes*.

15. Husserl, CES, pp. 51-52. For a discussion of mathematics as an idealizing object compatible with Husserl's phenomenology, see Hermann Weyl, *Philosophy of Mathematics and Natural Science*.

16. Gurwitsch, CPM, p. 300. For Heidegger's critique of modern science as the projection of a mathematical framework into the conceptualization of nature, see Martin Heidegger, *What Is a Thing?*, pp. 66-108. Hereafter cited as "WIT." Heidegger's discussion is concerned with the original meaning of the mathematical in Greek thought and the way in which it became transformed so as to constitute the foundation of knowledge in modern science (Galileo and Newton) and modern philosophy (Descartes).

17. Jacob Klein, *Greek Mathematical Thought and the Origin of Algebra*, p. 123. Hereafter cited as "GMT."

18. Ludwig Landgrebe, "The Phenomenological Concept of Experience," p. 1.

19. Robert Sokolowski, "Husserl's Protreptic," p. 81. Heinz Eulau typifies the behavioralist polarization of one's commitment to science and citizenship when he says: "I never concern myself with the problem of whether the result of research is critical or conformist; let us not confuse our role of responsible citizen with our role of scientist." See James C. Charlesworth (ed.), *A Design for Political Science: Scope, Objectives and Methods*, p. 115.

20. Schutz, CP, p. 59.

21. *Ibid.*, p. 59.

22. *Ibid.*, p. 57. A comparative study of Weber and Schutz is found in Robert Williame, *Les Fondements Phénoménologiques de la Sociologie Compréhensive: Alfred Schutz et Max Weber*. For an excellent collection of essays on the controversy of *Verstehen* in social inquiry, see Fred R. Dallmayr and Thomas A. McCarthy (eds.), *Understanding and Social Inquiry*.

23. Although he sees phenomenology as an alternative to positivist epistemology, Richard J. Bernstein is critical of Schutz's social phenomenology for lacking any *critical evaluation* of the different forms of social and political reality. See Richard J. Bernstein, *The Restructuring of Social and Political Theory*, pp. 115–69. Cf. Robert A. Gorman, *The Dual Vision: Alfred Schutz and the Myth of Phenomenological Social Science*. In all fairness, it should be noted that Schutz's concern is primarily a phenomenological clarification of the methodology of the social sciences. The question of this critical evaluation concerning the different forms of social and political reality Bernstein has in mind is implicit in this book. Because it is most fundamental in political theory, it requires special attention in any future work on a phenomenological critique of politics. In this regard, Schutz's *descriptive* phenomenology of social reality constitutes the indispensable *foundation* of *any* critical theory of politics and society. Any critic who ignores this fails to fathom the depth of phenomenological description. It must further be pointed out that the absence of critical evaluation in Schutz's phenomenology does by no means imply that phenomenology as such is intrinsically incapable of critical evaluation. Merleau-Ponty's phenomenology alone would dispel at once such a misunderstanding.

24. This section is taken from my previously published article, "A Hermeneutical Accent on the Conduct of Political Inquiry." The first section of it (pp. 48–62) has been shortened, revised, and adapted for this section. Hereafter cited as "HA."

25. For a discussion on the humanistic tradition of Vico's philosophy of language, see Karl-Otto Apel, *Die Idee der Sprache in der Tradition des Humanismus von Dante bis Vico*, pp. 318–80.

26. Among the political theorists in the English-speaking world, so far Quentin Skinner appears to be most promising to carry on a dialogue with the continental tradition of hermeneutics. See particularly Quentin Skinner, "Hermeneutics and the Role of History" and "Political Language and the

Explanation of Political Action." For a discussion of the hermeneutics of politics, see Kazuhiko Okuda, *Hermeneutics and Politics: A Study in Political Symbolism and Communication.*

27. It is interesting to note that recently David E. Apter describes his position as the "hermeneutic" or interpretive approach which constitutes an alternative to the "behavioral" and the "paradigmatic" approach in political science. "In my view," he suggests, "the danger of the behavioral position, with its emphasis on quantitative detail, specialization, and fine applications, is that it will engage small minds on small issues, while the paradigmist position with its emphasis on grand solutions will engineer empty architectural plans for buildings that can never be built." David E. Apter, *Introduction to Political Analysis*, p. 537.

28. Merleau-Ponty, SI, p. 84.

29. Paul Ricoeur, "The Model of the Text: Meaningful Action Considered as a Text," p. 529.

30. This *magnum opus* of Gadamer is supplemented here by his later writings on philosophical hermeneutics. See Hans-Georg Gadamer, *Philosophical Hermeneutics.* Hereafter cited as "PH." In the context of this section, the following works are also useful: Paul Ricoeur, CI; *Freud and Philosophy: An Essay on Interpretation; Interpretation Theory: Discourse and the Surplus Meaning;* and James M. Edie, *Speaking and Meaning: The Phenomenology of Language.*

31. Some of Gadamer's hermeneutical themes in relation to the human sciences were dealt with by Wilhelm Dilthey. See Wilhelm Dilthey, *Selected Writings*, particularly pp. 247–63. Hereafter cited as "SW." Dilthey's thought is most significant for developing the epistemology of the human sciences alternative to scientism. Ricoeur captures the spirit of Dilthey's ambition in the historical context of the nineteenth century when he writes: "Dilthey's times were those of the complete refusal of Hegelianism and an apologetic for experimental knowledge. Thus the only way of doing justice to historical knowledge seemed to be to give it a scientific dimension, comparable to the dimension which [the] natural sciences had conquered. So it was in order to reply to positivism that Dilthey undertook to endow the cultural sciences with an epistemology and a methodology just as respectable as those belonging to the natural sciences." Paul Ricoeur, "The Task of Hermeneutics," p. 117.

32. Gadamer, TM, pp. 401–2.

33. Steiner, EX, p. 133.

34. Norman O. Brown, *Closing Time*, p. 105.

35. Paul Ricoeur, "New Developments in Phenomenology in France: The Phenomenology of Language," p. 30.

36. E. D. Hirsch, Jr. treats the question of validity (in interpretation) as an epistemological problem in which he hopes to save literary interpretation from the "shackles" of subjectivism and historicism. His critique of Gadamer's hermeneutics as subjectivism, however, is misconceived and misguided on two grounds: first, it ignores the "ontological" dimension of Gadamer's endeavor and fails to see its ultimate consequences and second, interpretation as a

hermeneutical *event*, as Gadamer himself repeatedly stresses, has nothing to do with subjectivism or historicism. For Hirsch's critique of Gadamer's hermeneutics, see E. D. Hirsch, Jr., *Validity in Interpretation*, pp. 245-64. Hirsch's conception of hermeneutics is further elaborated on and developed in a collection of essays: E. D. Hirsch, Jr., *The Aims of Interpretation* which, unlike *Validity in Interpretation*, stresses the idea that the processes of understanding and validation are inseparable. Even though it is impossible for me to offer here a systematic critique of Hirsch in defense of Heidegger and Gadamer who, contrary to Hirsch's allegation, are by no means epistemological or cognitive "atheists," "relativists," or "skeptics," one critical point must be emphasized. For Hirsch but not for Heidegger and Gadamer, the aim of hermeneutics is epistemological rather than ontological, that is, the aim of interpretation is to yield *valid knowledge* which is identified with truth. The point is simply that the depth of an ontological sea cannot be fathomed or validated by the shallowness of an epistemological lagoon. The most lucid exposition and eloquent defense of Gadamer's hermeneutics against his critics are fouond in David Couzens Hoy, *The Critical Circle: Literature and History in Contemporary Hermeneutics* which came to my attention after this book had been completed. For the defense of Gadamer against Hirsch's critique, see pp. 11-40. Hereafter cited as "CC." A short critical analysis of Hirsch in terms of Husserl's phenomenology is found in Robert R. Magliola, *Phenomenology and Literature: An Introduction*, pp. 97-106.

37. Gadamer, TM, pp. 267-70.

38. Ricoeur, CI, p. 27.

39. Steiner, EX, p. 62.

40. See further Hans-Georg Gadamer, "The Problem of Historical Consciousness." Hereafter cited as "PHC." The term "historically operative consciousness" is Richard E. Palmer's translation of *wirkungsgeschichtliches Bewusstsein* whose more literal translation is "effect-historical consciousness." See Richard E. Palmer, *Hermeneutics: Interpretation Theory in Schleiermacher, Dilthey, Heidegger, and Gadamer*, p. 191. Hereafter cited as "HE." The term "effect" in relation to the interpretation of "tradition" must be taken to mean "tracing," "taking into account," or "soliciting" rather than "causal." "Effective history" may be likened to investment which produces dividends from the initial capital (i.e., tradition). See Derrida, SP, pp. 140-41, 155, 156.

41. Gadamer, TM, p. 238.

42. *Ibid.*, pp. 239-40.

43. Gadamer, PH, pp. 26-42 and TM, pp. 491-98. Hoy briefly recounts the Gadamer-Habermas debate and clarifies Gadamer's claim that hermeneutics has universal application to all areas of human conduct against Habermas's contention that the hermeneutical dimension is subordinate to the "critique of ideology." See Hoy, CC, pp. 117-28.

44. For an analysis of Heidegger and Husserl in relation to Dilthey, see Georg Misch, *Lebensphilosophie und Phänomenologie*.

45. Gadamer, TM, pp. xvi-xvii.

46. For Husserl's critique of Dilthey's "psychologism" and "historicism," see Edmund Husserl, *Phenomenology and the Crisis of Philosophy*, pp. 71-147. Hereafter cited as "PCP."

47. Gadamer, TM, p. 264.

48. *Ibid.*, p. 88.

49. *Ibid.*, p. 147. Cf. Paul Ricoeur, "History and Hermeneutics."

50. For the application of hermeneutical phenomenology to the study of cross-cultural phenomena, see Hwa Yol Jung and Petee Jung, "The Hermeneutics of Political Ideology and Cultural Change: Maoism as the Sinicization of Marxism" and "Revolutionary Dialectics: Mao Tse-tung and Maurice Merleau-Ponty." Pages 165-69 of the former and pages 35-37 of the latter are incorporated into what follows in this section. For a phenomenology of modernization and an interpretive theory of cultures, see Peter Berger, Brigitte Berger, and Hansfried Kellner, *The Homeless Mind: Modernization and Consciousness* and Clifford Geertz, *The Interpretation of Cultures: Selected Essays*. The phenomenon of "seeing" an esoteric Indian culture by Carlos Castaneda is no less relevant to the study of comparative cultures than these two works when he writes: "Obviously that event or any event that occurred within this alien system of sensible interpretation could be explained or understood only in terms of the units of meaning proper to that system. This work is, therefore, a reportage and should be read as a reportage.... In this respect I have adopted the phenomenological method and have striven to deal with sorcery solely as phenomena that were presented to me. I, as the perceiver, recorded what I perceived, and at the moment of recording I endeavored to suspend judgment." Carlos Castaneda, *A Separate Reality: Further Conversations with Don Juan*, p. 25.

51. A. L. Kroeber and Clyde Kluckhohn, *Culture: A Critical Review of Concepts and Definitions*, p. 338.

52. Charles Taylor, "Interpretation and the Sciences of Man," p. 16. Hereafter cited as "ISM." Eric Voegelin maintains that the notion of self-interpretation is part of man's historical existence when he writes: "Political science is suffering from a difficulty that originates in its very nature as a science of man in historical existence. For man does not wait for science to have his life explained to him, and when the theorist approaches social reality he finds the field pre-empted by what may be called the self-interpretation of society. Human society is not merely a fact, or an event, in the external world to be studied by an observer like a natural phenomenon. Though it has externality as one of its important components, it is as a whole, a little world, a cosmion, illuminated with meaning from within by the human beings who continuously create and bear it as the mode and condition of their self-realization." Eric Voegelin, *The New Science of Politics*, p. 27. Hereafter cited as "NSP."

53. Taylor, ISM, p. 30.

54. *Ibid.*, p. 34. The theory of political development Taylor cites is the functionalist framework of Gabriel A. Almond and G. Bingham Powell, Jr., *Comparative Politics: A Developmental Approach*. This functionalist approach of Al-

mond is fully elaborated from its inception in Gabriel A. Almond, *Political Development: Essays in Heuristic Theory*. For a critique of the contemporary theory of comparative politics similar to Taylor, see Alasdair MacIntyre, *Against the Self-Image of the Age: Essays on Ideology and Philosophy*, pp. 260-79.

55. For the development of a phenomenology of socialization, the following work of Merleau-Ponty is indispensable: "The Child's Relations with Others," trans. William Cobb, in PPE, pp. 96-155.

56. See G. W. F. Hegel, *The Philosophy of History*, pp. 105-6, 116-38.

57. Edward W. Said, *Beginnings: Intention and Method*, p. 357.

58. Merleau-Ponty, VI, p. 224.

59. Merleau-Ponty, SI, p. 120. What Lévi-Strauss impresses us most with is not his structuralist theory or techniques, but the homage he pays to the "savage mind" of the "primitives," whose "pupil" and "witness" he is, to the end of preserving the *lateral* continuity of humanity in the same spirit of Merleau-Ponty. See Claude Lévi-Strauss *Structural Anthropology*, p. 32.

60. Merleau-Ponty, SI, p. 120.

61. *Ibid.*, p. 138.

62. *Ibid.*, p. 133.

63. *Ibid.*, p. 139.

64. *Ibid.*, p. 128.

65. *Ibid.*, p. 139. Arendt believes that Chinese philosophy "may well rank with the philosophy of the Occident" (LM, 1: 100). The following two works exemplify in spirit the notion of truth as lateral: Karl Jaspers, *The Great Philosophers* and Tetsuro Watsuji, *Rinri Gaku* (Ethics).

66. Husserl, CES, p. 380.

67. Schutz, CP, pp. 65-66.

68. Gurwitsch, PTS, pp. 148-49. Cf. Hesse who suggests that "Natural scientific inference has rational grounds, but these are essentially finite and local in application, and determined by empirical conditions of testability and self-correction. If we wish to go beyond this form of rationality, we must look to the studies of man, society and history, which in all European languages except English are still called 'science', and whose methods and aims are not exhausted by those of natural science" (SSI, p. 302). For an extensive collection of essays on phenomenology and the nature of natural science, see Joseph J. Kockelmans and Theodore J. Kisiel, *Phenomenology and the Natural Sciences: Essays and Translations*.

69. For a discussion of the movement of unified knowledge in terms of some important individual thinkers in Western philosophy, see Robert McRae, *The Problem of the Unity of the Sciences: Bacon to Kant*.

70. Albert William Levi proposes a new mode of analyzing philosophy or the history of ideas in its social anchorage. However, he is critical of an "over-sociologizing" tendency in the sociology of knowledge (*Wissenssoziologie*). See Albert William Levi, *Philosophy as Social Expression*, particularly pp. 1-37. While he recognizes the useful function of a "critique of ideology," Hans Barth points out the tension in Marx's thought between the creative autonomy of human consciousness—including that of knowledge—and its "ide-

ological" dependency on the material and social conditions of life. See Hans Barth, *Truth and Ideology*, pp. 100 ff.

71. Husserl, CES, pp. 130-31.

72. For a discussion of this point in relation to the human sciences, see Merleau-Ponty, "Phenomenology and the Sciences of Man," trans. John Wild, in PPE, pp. 43-95. Arendt suggests that the essential is "something generally *meaningful*" and that "the 'essential' is what is applicable everywhere, and this 'everywhere' that bestows on thought its specific weight is spatially speaking a 'nowhere.' The thinking ego, moving among universals, among invisible essences, is, strictly speaking, nowhere; it is homeless in an emphatic sense—which may explain the early rise of a cosmopolitan spirit among the philosophers" (LM, 1: 199). Speaking of overcoming relativism, Gurwitsch writes that "Whatever differences may obtain among the several cultural worlds and, correspondingly, among the several particular forms of conscious life in which the cultural worlds originate and of which they are the correlates, the general reference of every such world to the corresponding consciousness, which underlies all relativities, is not itself relative. The task arises of setting forth and elucidating the universal structures of consciousness which makes possible *any* cultural world as the life-world of a sociohistorical group. Only on the basis of a general theory of consciousness, as developed by Husserl in his several writings under the heading of intentionality, can the aforementioned program of understanding the various cultural worlds by referring each one of them to the corresponding mental life be realized and carried out, since all particularizations of consciousness here in question are variations within an invariant framework as delineated and defined by the essential and universal structure of consciousness" (PTS, p. 25).

73. Giambattista Vico, *On the Study of Methods of Our Time*, p. 23. Hereafter cited as "OSM." Gurwitsch maintains that "This [Galilean] science is certainly one of the greatest accomplishments of the human mind.... As a product of the mind, science of the Galilean style requires phenomenological clarification. Because of the role of the life-world as the presupposition of scientific construction, the problems which (if one is to be systematic) must be attacked first are those related to the life-world itself and the experience through which it presents itself, i.e., perceptual experience. Subsequently, a phenomenological account must be given of the higher intellectual processes which, like idealization, formalization, and so on, are basic to the construction of pure mathematics and the mathematization of nature" (PTS, p. 56).

74. Max H. Fisch and Thomas G. Bergin, "Introduction" to *The Autobiography of Giambattista Vico*, p. 60. R. G. Collingwood goes so far as to maintain that the knowledge of natural sciences depends on the knowledge of history or historical knowledge because scientific facts or events in the world of nature are a class of historical facts; and therefore unless we understand history, we cannot understand nature. See R. G. Collingwood, *The Idea of Nature*, pp. 176-77. Since for him we cannot adequately reflect upon the nature of the natural sciences without taking into account history, we should consult his philosophy of history in R. G. Collingwood, *The Idea of History*.

75. Abraham Kaplan, *The Conduct of Inquiry: Methodology for Behavioral Science*, p. 407. Hereafter cited as "CIM."
76. See Thomas S. Kuhn, "Second Thoughts on Paradigms."
77. Kuhn, SSR, p. 5.
78. Thomas S. Kuhn, "Logic of Discovery or Psychology of Research?," p. 21.
79. Kuhn, SSR, p. 146.
80. Michael Polanyi, *Knowing and Being*, pp.65–66.
81. Thomas A. Spragens, Jr. uses Polanyi's philosophy as a springboard in the hopes of creating a post-behavioral science of politics in his work: Thomas A. Spragens, Jr., *The Dilemma of Contemporary Political Theory: Toward a Postbehavioral Science of Politics*.
82. See Michael Polanyi, *The Tacit Dimension*. Hilary Putnam, too, is critical of scientism as an epistemology or "scientizing" the social sciences whose tradition, as he sees it, goes back to J. S. Mill's attempt to remedy their backwardness by applying and extending the methods of physical science. See Hilary Putnam, *Meaning and the Moral Sciences*, particularly pp. 66–77. Based on his primary distinction between "theoretical" and "practical" knowledge in the tradition of Aristotle and Kant, Putnam asserts the dependency of the former on the latter in his opposition to scientism. Like Polanyi's "tacit knowing," Putnam's practical knowledge is both "unformalized" and "unformalizable." Insofar as the knowing subject implicates himself in both "discovery" and "justification" of theoretical knowledge, Putnam insists that both social-scientific and natural-scientific knowledge depends on practical knowledge or *Verstehen:* "Physics may rest on *Verstehen* as much as the social sciences" (*ibid.*, p. 74). He invokes the notion of *Verstehen* or the "unformalizability of practical knowledge" as the necessary foundation of theoretical knowledge.
83. Michael Polanyi, *Science, Faith and Society*, p. 38.
84. *Ibid.*, p. 24.
85. *Ibid.* Paul K. Feyerabend more radically asserts that "the history of science, after all, consists not only of facts and conclusions drawn therefrom. It consists also of ideas, interpretations of facts, problems created by a clash of interpretations, actions of scientists, and so on. On closer analysis we even find that there are no 'bare facts' at all but that the facts that enter our knowledge are already viewed in a certain way and are therefore essentially ideational. This being the case the history of science will be as complex, as chaotic, as full of error, and as entertaining as the ideas it contains and these ideas in turn will be as complex, as chaotic, as full of error, and as entertaining as are the minds of those who invented them. Conversely, a little brainwashing will go a long way in making the history of science more simple, more uniform, more dull, more 'objective,' and more accessible to treatment by 'certain and infallible' rules: a theory of errors is superfluous when we are dealing with well-trained scientists who are kept in place by an internal slave master called 'professional conscience' and who have been convinced that it is good and rewarding to attain, and then to forever keep, one's 'professional integrity'." Paul K. Feyerabend, "Against Method: Outline of an Anarchistic Theory of Knowledge," p. 20.

CHAPTER 5. A CRITIQUE OF POLITICAL BEHAVIORALISM AS SCIENTIFIC
EPISTEMOLOGY

1. This chapter is based on and makes use of my previous work, "A Critique
of the Behavioral Persuasion in Politics: A Phenomenological View."
2. Robert A. Dahl, "The Behavioral Approach in Political Science: Epitaph
for a Monument to a Successful Protest," p. 770.
3. Heinz Eulau, *Micro-Macro Political Analysis,* p. 150. Hereafter cited as
"MMP."
4. Heinz Eulau, *The Behavioral Persuasion in Politics,* p. 32. Hereafter cited as
"BPP." It might also be suggested that an equally interesting task for
psychoanalysis is to determine *why* science and technology have become a
panacea for modern man, both the intellectual and the layman alike.
Abraham H. Maslow remarks that "these 'good,' 'nice' scientific words—
prediction, control, rigor, certainty, exactness, preciseness, neatness, orderli-
ness, lawfulness, quantification, proof, explanation, validation, reliability, rationality, organization, etc.—are all capable of being pathologized when
pushed to the extreme. All of them may be pressed into the service of the
safety needs, that is, they may become primarily anxiety-avoiding and anxi-
ety-controlling mechanisms." Abraham H. Maslow, *The Psychology of Science,*
p. 30.
5. Scheler, SPE, p. 12.
6. Eulau, BPP, pp. 5-6.
7. Graham Wallas, *Human Nature in Politics.* In this connection, see particularly David Hume, *A Treatise of Human Nature* and John Stuart Mill, *A System
of Logic: Ratiocinative and Inductive.* Hereafter cited as "SL."
8. Gadamer notes that the German translator of Mill's SL coined the term
"*Geisteswissenschaften*" in translating Mill's term "Moral Sciences" spurred by
romantic idealism (as in Book Six of *System der deduktiven und induktiven Logik:*
"*Von der Logik der Geisteswissenschaften oder moralischen Wissenschaften*"). See Gadamer, TM, p. 5; PHC, p. 12; and "Theory, Technology, Practice: The
Task of the Science of Man," pp. 559-60 which will be cited hereafter as
"TTP." Gadamer further notes that "we must, however, deny Mill the intention of having wishes to attribute to the 'moral sciences' a logic *of their own.* On
the contrary, Mill's science is also the only valid method for the domain of the
moral sciences" (PHC, p. 12). How Mill's inductive method of science is compatible with his normative philosophy of man is the same thorny question
raised in political behavioralism regarding the issue of fact and value or the
"is" and the "ought."
9. Eulau, MMP, p. 151.
10. See Robert E. Lane, *Political Thinking and Consciousness.*
11. Stanley Cavell, *Must We Mean What We Say?,* p. 22.
12. Merleau-Ponty, SNS, p. 97. See particularly Maurice Roche, *Phenomenology, Language and the Social Sciences,* one of whose main theses is that the
"humanistic" outlook of phenomenological philosophy (in, e.g., Heidegger,
Merleau-Ponty, Sartre, and Schutz) and its "sociological" component go hand

in hand. In the contemporary study of political thought, the following work of William T. Bluhm presents the most comprehensive effort to build a bridge between philosophy and science as well as between different theories and between the past and the present: William T. Bluhm, *Theories of the Political System: Classics of Political Thought and Modern Political Analysis.* Hereafter cited as "TPS."

13. Merleau-Ponty, PPE, p. 50.

14. See Don Ihde, *Experimental Phenomenology: An Introduction.*

15. Merleau-Ponty, SI, p. 101. See also Edmund Husserl, "Phenomenology and Anthropology."

16. Otto Neurath, "Sociology and Physicalism," p. 285.

17. Cf. Charles Taylor, *The Explanation of Behavior,* p. 272.

18. T. D. Weldon, *The Vocabulary of Politics.* The most comprehensive critique of logical positivism in political inquiry is found in John G. Gunnell, *Philosophy, Science, and Political Inquiry.*

19. Brian Barry, *Political Argument,* p. 290.

20. Anthony Downs, *An Economic Theory of Democracy.* Hereafter cited as "ETD."

21. Milton Friedman, *Essays in Positive Economics,* pp. 8–9. Hereafter cited as "EPE." In order to avoid the confusion of telling what will happen in the future and explaining an event that has already taken place, it may be useful to distinguish prediction (pre-dict the future) and postdiction (retro-dict the past). See Stephen Toulmin, *Foresight and Understanding,* p. 27. Hereafter cited as "FU." See also W. H. Walsh, *An Introduction to Philosophy of History,* p. 41. So-called prediction in the social sciences has largely been of a postdictive rather than a predictive nature.

22. Friedman, EPE, p. 9. Toulmin challenges this predictivist thesis and denies the idea that prediction is "the kernel of science." Rather, prediction is a craft or technical application of science: "the predictive success of a theory is only one test of its explanatory power and neither a necessary nor a sufficient one" (FU, pp. 35–36).

23. Merleau-Ponty, PPE, p. 194.

24. *Ibid.,* p. 84.

25. Peter Winch, *The Idea of a Social Science and Its Relation to Philosophy,* p. 12.

26. *Ibid.,* pp. 15, 17. Cf. Ludwig Wittgenstein, *Remarks on Colour,* pp. 9e, 15e, and 16e: "There is no such thing as phenomenology, but there are indeed phenomenological problems"; "Here the temptation to believe in a phenomenology, something midway between science and logic, is very great"; and "Phenomenological analysis (as e.g., Goethe would have it) is analysis of concepts and can neither agree with nor contradict physics." Precisely what Wittgenstein meant by "phenomenology" or "phenomenological" beyond what is apparent in the above passages as something "conceptual" or "mental" is beyond the scope of our inquiry here.

27. Merleau-Ponty, PP, p. viii (italics added).

28. Straus, PWS, pp. 111–12.

29. Edward Hallett Carr, *What Is History?,* p. 9.

30. Michael Oakeshott, *Experience and Its Modes*, p. 42.
31. Norwood R. Hanson, *Patterns of Discovery*, p. 31.
32. Kuhn, SSR, p. 55.
33. See Merleau-Ponty, PPE, pp. 43-95.
34. Sheldon S. Wolin, "Political Theory as a Vocation," p. 1073.
35. The following discussion on the dualism of fact and value in political behavioralism is adapted from my article, "The Place of Valuation in the Theory of Politics: A Phenomenological Critique of Political Behavioralism," pp. 18-22.
36. The view that fact and value are logically heterogeneous is stated most clearly in David Easton, *The Political System: An Inquiry into the State of Political Science*, pp. 219-32 and *A Framework of Political Analysis*, pp. 1-22 which will be cited hereafter as "FPA." It appears that some positivists in political science now wish to break away from the rigid separation of fact and value. William H. Riker and Peter C. Ordeshook, for example, state that "In a science . . . , one wishes to avoid both ideology and utopia; hence it is important to look for outcomes that are both desirable and possible. Currently there is much controversy over whether the science of politics has room for 'ought' sentences. Some wish to concentrate exlusively on normative imperatives, others to banish them altogether. Both sides err, for in a practical science the moral and the descriptive go . . . hand in hand." William H. Riker and Peter C. Ordeshook, *An Introduction to Positive Political Theory*, p. 6. The most fundamental phenomenological notion of moral experience is stated by Maurice Mandelbaum when he says: "If the system which the metaphysician deduces is not consonant with the judgments of values and obligation which.men actually make, no amount of argument will convince us that the system is valid and its metaphysical basis true." Maurice Mandelbaum, *The Phenomenology of Moral Experience*, p. 17.
37. Heinz Eulau, "Political Science," p. 210.
38. David Easton, FPA, p.7 and "The Current Meaning of 'Behavioralism'," p. 16.
39. Felix E. Oppenheim, *Moral Principles in Political Philosophy*, p. 10.
40. *Ibid.*, p. 12.
41. Austin, PPA, p. 222. It is interesting to note that Isaiah Berlin attributes to Vico the conception of language as "performative utterances." See Isaiah Berlin, *Vico and Herder: Two Studies in the History of Ideas*, p. 50.
42. J. O. Urmson, *The Emotive Theory of Ethics*, p. 147.
43. The term "personal" is used by Michael Polanyi who rejects the idea of "scientific detachment" and considers scientific activity as the personal participation of the knower in the act of establishing contact with reality. Thus to be "personal" means to be neither purely subjective nor purely objective. See Michael Polanyi, *Personal Knowledge: Towards a Post-Critical Philosophy*.
44. Kaplan, CIM, p. 401.
45. Heidegger, QT, p. 120.
46. Ludwig Wittgenstein, *Tractatus Logico-Philosophicus*, p. 119. Hereafter cited as "TLP."

CHAPTER 6. A CRITIQUE OF THE CYBERNETIC MODEL OF MAN IN POLITICAL
SCIENCE

1. Eulau, BPP, p. 32. Dante Germino detects in Eulau's "revisionist" approach the sign of "a changed temper of behavioralism in the future" because
of its respect for the nonbehavioral, normative tradition of political science.
Nevertheless, Germino rightly objects to Eulau's unwillingness to concede
natural limits on computer technology in political research and contends that
"It is rather difficult to see how any computer could even answer the question
of the *summum bonum* for man." Dante Germino, *Beyond Ideology: The Revival of
Political Theory*, p. 191. However, the fundamental problem of even Eulau's
"revisionism" is deeper. As indicated in chapter 5, it lies in the impossibility
of reconciling the ontology of man, which he recognizes as radically different
from that of nature, and political behavioralism as scientific epistemology.
2. Eulau often endorses Morris R. Cohen's views of science and liberalism as
two complementary systems of attitudes. See Morris R. Cohen, *The Faith of a
Liberal*, pp. 437–69. Like Morgenthau who in SM criticizes the dogmatic faith
of scientific rationalism reflected on the political philosophy of liberalism
affecting foreign policy and international politics, Merleau-Ponty is critical of
that "abstract," "rigid," "optimistic," and "moralistic" liberalaism which leads to
the belief that "in a State where the rights of man are guaranteed, no liberty
any longer encroaches on any other, and the co-existence of men as autonomous and reasonable subjects is assured. This is to suppose that violence
appears only episodically in human history, that economic relationships in
particular tend of themselves to effect harmony and justice, and, finally, that
the structure of the human and natural world is rational. We know today that
formal equality of rights and political liberty mask rather than eliminate relationships based on force. And the political problem is then to institute social
structures and real relationships among men such that liberty, equality, and
right become effective. The weakness of democratic thinking is that it is less
political than moral, since it poses no problem of social structure and considers the conditions for the exercise of justice to be given with humanity. In
opposition to that particular moralism we all rallied to realism, if by that one
means a politics concerned with realizing the conditions of existence for its
chosen values" (SNS, pp. 102–3). Cf. Sonia Kruks who summarizes Merleau-
Ponty's critique of liberalism: "Liberalism refuses to recognize the precon-
scious, the obscure, the half submerged aspects of life. It insists on the autonomy from the standpoint of logic and attempts to impose on the world
principles which do not derive from the world as it is, but from a rationalistic
idealization of it. As such, liberalism is doomed to remain abstract and un-
dialectical and, as a conception of the world, incompatible with the phenomenological philosophy which Merleau-Ponty defends throughout his work."
Sonia Kruks, "Merleau-Ponty: A Phenomenological Critique of Liberalism,"
p. 400.
3. For a critique of the "instrumental rationality" of political behavioralism,
see particularly Herbert G. Reid, "The Politics of Time: Conflicting

Philosophical Perspectives and Trends" and Herbert G. Reid and Ernest J. Yanarella, "Toward a Post-Modern Theory of American Political Science and Culture: Perspectives from Critical Marxism and Phenomenology."

4. See Maurice Merleau-Ponty, *L'Oeil et l'Esprit* (Paris: Gallimard, 1964) which has been translated by Carleton Dallery in PPE, pp. 159-90.

5. Victor C. Ferkiss, *Technological Man: The Myth and the Reality*, p. 90.

6. Thus Heidegger writes that "Technology, conceived in the broadest sense and in its manifold manifestations, is taken for the plan which man projects, the plan which finally compels man to decide whether he will become the servant of his plan or will remain its master." Martin Heidegger, *Identity and Difference*, p. 34.

7. Merleau-Ponty, PPE, p. 160.

8. *Ibid.*

9. James Joyce, *Ulysses*, p. 34.

10. Merleau-Ponty, PPE, pp. 159-61.

11. Hobbes, LE, pp. 25-26.

12. *Ibid.*, p. 5.

13. Husserl, CES, p. 63.

14. Speaking of the role of mathematics in comparative politics, Robert T. Holt and John M. Richardson, Jr. remark that "It is not unlikely that the mathematics that presently exists is unsuitable for handling our problems, in which case the development of theory in comparative politics may depend upon innovative work in pure mathematics." Robert T. Holt and John M. Richardson, Jr., "Competing Paradigms in Comparative Politics," p. 70. Those social scientists who have an unblemished faith in the deductive and predictive power of mathematics and in building the mathematics *of* society should be aware of the following warning of Bertrand de Jouvenel: "A mathematical formula is never more than a precise statement. It must not be made into a Procrustean bed—and that is what one is driven to by the desire to quantify at any cost. It is utterly implausible that a mathematical formula should make the future known to us, and those who think it can would once have believed in witchcraft. The chief merit of mathematicization is that it compels us to become conscious of what we are assuming." Bertrand de Jouvenal, *The Art of Conjecture*, p. 173.

15. Karl W. Deutsch, *The Nerves of Government* and Herbert A. Simon, *The Sciences of the Artificial.* Hereafter cited as "NG" and "SA," respectively.

16. Norbert Wiener, *Cybernetics*, p. 164.

17. Simon, SA, p. 15.

18. Deutsch, NG, p. 38.

19. *Ibid.*, p. 133.

20. Michael Oakeshott, "Introduction" to Hobbes, LE, p. lv.

21. B. F. Skinner is critical of cybernetics because it assumes the existence of an "inner processor." B. F. Skinner, *Beyond Freedom and Dignity*, p. 18. Hereafter cited as "BFD."

22. Simon, SA, pp. 51-52. For a discussion of Cartesianism different from

that of Simon here, see Noam Chomsky, *Cartesian Linguistics*. Cf. Steiner, EX, 102–25.

23. For a teleological argument against cybernetics, see Hans Jonas, *The Phenomenon of Life*, pp. 108–34.

24. Simon, SA, p. 3.

25. *Ibid.*, p. 13.

26. Hubert L. Dreyfus, *What Computers Can't Do: A Critique of Artificial Reason*, p. 105. Hereafter cited as "WC." In an excellent *précis* of the mind-body problem today, John Beloff reproaches Dreyfus for removing the threat to the mind's autonomy from the contemporary philosophy of artificial intelligence: "What matters in this context are the negative implications of his thesis which, if it has any force, would remove the threat which artificial intelligence otherwise poses to a belief in the autonomy of mind." John Beloff, "The Mind-Body Problem as It Now Stands," p. 264. However, Beloff seems to have missed an essential point of Dreyfus's phenomenological argument against artificial reason. By eliminating the dualism of mind and body, his phenomenological critique affirms the creative autonomy of man (or self) as an integral unity of mind and body rather than of mind alone. According to Dreyfus, it was precisely the Cartesian philosophy of the disembodied mind that laid the foundation for the contemporary philosophy of artificial intelligence.

27. Jean-Paul Sartre, "Faces," p. 160.

28. Simon, SA, p. 107.

29. Merleau-Ponty, PPE, p. 99.

30. Wittgenstein, PI, p. 4e.

31. See Merleau-Ponty, SI, p. 88 and Paci, FS, pp. 212, 218. For an intensive and comprehensive discussion on the inner or idiolectic dimension of language, see George Steiner, *After Babel: Aspects of Language and Translation*.

32. Dreyfus, WC, p. 110.

33. Gadamer, PH, p. 15.

34. Cited in Dreyfus, WC, p. 115.

35. Michael Oakeshott, *On Human Conduct*, p. 120. Hereafter cited as "OHC." Stephen A. Erickson distinguishes a *rule* and a *regularity*. The former is intentional (noncausal) whereas the latter is nonintentional (causal): "A rule is something in accordance with which intentional activity is guided. Through appeal to rules predictions and explanations are possible on conceptual grounds. A regularity on the other hand is something in accordance with which nonintentional activity is described." Stephen A. Erickson, *Language and Being: An Analytic Phenomenology*, p. 158.

36. Dreyfus, WC, p. 113.

37. Merleau-Ponty, PW, p. 46.

38. See Dreyfus, WC, p. 123.

39. *Ibid.*, p. 117.

40. Merleau-Ponty, PP, p. 28.

41. William James, *The Principles of Psychology*, 1:222. Cf. Hampshiré, TA, p.

143: "The 'reduction' of moral judgments to quasi-orders and recommendations is like the behaviourist's reduction of inner thoughts and feelings to their natural expression in behaviour: it is a confusion between a necessary precondition and the essential nature of that which develops from it."
42. Eugene T. Gendlin, *Experiencing and the Creation of Meaning.*
43. Lev Semenovich Vygotsky, *Thought and Language.*
44. Mill, SL, p. 547.
45. Simon suggests that "only human pride argues that the apparent intricacies of our path stem from a quite different source than the intricacy of the ant's path" (SA, p. 53).
46. Sartre, BN, p. 233.
47. Oakeshott, OHC, p. 53.
48. Arendt, HC, p. 23.
49. Alfred Schutz, *Collected Papers,* vol. 3: *Studies in Phenomenological Philosophy,* p. 82.
50. The important work of this neglected philosopher is found in John Macmurray, *The Self as Agent* and *Persons in Relation.*
51. The following critique of sociologism incorporates my previously published article, "Embodiment and Political Action," pp. 367–68, 371, 374–80.
52. See Ernst H. Kantorowicz, *The King's Two Bodies: A Study in Mediaeval Political Theology.*
53. Voegelin, NSP, pp. 42 ff.
54. Merleau-Ponty, SI, p. 97.
55. Skinner, BFD, p. 18.
56. Simon, SA, p. 83.
57. *Ibid.*, p. 81.
58. *Ibid.*, p. 26.
59. B. F. Skinner, "Behaviorism at Fifty," p. 85.
60. Simon, SA, p. 25.
61. *Ibid.*, p. 11.
62. *Ibid.*, p. 35.
63. Eulau, MMP, pp. vii–viii.
64. Ralf Dahrendorf, *Essays in the Theory of Society,* pp. 24–25. Hereafter cited as "ETS."
65. *Ibid.*, pp. 56–57.
66. *Ibid.*, p. 57.
67. Anton C. Zijderveld, *The Abstract Society,* p. 36.
68. Dahrendorf, ETS, p. 26.
69. For an attempt to reconcile two models of man, "Plastic Man" and "Autonomous Man" which differs from but, in certain respects, is sympathetic with our presentation here, see Martin Hollis, *Models of Man: Philosophical Thoughts on Social Action.*
70. Maurice Natanson, "The Nature of Social Man," p. 270.
71. Maurice Natanson, *The Journeying Self,* p. 33.
72. Jürgen Habermas, "A Review of Gadamer's *Truth and Method,*" p. 341. Cf. Herbert Marcuse, *The Aesthetic Dimension: Toward a Critique of Marxist*

Aesthetics, pp. 38-39. "Today, the rejection of the individual as a 'bourgeois' concept recalls and presages fascist undertakings. Solidarity and community do not mean absorption of the individual. They rather originate in autonomous individual decision; they unite freely associated individuals, not masses." In his critical comparison of Georg Lukács and Martin Heidegger, Lucien Goldmann too is concerned with the way to overcome the traditional dichotomy between the individual and society as well as between theory and practice. It is worth noting here that he is critical of structuralism for eliminating the diachronic dimensions of man in favor of synchronic structures, that is to say, dissolving man as the signifying subject and actor. See Lucien Goldmann, *Lukács and Heidegger: Towards a New Philosophy*. The phenomenological notion of intersubjectivity I propound here as the dialectical process of internalization and externalization is capable of resolving fallacies of misplaced sociocentric and psychocentric orientations as diagnosed in recent years by the American sociologists David Riesman and Richard Sennet, respectively. See David Riesman, *The Lonely Crowd: A Study of the Changing American Character* and Richard Sennett, *The Fall of Public Man*. For a classical account of society as the dialectic of internalization and externalization in the tradition of Alfred Schutz's social phenomenology, see Peter L. Berger and Thomas Luckmann, *The Social Construction of Reality: A Treatise in the Sociology of Knowledge*.

CHAPTER 7. ONTOLOGY AND TECHNOLOGY: A CRITIQUE OF C. B.
MACPHERSON'S THEORY OF DEMOCRATIC POLITY

1. See Michael A. Weinstein, "C. B. Macpherson: The Roots of Democracy and Liberalism." Hereafter cited as "CBM." This chapter is a shortened and revised version of my article, "Democratic Ontology and Technology: A Critique of C. B. Macpherson."
2. See particularly Macpherson's works: *Democratic Theory: Essays in Retrieval* which will be cited hereafter as "DT"; *The Political Theory of Possessive Individualism: Hobbes to Locke* which will be cited hereafter as "PT"; *The Real World of Democracy;* and *The Life and Times of Liberal Democracy* which will be cited hereafter as "LT." In the recent development of democratic theory, a comparison of Macpherson, John Rawls, Robert Paul Wolff, and Robert Nozick would be an interesting study. I have in mind a comparison of the following four works: Macpherson, DT; John Rawls, *A Theory of Justice;* Robert Paul Wolff, *In Defense of Anarchism;* and Robert Nozick, *Anarchy, State, and Utopia.*
3. Another critic of liberalism, Sheldon Wolin, also focuses on the substantive issues of Locke's liberalism as having contributed to the decline of political philosophy and the sublimation of politics by subordinating *homo politicus* to *homo economicus.* For Wolin, as has been already said in chapter 3, Locke alone is the villain whose economic categories usurped political ones when he regarded the chief purpose of civil government to be the protection of private property—life, liberty, and estate, whereas Hobbes is the philosopher of the political *par excellence* because of his vigorous assertion of the distinctiveness

of the political and of making the concepts of authority, political obligation, and the system of common rules central to this thought. See Wolin, PV, pp. 286–434.

4. Macpherson, LT, p. 4.

5. Cited in Weinstein, CBM, p. 252.

6. Macpherson, DT, p. 192.

7. Macpherson, PT, pp. 263–64.

8. Macpherson writes that "We should not shrink from either the populist teaching of Rousseau or the radical teaching of Marx. Neither will suit us, but we may have more to learn from them than we think. It may even be—if the economists present will permit me an intertemporal comparison of utilities— that the utility of Marxism as a means of understanding the world is increasing over time" (DT, p. 184). The logic of Macpherson's sociologistic reasoning makes self-serving his observation on how relevant Rousseau's and Marx's thought is to the world today.

9. Karl Marx, *Grundrisse: Foundations of the Critique of Political Economy*.

10. Cf. Leo Strauss who says: "The 'invisible hand' remains ineffectual if it is not supported by the *Leviathan* or, if you wish, by the *Wealth of Nations*" (NRH, p. 201).

11. Macpherson, DT, pp. 246–47. Cf. Jürgen Habermas who considers Hobbes as both the originator of scientism in politics and the founder of liberalism. See Habermas, TP, pp. 56–76.

12. For an excellent general discussion of the development of early scientism in this context, see Paolo Rossi, *Philosophy, Technology and the Arts in the Early Modern Era*. Paul Valéry advanced in 1897 a visionary critique of scientific and technological transformation and its rationality. See Valéry, HP, pp. 46–66. Benjamin Nelson outlines an important argument that the breakthroughs for modernity are due to the broad effects of a fusion of the Protestant Reformation and the Scientific Revolution rather than the spirit of capitalism and its profit motive as narrowly defined by Max Weber. The Protestant Reformation bears its impact on the new orientation of self and society and the Scientific Revolution propels the development of mathematical science and technology, the fusion of which has now reached the point of exponential growth. See Benjamin Nelson, "Scholastic *Rationales* of 'Conscience', Early Modern Crises of Credibility, and the Scientific-Technocultural Revolution of the 17th and 20th Centuries."

13. On the twofold account of possessive individualism and scientism, today Anthony Downs is the most faithful student of Hobbes. See Downs, ETD. Cf. Bluhm, TPS, pp. 274–82.

14. For the treatment of ideology as a self-conscious, theoretical construct of man's thought and its consequences on his action, see David Gauthier, "The Social Contract as Ideology."

15. Heisenberg, PCN, p. 18.

16. Merleau-Ponty, PP, p. 171. Ellen Meiksins Wood also attempts to establish a linkage between epistemological atomism and liberal individualism. See Ellen Meiksins Wood, *Mind and Politics: An Approach to the Meaning of Liberal and Socialist Individualism*, especially pp. 19–46.

17. Macpherson, DT, p. 37.

18. *Ibid.*, p. 38.

19. *Ibid.*

20. What is ignored by Macpherson is brought to a sharp focus in Ferkiss, FTC.

21. The excellent accounts for creative human development in terms of the noninstrumental conception of nature and the recognition of the psychological and material limits of satisfaction are William Leiss, *The Limits to Satisfaction;* William Ophuls, *Ecology and the Politics of Scarcity: Prologue to a Political Theory of the Steady State;* and Mulford Q. Sibley, *Nature and Civilization: Some Implications for Politics.* For a discussion on the ethics of human development and the social consequences of economic growth on the basis of the earth as a finite planet, see Denis Goulet, *The Cruel Choice: A New Concept in the Theory of Development.*

22. See Lynn White, Jr., *Machina ex Deo: Essays in the Dynamism of Western Culture,* pp. 75–105.

23. William Coleman, "Providence, Capitalism, and Ecologic Crisis: English Apologetics in an Era of Economic Revolution," p. 44.

24. Macpherson, DT, p. 38.

25. For Sartre's view of scarcity, see CDR, pp. 735 ff.

26. Macpherson, DT, p. 61.

27. For a classical analysis of the Marxian concept of reification, see Georg Lukács, *History and Class Consciousness.* See also Joachim Israel, *Alienation from Marx to Modern Sociology: A Macrosociological Analysis,* pp. 255–342.

28. The classical views that separate leisure from labor or work are found in Josef Pieper, *Leisure: The Basis of Culture* and Johan Huizinga, *Homo Ludens: A Study of the Play-Element in Culture.*

29. Similarly, Calvin O. Schrag says of *praxis*-oriented Marxist theory that "it may well be that within this Marxian ethical critique praxis functions more as a negative principle of *redress* than as a positive foundation for social theory and practice." Calvin O. Schrag, "Praxis and Structure: Conflicting Models in the Science of Man," p. 26.

30. Sigmund Freud, *Civilization and Its Discontents,* p. 92. A sociologistic explanation may lead to the conclusion that Freud's observation of the inherent repressiveness of civilization in general is abstracted from the conditions of the industrial and technological civilization of his or our own time. John Murray Cuddihy analyzes Freud's thought (as well as Marx's) as an expression of the agonizing Jewish initiation into modernization. See John Murray Cuddihy, *The Ordeal of Civility: Freud, Marx, Lévi-Strauss, and the Jewish Struggle with Modernity,* pp. 17–116.

CHAPTER 8. THE LIFE-WORLD, HISTORICITY, AND TRUTH: LEO STRAUSS'S ENCOUNTER WITH HEIDEGGER AND HUSSERL

1. See my article, "Leo Strauss's Conception of Political Philosophy: A Critique." This chapter is a revised version of my previously published article,

"The Life-World, Historicity, and Truth: Reflections on Leo Strauss's Encounter with Heidegger and Husserl."

2. Leo Strauss, "An Epilogue," p. 327.

3. For an application of this Straussian thought to a critique of contemporary political inquiry, see Eugene F. Miller, "Positivism, Historicism, and Political Inquiry." For a general discussion of Strauss's thought, see also Eugene F. Miller, "Leo Strauss: The Recovery of Political Philosophy."

4. Leo Strauss, *What Is Political Philosophy? And Other Studies*, p. 11.

5. See Jacob Klein and Leo Strauss, "A Giving of Accounts" and Leo Strauss, "Philosophy as Rigorous Science and Political Philosophy." Hereafter cited as "GA" and "PRS," respectively. Also useful is Leo Strauss's "Preface to the English Translation," in *Spinoza's Critique of Religion*, pp. 1-31. Hereafter cited as "SCR."

6. Cf. Emil L. Fackenheim, *Metaphysics and Historicity*. Fackenheim cites Strauss's definition of historicism as a classical one (*ibid.*, p. 61), and Strauss once remarked that Fackenheim's work is the best critique of historicism.

7. Strauss somehow overlooks what he calls historicism as the prime movement against positivism or scientism. For a clash of these classical and modern philosophical ideas, see Karl Löwith, *Nature, History, and Existentialism and Other Essays in the Philosophy of History*. To counter Strauss's claim for the continuity between positivism and historicism, we may revert to Heidegger's mode of questioning Being (*Seinsfrage*) which reveals the metaphysical continuity between Strauss's search for timeless "essence" and the positivist search for "objectivity." The aim of Heidegger's ontology is to think what is unthought in the tradition of Western metaphysics. The postulate of "human nature" itself as timeless essence which constitutes the basis of Strauss's critique of historicism ought to be examined in terms of what Heidegger calls the historicity of what is natural or a historical destiny of Being (*Seinsgeschick*) as the "event of appropriation" (*Ereignis*). Only then do we discover that whatever is natural is never "self-evident" but always questionable. See Heidegger, WIT, pp. 39 ff. As Otto Pöggeler says of the questioning spirit of Heidegger's thought, "The understanding of Being as Idea, *energeia*, objectivity, will to power, etc. must be thought through on the basis of what was not thought in it, i.e. time as the horizon of the understanding of Being. In this manner, thought, as it has been understood up until now, is to be placed back onto its own ground. Heidegger, however, does not think that which metaphysics left unthought by placing himself at the 'end' of history and making the law of a self-contained system into the law of history, and thus superseding history (Hegel). Much more, Heidegger's thinking places itself into history in the full knowledge that it itself is finite and historical. The reflection which brings to completion the step backwards into that which has always at any given time been left unthought, does not itself arrive at a final end or absolute completion." Otto Pöggeler, "Being as Appropriation," p. 177.

8. According to Samuel J. Todes and Hubert L. Dreyfus, the traditional metaphysical characterization of "objective" knowledge is fivefold: "(1) impersonal, i.e., invariant from knower to knower; (2) disinterested, without any

interest the knower may have that something be so; (3) universal, i.e., applicable to all times and places; (4) eternal, i.e., not perishable like temporal things; (5) necessary, i.e., not conceivably otherwise, so that alternative conceptions would be logically unintelligible or would leave experience unintelligible." Samuel J. Todes and Hubert L. Dreyfus, "The Existentialist Critique of Objectivity," p. 347. Todes and Dreyfus are concerned particularly with the criticisms of Kierkegaard, Nietzsche, and Heidegger on the traditional "objectivist" view of impersonality, disinterestedness, and universality.

9. So Simone de Beauvoir remarks that "I remember having experienced a great feeling of calm on reading Hegel in the impersonal framework of the Bibliothèque Nationale in August 1940. But once I got into the street again, into my life, out of the system, beneath a real sky, the system was no longer of any use to me: what it had offered me, under a show of the infinite, was the consolations of death; and I again wanted to live in the midst of living men. I think that, inversely, existentialism does not offer to the reader the consolations of an abstract evasion: existentialism proposes no evasion. On the contrary, its ethics is experienced in the truth of life, and it then appears as the only proposition of salvation which one can address to men" (EA, pp. 158-59).

10. Echoing Merleau-Ponty in his interpretation of Hegel, Charles Taylor comments that "Complete freedom would be a void in which nothing would be worth doing, nothing would deserve to count for anything. The self which has arrived at freedom by setting aside all external obstacles and impingements is characterless, and hence without defined purpose, however much this is hidden by such seemingly positive terms as 'rationality' or 'creativity'." Charles Taylor, *Hegel*, p. 561. The same point was persistently argued by Merleau-Ponty against Sartre throughout his philosophical career. See particularly Merleau-Ponty, PP, pp. 434-56.

11. Cf. Marvin Zetterbaum who contends that "A radical separation of man and nature in which man forgets the origin of man out of nonhuman, be it God or nature, is forgetful also of an aspect of human reality, and it verges on the arbitrary to identify the 'genuinely human' with that which is said to be of man's own making as if that making is wholly free of any natural component." Marvin Zetterbaum, "Human Nature and History," p. 245. Cf. Eugene F. Miller, "Political Philosophy and Human Nature."

12. In addition to Merleau-Ponty's writings cited throughout this book on this subject, see particularly Paul Ricoeur, *Freedom and Nature: The Voluntary and the Involuntary*.

13. From a perspective of Husserl's phenomenology, Robert Sokolowski also comes to the conclusion that "Heidegger situates Husserlian themes within the wider context of the question of being, but he does not sufficiently consider the context of political philosophy. And even the question of being appears different if the political context is taken into account. Heidegger advances beyond Husserl by explicitly raising the question of being in ways Husserl did not, and by raising the issue of publicness in a more appropriate way than Husserl, with his stress on the discourse of science, was able to do. But Heidegger's conception of the public is not adequate for political life; in

terms of the kinds of human association distinguished by Aristotle in *Politics* I.2—family, village, city—Heidegger's thoughts are most appropriate for the village, not the city. A village is not based on any kind of constitution or 'social contract.'" Robert Sokolowski, *Husserlian Meditations: How Words Present Themselves*, pp. 212-13, n. 7.

14. Strauss relates an episode about Heidegger: "One of the unknown young men in Husserl's entourage was Heidegger. I attended his lecture course from time to time without understanding a word, but sensed that he dealt with something of the utmost importance to man as man. I understood something on one occasion: when he interpreted the beginning of the [Aristotle's] *Metaphysics*. I had never heard nor seen such a thing—such a thorough and intensive interpretation of a philosophic text. On my way home I visited Rosenzweig and said to him that compared to Heidegger, Max Weber, till then regarded by me as the incarnation of the spirit of science and scholarship, was an orphan child" (Klein and Strauss, GA, p. 3). Cf. Marcuse, HPI, p. 37 and Hannah Arendt, "Martin Heidegger at Eighty," p. 51.

15. Strauss, SCR, p. 9.

16. Heidegger, EP, p. 96. Strauss states that "Above all, according to Heidegger all thinkers prior to him have been oblivious to the true ground of all grounds, the fundamental abyss. This assertion implies the claim that in the decisive respect Heidegger understands his great predecessors better than they understood themselves" and that "The character of the historicist insight must correspond to the character of the period to which it belongs. The historicist insight is the final insight in the sense that it reveals all earlier thought as radically defective in the decisive respect and that there is no possibility of another legitimate change in the future which would render obsolete or as it were mediative the historicist insight" (PRS, pp. 2, 3). Thus Strauss seems to be objecting to not only Heidegger's claim for the historicity of thought but also, more importantly, what appears to Strauss to be Heidegger's revisionary claim against the shortcomings and irrelevances of all past philosophy, that is, Heidegger's claim to end all (Western) philosophy. For a definitive discussion on Heidegger's revisionary intention and the tradition of Western philosophy, see Werner Marx, *Heidegger and the Tradition*. For an exposition of Heidegger's intent to uproot the traditional metaphysical foundations and rebuild a new ontological foundation of value, that is, the notion of value grounded in Being, see Henri Mongis, *Heidegger et la Critique de la Notion de Valeur*.

17. Martin Heidegger, "Preface" to William J. Richardson, S. J., *Heidegger: Through Phenomenology to Thought*, p. xvi.

18. For the work that brings out most clearly the continuity of Heidegger's ontology, see J. L. Mehta, *Martin Heidegger: The Way and the Vision*.

19. See Joseph Cropsey who writes: "While Nietzsche spoke of the will to power, the overman, and the invitation to the eternal recurrence of the nauseous; and Heidegger proclaimed the authentic separation of *Dasein* from the dominance of the mass called 'Them' or 'They' (*der Man*) [*sic*] with an intention that was compatible with his own National Socialism, it cannot be

doubted that the project of authentic existentialism is to harden—perhaps into petrification—the liberalized spirit of modern man and not to license it for petulant or hedonistic self-assertions. What exists among us now, as part of the extended regime that forms us and shapes our existence, is the ominous human discipline of high existentialism, passed through the medium of the liberalistic modernity it is intended to reform, and transformed by it into willfulness, consciousness-raising, and moral latitudinarianism. It would be morally wrong to pass from the subject of the vulgarization of existentialism without referring to the Nazism to which it lent itself, as well as to the attempts to turn it to the uses of communism that have an especial prestige in Europe." Joseph Cropsey, *Political Philosophy and the Issues of Politics,* p. 11. See also Allan Bloom, "Leo Strauss: September 20, 1899–October 18, 1973," p. 389 which will be cited hereafter as "LS" and Emil L. Fackenheim, *Encounters between Judaism and Modern Philosophy,* pp. 217, 223. Strauss cites 1933 as the year in which Heidegger became involved in German National Socialism, and then more than any other man Heidegger learned a lesson which left him with no political philosophy. The year 1953 Strauss mentions is the year when *Einführung in die Metaphysik* was published with "no change in the content" from the reworked text of the lecture Heidegger gave in the summer of 1935 at Freiburg. The English translation is *An Introduction to Metaphysics.* If we read the general tone of this work of Heidegger correctly, we will sense that he bemoans the spiritual disintegration of European culture (e.g., the technologization of the earth, the standardization of man, and the preeminence of the mediocre). This is not, Heidegger assures us, an expression of "cultural pessimism" (*Kulturpessimismus*). For Heidegger, the respiritualization of European culture is tied to the destiny of Being itself which is fundamentally a philosophical task. As history is not synonymous with the past, the regeneration of European culture is a task yet to be achieved (a task of and for the *future*); and the spirit of Germany and its historical mission are not necessarily those of Nazi Germany but are those of Germany in a cultural and historical sense. The best accounts of Heidegger's political writings are found in Jean-Michel Palmier, *Les Écrits Politiques de Heidegger* and Otto Pöggeler, *Philosophie und Politik bei Heidegger.* Heidegger's own account of his involvement with German National Socialism is found in the invited interview on September 23, 1966 conducted by the Senior Editors of *Der Spiegel,* Rudolf Augstein and George Wolff, which was published shortly after Heidegger's death in 1976. See "Nur noch ein Gott kann uns retten," *Der Spiegel,* No. 23 (May 31, 1976): 193–219 which has been translated by David Schendler as "Only a God Can Save Us Now."

20. Klein and Strauss, GA, p. 1.

21. With regard to Nazi totalitarianism, one can very well argue that it originated from the anonymity of mass man (*das Man*) rather than from existential resoluteness which Heidegger characterized as the authenticity of *Dasein* in BT. Following Heidegger, Hannah Arendt argues against the atomization of individuals or the loss of selfhood that kills human dignity and constitutes the psychological basis of Nazi totalitarianism. See Hannah Arendt, *The Ori-*

gins of Totalitarianism. Cf. also Erich Fromm, *Escape from Freedom.* A prognostic analysis of the rise of totalitarian politics in Nazi Germany based on the anonymity of mass man manipulated by technocracy in the twentieth century is found in Karl Jaspers, *Man in the Modern Age.*

22. Stanley Rosen too attempts to show that Heidegger's political nihilism has its roots in his ontology and epistemology. See Stanley Rosen, *Nihilism: A Philosophical Essay,* pp. 94–139.

23. Allan Bloom states that "His [Strauss's] attachment to the American regime was deep. He studied its history and was charmed by its particular genius. Practically, he was grateful for the refuge it gave him, and he was aware that the liberal democrats are the surest friends of his people" (LS, p. 374). Since I am fully aware of the danger of committing what Peter Gay calls "comparative trivialization," I certainly do not wish to minimize the difference in magnitude of Hitler's calculated policy of mass extermination and Nixon's politics of deception. For Gay's critique of comparative trivialization, see Peter Gay, *Freud, Jews and Other Germans: Masters and Victims in Modernist Culture,* pp. xi–xiv. The point I make here is simply that both Heidegger and Strauss misread practical politics and that their misreadings are illustrative once again of an ambiguity between theory and practice.

24. Arendt speculates that Heidegger's "reversal" turned primarily against Nietzsche's affirmation of "the will-to-power." "In Heidegger's understanding," she writes, "the will to rule and to dominate is a kind of original sin, of which he found himself guilty when he tried to come to terms with his brief past in the Nazi movement" (LM, 2: 174). As the will-to-will whose total destructiveness is inherent in modern technology, Arendt suggests that Heidegger's ultimate solution lies in the "will-not-to-will." According to her, the alternative to the "subjectivized" will-to-will (domination) for Heidegger is the "desubjectivized" thinking which is obedient to the call of Being—that is, the mode of *thinking* which is not a willing. Whether or not the alternative to "politology" or political technocracy is anarchism, or if indeed the conception of political philosophy itself is nugatory, in Heidegger's ontology is an interesting question to pursue further in a future study. For the beginning of an exploration into the relevance of Heidegger's thought to politics, see Bernard P. Dauenhauer, "Renovating the Problem of Politics"; Karsten Harries, "Heidegger as a Political Thinker"; Reiner Schürmann, "Political Thinking in Heidegger" and "The Ontological Difference and Political Philosophy." The views of all these three authors are interesting interpolations of Heidegger's political thinking based on his ontology.

25. Klein and Strauss, GA, p. 2.

26. *Ibid.,* and Strauss, PRS, pp. 2–3.

27. The English translation is found in Husserl, PCP, pp. 71–147.

28. *Ibid.,* p. 122.

29. Strauss mistakenly identifies this Vienna Lecture with a Prague lecture. Six months later (in November) Husserl delivered lectures in Prague which were based on the Vienna Lecture. They were in turn the basis of his *Krisis*

manuscript, which was published posthumously by Martinus Nijhoff in 1953 as *Die Krisis der europäischen Wisseschaften und die transzendentale Phänomenologie: Eine Einleitung in die phänomenologische Philosophie,* Husserliana, vol. 6 under the editorship of Walter Biemel. Strauss uses the second edition of the *Krisis* (1962). The 1970 English translation has been cited as CES throughout this book. For a discussion of Husserl's *Krisis* text, see Philip J. Bossert, "A Common Misunderstanding Concerning Husserl's *Crisis* Text."

30. Husserl, PCP, p. 141.

31. Husserl, CES, p. 289.

32. *Ibid.,* p. 296. One of the most prominent students of Husserl, Roman Ingarden, writes that " . . . a striking feature of the *Crisis* and of the connected *Essays* is that a perspective is given, within a phenomenological context, of problems in the philosophy of history, and of the historicity of pure transcendental consciousness itself. There is a certain similarity here with a historico-philosophical world-view which Husserl had firmly rejected in discussions with Dilthey (1911). This is obviously connected with the strengthening of the influence of Dilthey in Germany, even in Husserl's immediate surroundings, toward the end of the twenties and the beginning of the thirties." Ingarden reports that when Oskar Becker once said to Heidegger that "Actually, we are all Dilthey-people," Heidegger did not object. Roman Ingarden, "What Is New in Husserl's 'Crisis'," pp. 24, 46.

33. Husserl, CES, p. 288.

34. Leo Strauss, *The Political Philosophy of Hobbes: Its Basis and Its Genesis,* p. 2. Strauss maintains that his conclusion was reached by the fact that the most mature presentation of Hobbes's philosophy, that is, the *Leviathan,* "is by no means an adequate source for an understanding of Hobbes's moral and political ideas" (*ibid.,* p. 170).

35. See Husserl, CES, pp. 230 ff.

36. In CES, Husserl traces the crisis of modern philosophy in Galilean physics. Strauss echoes the philosophical mood of Husserl when in 1964 he attributes "the crisis of our time" to "the modern project" which emerged in the philosophical thought of the sixteenth and seventeenth centuries (i.e., the thought of Bacon, Descartes, and Hobbes). As Husserl sets the standard of the *telos* of Western philosophy in ancient Greece, so does Strauss judge the crisis of the modern project in terms of Greek thought. See Leo Strauss, "Political Philosophy and the Crisis of Our Time."

37. Strauss, PRS, p. 3.

38. Strauss, NRH, pp. 77, 79–80.

39. Klein, GMT, p. 120.

40. Strauss, NRH, pp. 79–80.

41. David Carr, *Phenomenology and the Problem of History,* particularly pp. 190–211. Hereafter cited as "PPH."

42. *Ibid.,* p. 242.

43. *Ibid.,* p. 277.

44. Husserl, CES, p. 347.

45. Carr, PPH, p. 263.

46. This comment is found in a letter from Strauss to Gadamer dated February 26, 1961. A direct exchange of views between Strauss and Gadamer is found in the following three letters: the initial letter from Strauss to Gadamer which contains the former's commentary on the latter's *Wahrheit und Methode* dated February 26, 1961; Gadamer's reply to Strauss dated April 5, 1961; and then Strauss's response to Gadamer dated May 14, 1961. I am grateful to Professor George Elliott Tucker for sending me copies of these letters. They will be published in Leo Strauss and Hans–Georg Gadamer, "Correspondence Concerning *Wahrheit und Methode.*"

47. Dilthey, SW, pp. 259–60. What follows is adapted from my work, HA, pp. 65–67.

48. It is important to note here that Gadamer is critical of Strauss who, in defending the tradition of classical philosophy as a unity, fails to recognize the existence of the extreme contrast between Plato and Aristotle concerning the question of the good. See Gadamer, TM, pp. 489–90. Aristotle's conception of practical philosophy—his notion of *phronesis* (practical wisdom) in particular— is extremely relevant to the development of Gadamer's philosophical hermeneutics and human, moral sciences. For Gadamer but not for Strauss, the idea of natural law in Aristotle's moral and political thought plays a "critical" rather than "dogmatic" function. See *ibid.*, pp. 278–89. However important they may be, the theoretical ramifications of Gadamer's views on the substance of political thought cannot be discussed here. For a critique of the myth of the tradition and its historical etiology as "academic folklore" in reference to Strauss's thought, see John G. Gunnell, "The Myth of the Tradition." The most interesting collection of essays on the nature of exegesis by Strauss is found in his work: Leo Strauss, *Persecution and the Art of Writing* which, for example, deals with the relation between philosophy and its social and political environments. It deals with the "sociology of philosophy"—to use his own term—by focusing on the problem of exegesis, that is, how to read the truth of things presented exclusively in between the lines for the reason of persecution.

49. Gadamer, TM, p. 264.

50. *Ibid.*, p. 267.

51. *Ibid.*, p. 484.

CHAPTER 9. THE TRIUMPH OF SUBJECTIVITY IN THE CONDUCT OF POLITICAL INQUIRY

1. Merleau-Ponty, VI, p. 177.

2. Kenneth E. Boulding, *The Image,* pp. 3–18.

3. Alan F. Blum, "Theorizing," p. 313. Cf. Ihde, SS, p. 19: "Phenomenology is both an experience of the world and a questioning of that experience. But the philosopher's experience of the world is also a transformation of the meaning of the world. In that lies the excitement of philosophical investigation." Similarly, Herbert Fingarette also declares that " . . . concepts do not only 're-

flect' and report our experience; as meanings, not merely as verbalistic structures, they are *constitutive* of experience. Human experience is further distinguished from all other biological behavior in that meaning-structure is not only constitutive of the experience-content, it is efficacious with regard to the course of that content's transformations." Herbert Fingarette, *The Self in Transformation: Psychoanalysis, Philosophy and the Life of the Spirit*, p. 22.

4. Arendt, LM, 1: 178.

5. Palmer, HE, p. 116.

6. Merleau-Ponty, PP, pp. 170-71.

7. Arendt, HC, p. 8.

8. *Ibid.*, pp. 175-76.

9. *Ibid.*, p. 9.

10. Husserl, CES, p. 72.

11. Gadamer, PH, p. 93.

12. Scheler, MP, p. 4. A systematic inquiry into the nature of the human sciences based on the notion of philosophical anthropology and the radical reflection of phenomenology is found in Calvin O. Schrag, *Radical Reflection and the Origin of the Human Sciences*. Despite our shared concern and themes, it was too late for me to incorporate his important insights into my present inquiry.

13. Gadamer, TTP, p. 556.

14. Ernest Nagel, *Logic without Metaphysics*, p. 382. This passage is found in Nagel's critical review of Morgenthau, SM.

15. Friedrich Waismann, "How I See Philosophy," p. 380.

16. This phrase is Hannah F. Pitkin's in *Wittgenstein and Justice*, p. 337.

17. Wittgenstein, TLP, p. 151.

18. Allan Janik and Stephen Toulmin, *Wittgenstein's Vienna*, p. 220. Hereafter cited as "WV."

19. See Dreyfus, WC, p. 124.

20. In the same spirit, Karl-Otto Apel critically compares Wittgenstein's "analytical philosophy of language" with the continental tradition of "hermeneutics." "Now we can . . . see," Apel writes, "in which respect the methodical presupposition of Analytical Philosophy, that all understanding must be explicated as 'clarification of language', is correct: not as clarification of either the logical form of a single ideal language, or of monadic and static language games, but as hermeneutical development (widening and deepening) of that dialogue, which we human beings—to quote Hölderlin—'are'." Karl-Otto Apel, *Analytic Philosophy of Language and the Geisteswissenschaften*, p. 57.

21. Janik and Toulmin, WV, p. 220.

22. Søren Kierkegaard, *The Concept of Irony*, p. 47.

23. Søren Kierkegaard, *Concluding Unscientific Postscript*, p. 311.

24. *Ibid.*, p. 314. For an interesting comparison between Kierkegaard and Wittgenstein, see Stanley Cavell, "Existentialism and Analytical Philosophy." pp. 957 ff.

25. Husserl, CES, p. 299.

26. Carr, PPH, p. 187.

27. For an attempt to clarify normative issues in political life on this line, see Fred R. Dallmayr, "Beyond Dogma and Despair: Toward a Ciritical Theory of Politics."

28. Vico, OSM, p. 33.

29. Ricoeur, CI, p. 5.

30. Merleau-Ponty, AD, p. 11.

Bibliography: Cited Works

Adorno, Theodor W. *The Jargon of Authenticity,* trans. Knut Tarnowski and Frederic Will. Evanston, Ill.: Northwestern University Press, 1973.

Almond, Gabriel A. *Political Development: Essays in Heuristic Theory.* Boston: Little, Brown, 1970.

—— and G. Bingham Powell, Jr. *Comparative Politics: A Developmental Approach.* Boston: Little, Brown, 1966.

Apel, Karl-Otto. *Analytic Philosophy of Language and the Geisteswissenschaften,* trans. Harald Holstelilie. Dordrecht, The Netherlands: D. Reidel, 1967.

——. *Die Idee der Sprache in der Tradition des Humanismus von Dante bis Vico,* 2nd ed. Bonn, Germany: Bouvier Verlag, 1975.

Apter, David E. *Introduction to Political Analysis.* Cambridge, Mass.: Winthrop, 1977.

Arendt, Hannah. *Crises of the Republic.* New York: Harcourt Brace Jovanovich, 1972.

——. *The Human Condition.* Chicago: University of Chicago Press, 1958. Cited as "HC."

——. *The Life of the Mind.* 2 vols. New York: Harcourt Brace Jovanovich, 1978. Cited as "LM."

——. "Martin Heidegger at Eighty," trans. Albert Hofstadter, *The New York Review of Books,* 17 (October 21, 1971): 50–54.

——. *On Violence.* New York: Harcourt, Brace and World, 1970.

——. *The Origins of Totalitarianism,* new ed. New York: Harcourt, Brace and World, 1966:

Austin, J. L. *How to Do Things with Words,* ed. J. O. Urmson. New York: Oxford University Press, 1962.

——. "Performative-Constative," trans. G. J. Warnock, in *Philosophy and Ordinary Language,* ed. Charles E. Caton. Urbana, Ill.: University of Illinois Press, 1963, pp. 22–54.

——. *Philosophical Papers,* ed. J. O. Urmson and G. J. Warnock. Oxford, England: Clarendon Press, 1961. Cited as "PPA."

Axelos, Kostas. *Alienation, Praxis, and Technē in the Thought of Karl Marx,* trans. Ronald Bruzina. Austin, Texas: University of Texas Press, 1976.

Barry, Brian. *Political Argument.* New York: Humanities Press, 1965.

Barth, Hans. *Truth and Ideology,* trans. Frederic Lilge. Berkeley, Calif.: University of California Press, 1976.

Beauvoir, Simone de. *The Coming of Age,* trans. Patrick O'Brian. New York: G. P. Putnam's Sons, 1972.

———. *The Ethics of Ambiguity*, trans. Bernard Frechtman. New York: Citadel Press, 1962. Cited as "EA."

———. *The Second Sex*, trans. and ed. H. M. Parshley. New York: Alfred A. Knopf, 1952.

Bell, Daniel. *The Coming of Post-Industrial Society: A Venture in Social Forecasting.* New York: Basic Books, 1973.

Beloff, John. "The Mind-Body Problem as It Now Stands," *Virginia Quarterly Review*, 49 (Spring 1973): 251-64.

Benthall, Jonathan and Ted Polhemus (eds.). *The Body as a Medium of Expression.* New York: E. P. Dutton, 1975.

Berger, Peter, Brigitte Berger, and Hansfried Kellner. *The Homeless Mind: Modernization and Consciousness.* New York: Random House, 1973.

Berger, Peter L. and Thomas Luckmann. *The Social Construction of Reality: A Treatise in the Sociology of Knowledge.* Garden City, N.Y.: Doubleday, 1967.

Bergson, Henri. *Matter and Memory*, trans. Nancy M. Paul and W. Scott Palmer. London: George Allen and Unwin, 1911.

Berlin, Isaiah. *Vico and Herder: Two Studies in the History of Ideas.* New York: Random House, 1976.

Bernstein, Richard J. *The Restructuring of Social and Political Theory.* New York: Harcourt Brace Jovanovich, 1976.

Biemel, Walter. *Martin Heidegger: An Illustrated Study*, trans. J. L. Mehta. New York: Harcourt Brace Jovanovich, 1976.

Bloom, Allan. "Leo Strauss: September 20, 1899 – October 18, 1973,"' *Political Theory*, 2 (November 1974): 372-92. Cited as "LS."

Bluhm, William T. *Theories of the Political System: Classics of Political Thought and Modern Political Analysis*, 3rd ed. Englewood Cliffs, N.J.: Prentice-Hall, 1978. Cited as "TPS."

Blum, Alan F. "Theorizing," in *Understanding Everyday Life*, ed. Jack D. Douglas. Chicago: Aldine, 1970, pp. 301-19.

Bonifazi, Conrad. *A Theology of Things.* Philadelphia: J. B. Lippincott, 1967.

Bossert, Philip J. "A Common Misunderstanding Concerning Husserl's *Crisis* Text," *Philosophy and Phenomenological Research*, 35 (September 1974): 20-33.

Boulding, Kenneth E. *The Image.* Ann Arbor, Mich.: University of Michigan Press, 1956.

Brand, Gerd. *Die Lebenswelt: Eine Philosophie des konkreten A Priori.* Berlin: Walter de Gruyter, 1971.

Brecht, Arnold. *Political Theory: The Foundations of Twentieth-Century Political Thought.* Princeton, N.J.: Princeton University Press, 1959.

Brown, Norman O. *Closing Time.* New York: Random House, 1973.

———. *Life against Death.* Middletown, Conn.: Wesleyan University Press, 1959.

———. *Love's Body.* New York: Random House, 1968.

Buber, Martin. *I and Thou*, trans. Walter Kaufmann. New York: Charles Scribner's Sons, 1970.

————. *The Knowledge of Man,* ed. Maurice Friedman. New York: Harper and Row, 1965.

Buck-Morss, Susan. *The Origin of Negative Dialectics: Theodor W. Adorno, Walter Benjamin, and the Frankfurt Institute.* New York: Free Press, 1977.

Bugbee, Henry, Jr. *The Inward Morning.* State College, Pa.: Bald Eagle Press, 1958.

Buytendijk, F. J. J. *Pain: Its Modes and Functions,* trans. Eda O'Shiel. Chicago: University of Chicago Press, 1962.

Carr, David. *Phenomenology and the Problem of History.* Evanston, Ill.: Northwestern University Press, 1974. Cited as "PPH."

Carr, Edward Hallett. *What Is History?* New York: Alfred A. Knopf, 1962.

Cassirer, Ernst. *The Myth of the State.* New Haven, Conn.: Yale University Press, 1946.

Castaneda, Carlos. *A Separate Reality: Further Conversations with Don Juan.* New York: Simon and Schuster, 1971.

Cavell, Stanley. "Existentialism and Analytical Philosophy," *Daedalus,* 93 (Summer 1964): 946–74.

————. *Must We Mean What We Say?* New York: Charles Scribner's Sons, 1969.

Charlesworth, James C. (ed.). *A Design for Political Science: Scope, Objectives and Methods.* Philadelphia: American Academy of Political and Social Science, 1966.

Chomsky, Noam. *Cartesian Linguistics.* New York: Harper and Row, 1966.

Cohen, Morris R. *The Faith of a Liberal.* New York: Holt, 1946.

Coleman, William. "Providence, Capitalism, and Ecologic Crisis: English Apologetics in an Era of Economic Revolution," *Journal of the History of Ideas,* 37 (January–March 1976): 27–44.

Collingwood, R. G. *The Idea of History.* Oxford, England: Clarendon Press, 1946.

————. *The Idea of Nature.* Oxford, England: Clarendon Press, 1945.

Collins, James. *Descartes' Philosophy of Nature.* Oxford, England: Basil Blackwell, 1971.

Commoner, Barry. *The Closing Circle: Nature, Man and Technology.* New York: Alfred A. Knopf, 1971.

Cropsey, Joseph. *Political Philosophy and the Issues of Politics.* Chicago: University of Chicago Press, 1977.

Cuddihy, John Murray. *The Ordeal of Civility: Freud, Marx, Lévi-Strauss, and the Jewish Struggle with Modernity.* New York: Basic Books, 1974.

Cumming, Robert Denoon. *Human Nature and History,* 2 vols. Chicago: University of Chicago Press, 1969.

Dahl, Robert A. "The Behavioral Approach in Political Science: Epitaph for a Monument to a Successful Protest," *American Political Science Review,* 55 (December 1961): 763–72.

Dahrendorf, Ralf. *Essays in the Theory of Society.* Stanford, Calif.: Stanford University Press, 1969. Cited as "ETS."

Dallmayr, Fred. R. "Beyond Dogma and Despair: Toward a Critical Theory of Politics," *American Political Science Review,* 70 (March 1976): 64–79.

_____. "Phenomenology and Marxism: A Salute to Enzo Paci." in *Phenomenological Sociology,* ed. George Psathas. New York: John Wiley, 1973, pp. 305–56.

_____ (ed.). *Materialien zu Habermas' "Erkenntnis und Interesse,"* Frankfurt am Main, Germany: Suhrkamp Verlag, 1974.

_____ and Thomas A. McCarthy (eds.). *Understanding and Social Inquiry.* Notre Dame, Ind.: University of Notre Dame Press, 1977.

Dauenhauer, Bernard P. "Renovating the Problem of Politics," *The Review of Metaphysics,* 29 (June 1976): 626–41.

Derrida, Jacques. *Speech and Phenomena and Other Essays on Husserl's Theory of Signs,* trans. David B. Allison. Evanston, Ill.: Northwestern University Press, 1973. Cited as "SP."

Des Pres, Terrence. *The Survivor: An Anatomy of Life in the Death Camps.* New York: Oxford University Press, 1976.

Deutsch, Karl W. *The Nerves of Government.* New York: Free Press, 1966. Cited as "NG."

Dewey, John. *Human Nature and Conduct.* New York: Modern Library, 1957.

Diamond, Stanley. *In Search of the Primitive: A Critique of Civilization.* New Brunswick, N.J.: Transaction Books, 1974.

_____. "The Search of the Primitive," in *Sources,* ed. Theodore Roszak. New York: Harper and Row, 1972, pp. 212–36. Cited as "SPR."

Dilthey, Wilhelm. *Selected Writings,* ed. and trans. H. P. Rickman. Cambridge, England: University Press, 1976. Cited as "SW."

Douglas, Mary. *Natural Symbols: Explorations in Cosmology.* New York: Pantheon Books, 1970.

Downs, Anthony. *An Economic Theory of Democracy.* New York: Harper and Row, 1957. Cited as "ETD."

Dreyfus, Hubert L. *What Computers Can't Do: A Critique of Artificial Reason.* New York: Harper and Row, 1972. Cited as "WC."

Dufrenne, Mikel. *Jalons.* La Haye: Martinus Nijhoff, 1966.

_____. *The Notion of the A Priori,* trans. Edward S. Casey. Evanston, Ill.: Northwestern University Press, 1966.

Earle, William. "Phenomenology and Existentialism," *The Journal of Philosophy,* 57 (January 21, 1960): 74–84.

Easton, David. "The Current Meaning of 'Behavioralism'," in *Contemporary Political Analysis,* ed. James C. Charlesworth. New York: Free Press, 1967, pp. 11–31.

_____. *A Framework of Political Analysis.* Englewood Cliffs, N.J.: Prentice-Hall, 1965. Cited as "FPA."

_____. "The New Revolution in Political Science," *American Political Science Review,* 63 (December 1969): 1051–61.

_____. *The Political System: An Inquiry into the State of Political Science,* 2nd ed. New York: Alfred A. Knopf, 1971.

Edelman, Murray. *Political Language: Words That Succeed and Policies That Fail.* New York: Academic Press, 1977.

———. *Politics as Symbolic Action.* Chicago: Markham, 1971.

———. *The Symbolic Uses of Politics.* Urbana, Ill.: University of Illinois Press, 1964.

Edie, James M. *Speaking and Meaning: The Phenomenology of Language.* Bloomington, Ind.: Indiana University Press, 1976.

Eiseley, Loren. *The Invisible Pyramid.* New York: Charles Scribner's Sons, 1970.

Eliade, Mircea. *The Myth of the Eternal Return,* trans. Willard R. Trask. New York: Pantheon Books, 1954.

Ellul, Jacques. *The Technological Society,* trans. John Wilkinson. New York: Alfred A. Knopf, 1964.

Erickson, Stephen A. *Language and Being: An Analytic Phenomenology.* New Haven, Conn.: Yale University Press, 1970.

Eulau, Heinz. *The Behavioral Persuasion in Politics.* New York: Random House, 1963. Cited as "BPP."

———. *Micro-Macro Political Analysis.* Chicago: Aldine, 1969. Cited as "MMP."

———. "Political Science," in *A Reader's Guide to the Social Sciences,* ed. Bert F. Hoselitz, rev. ed. New York: Free Press, 1967, pp. 129–237.

Fackenheim, Emil L. *Encounters between Judaism and Modern Philosophy.* New York: Basic Books, 1973.

———. *Metaphysics and Historicity.* Milwaukee: Marquette University Press, 1961.

Ferkiss, Victor C. *The Future of Technological Civilization.* New York: George Braziller, 1974. Cited as "FTC."

———. *Technological Man: The Myth and the Reality.* New York: George Braziller, 1969.

Feuerbach, Ludwig. *Principles of the Philosophy of the Future,* trans. Manfred H. Vogel. Indianapolis: Bobbs-Merrill, 1966.

Feyerabend, Paul K. "Against Method: Outline of an Anarchistic Theory of Knowledge," in *Minnesota Studies in the Philosophy of Science,* vol. 4, ed. Michael Radner and Stephen Winokur. Minneapolis: University of Minnesota Press, 1970, pp. 17–130.

Fichte, Johann Gottlieb. *The Vocation of Man,* trans. William Smith. La Salle, Ill.: Open Court, 1946.

Fingarette, Herbert. *The Self in Transformation: Psychoanalysis, Philosophy and the Life of the Spirit.* New York: Basic Books, 1963.

Fisch, Max H. and Thomas G. Bergin. "Introduction" to *The Autobiography of Giambattista Vico,* trans. Max H. Fisch and Thomas G. Bergin. Ithaca, N.Y.: Cornell University Press, 1944, pp. 1–107.

Frankfurt Institute for Social Research. *Aspects of Sociology,* trans. John Viertel. Boston: Beacon Press, 1972.

Frankl, Viktor E. *Man's Search for Meaning: An Introduction to Logotherapy,* trans. Ilse Lasch. New York: Washington Square Press, 1963.

Freeman, Donald M. (ed.). *Foundation of Political Science: Research, Methods, and Scope,* New York: Free Press, 1977.

Freud, Sigmund. *Civilization and Its Discontents,* trans. and ed. James Strachey. New York: W. W. Norton, 1962.

Friedman, Milton. *Essays in Positive Economics.* Chicago: University of Chicago Press, 1953. Cited as "EPE."

Friedrich, Carl J. "Phenomenology and Political Science," in *Phenomenology and the Social Sciences,* ed. Maurice Natanson, 2 vols. Evanston, Ill.: Northwestern University Press, 1973, 2:175–95.

Fromm, Erich. *The Anatomy of Human Destructiveness.* New York: Holt, Rinehart and Winston, 1973.

———. *Escape from Freedom.* New York: Rinehart, 1941.

Gadamer, Hans-Georg. *Philosophical Hermeneutics,* trans. and ed. David E. Linge. Berkeley, Calif.: University of California Press, 1976. Cited as "PH."

———. "The Problem of Historical Consciousness," trans. Jeff L. Close, *Graduate Faculty Philosophy Journal,* 5 (Fall 1975): 2–52. Cited as "PHC."

———. "Theory, Technology, Practice: The Task of the Science of Man," trans. Howard Brotz, *Social Research,* 44 (Autumn 1977): 529–61. Cited as "TTP."

———. *Truth and Method.* New York: Seabury Press, 1975. Cited as "TM."

Gauthier, David. "The Social Contract as Ideology," *Philosophy and Public Affairs,* 6 (Winter 1977): 130–64.

Gay, Peter. *Freud, Jews and Other Germans: Masters and Victims in Modernist Culture.* New York: Oxford University Press, 1978.

Geertz, Clifford. *The Interpretation of Cultures: Selected Essays.* New York: Basic Books, 1973.

Gendlin, Eugene T. *Experiencing and the Creation of Meaning.* Glencoe, Ill.: Free Press, 1962.

Germino, Dante. *Beyond Ideology: The Revival of Political Theory.* New York: Harper and Row, 1967.

Gillan, Garth. "In the Folds of the Flesh: Philosophy and Language," in *The Horizons of the Flesh: Critical Perspectives in the Thought of Merleau-Ponty,* ed. Garth Gillan. Carbondale, Ill.: Southern Illinois University Press, 1973, pp. 1–60.

Goldmann, Lucien. *Lukács and Heidegger: Towards a New Philosophy,* trans. William Q. Boelhower. London: Routledge and Kegan Paul, 1977.

Gorman, Robert A. *The Dual Vision: Alfred Schutz and the Myth of Phenomenological Social Science.* London: Routledge and Kegan Paul, 1977.

Gouldner, Alvin W. *The Coming Crisis of Western Sociology.* New York: Basic Books, 1970.

———. *For Sociology: Renewal and Critique in Sociology Today.* New York: Basic Books, 1973.

Goulet, Denis. *The Cruel Choice: A New Concept in the Theory of Development.* New York: Atheneum, 1973.

Gray, J. Glenn. "Heidegger on Remembering and Remembering Heidegger," *Man and World,* 10 (1977): 62–78. Cited as "HR."

———. "Heidegger's Course: From Human Existence to Nature," *The Journal of Philosophy,* 56 (April 11, 1957): 197–207.

———. *On Understanding Violence Philosophically and Other Essays.* New York: Harper and Row, 1970.

Greenstein, Fred I. and Nelson W. Polsby (eds.). *Handbook of Political Science,* 8 vols. Reading, Mass.: Addison-Wesley, 1975.

Grene, Marjorie. "Merleau-Ponty and the Renewal of Ontology," *The Review of Metaphysics,* 29 (June 1976): 605–25.

Gunnell, John G. "The Myth of the Tradition," *American Political Science Review,* 72 (March 1978): 122–34.

———. *Philosophy, Science, and Political Inquiry.* Morristown, N.J.: General Learning Press, 1975.

Gurwitsch, Aron. "Comment on the Paper by H. Marcuse," in *Boston Studies in the Philosophy of Science,* vol. 2, ed. Robert S. Cohen and Marx W. Wartofsky. New York: Humanities Press, 1965, pp. 291–306. Cited as "CPM."

———. *Phenomenology and the Theory of Science,* ed. Lester Embree. Evanston, Ill.: Northwestern University Press, 1974. Cited as "PTS."

Habermas, Jürgen. *Knowledge and Human Interests,* trans. Jeremy J. Shapiro. Boston: Beacon Press, 1971.

———. *Legitimation Crisis,* trans. Thomas McCarthy. Boston: Beacon Press, 1975.

———. "A Review of Gadamer's *Truth and Method,*" in *Understanding and Social Inquiry,* ed. Fred R. Dallmayr and Thomas A. McCarthy. Notre Dame, Ind.: University of Notre Dame Press, 1977, pp. 335–63.

———. *Theory and Practice,* trans. John Viertel. Boston: Beacon Press, 1973. Cited as "TP."

———. *Toward a Rational Society,* trans. Jeremy J. Shapiro. Boston: Beacon Press, 1970.

Hampshire, Stuart. *Thought and Action.* New York: Viking Press, 1959. Cited as "TA."

Hanson, Norwood R. *Patterns of Discovery.* Cambridge, England: University Press, 1969.

Harries, Karsten. "Heidegger as a Political Thinker," *The Review of Metaphysics,* 29 (June 1976): 642–69.

Hegel, G. W. F. *Hegel's Philosophy of Right,* trans. T. M. Knox. Oxford, England: Clarendon Press, 1942.

———. *The Philosophy of History,* trans. J. Sibree. New York: Dover, 1956.

Heidegger, Martin. *Basic Writings,* ed. David Farrell Krell. New York: Harper and Row, 1976. Cited as "BW."

———. *Being and Time,* trans. John Macquarrie and Edward Robinson. New York: Harper, 1962. Cited as "BT."

———. *Discourse on Thinking,* trans. John M. Anderson and E. Hans Freund. New York: Harper and Row, 1966.

———. *The End of Philosophy,* trans. Joan Stambaugh. New York: Harper and Row, 1973. Cited as "EP."

———. *Identity and Difference,* trans. Joan Stambaugh. New York: Harper and Row, 1969.

———. *An Introduction to Metaphysics,* trans. Ralph Manheim. New Haven, Conn.: Yale University Press, 1959.

———. *On the Way to Language,* trans. Peter D. Hertz. New York: Harper and Row, 1971.

———. *On Time and Being,* trans. Joan Stambaugh. New York: Harper and Row, 1972.

———. "Only a God Can Save Us Now," trans. David Schendler, *Graduate Faculty Philosophy Journal,* 6 (Winter 1977): 5–27.

———. *The Piety of Thinking,* trans. James G. Hart and John C. Maraldo. Bloomington, Ind.: Indiana University Press, 1976.

———. *Poetry, Language, Thought,* trans. Albert Hofstadter, New York: Harper and Row, 1971.

———. "Preface" to William J. Richardson, S. J., *Heidegger: Through Phenomenology to Thought.* The Hague: Martinus Nijhoff, 1963, pp. viii–xxiii.

———. *The Question Concerning Technology and Other Essays,* trans. William Lovitt. New York: Harper and Row, 1977. Cited as "QT."

———. *What Is a Thing?,* trans. W. B. Barton, Jr. and Vera Deutsch. Chicago: Henry Regnery, 1967. Cited as "WIT."

———. *What Is Called Thinking?,* trans. Fred D. Wieck and J. Glenn Gray. New York: Harper and Row, 1968. Cited as "WCT."

Heisenberg, Werner. *The Physicist's Conception of Nature,* trans. Arnold J. Pomerans. New York: Harcourt, Brace, 1958. Cited as "PCN."

Hesse, Mary. *The Structure of Scientific Inference.* Berkeley, Calif.: University of California Press, 1974. Cited as "SSI."

Hirsch, E. D., Jr. *The Aims of Interpretation.* Chicago: University of Chicago Press, 1976.

———. *Validity in Interpretation.* New Haven, Conn.: Yale University Press, 1967.

Hobbes, Thomas. *Leviathan,* ed. Michael Oakeshott. Oxford, England: Basil Blackwell, 1960. Cited as "LE."

Hollis, Martin. *Models of Man: Philosophical Thoughts on Social Action.* Cambridge, England: University Press, 1977.

Holt, Robert T. and John M. Richardson, Jr. "Competing Paradigms in Comparative Politics," in *The Methodology of Comparative Research,* ed. Robert T. Holt and John E. Turner. New York: Free Press, 1970, pp. 21–71.

Horkheimer, Max. *Eclipse of Reason.* New York: Oxford University Press, 1947.

Howard, Dick. *The Marxian Legacy.* New York: Urizen Books, 1977.

Hoy, David Couzens. *The Critical Circle: Literature and History in Contemporary Hermeneutics.* Berkeley, Calif.: University of California Press, 1978. Cited as "CC."

Huizinga, Johan. *Homo Ludens: A Study of the Play-Element in Culture.* London: Routledge and Kegan Paul, 1950.

Humboldt, Wilhelm von. *Humanist without Portfolio: An Anthology of the Writings of Wilhelm von Humboldt,* trans. Marianne Cowan. Detroit: Wayne State University Press, 1963.

Hume, David. *A Treatise of Human Nature,* ed. L. A. Selby-Bigge. Oxford, England: Clarendon Press, 1960.

Husserl, Edmund. *Cartesian Meditations: An Introduction to Phenomenology,* trans. Dorion Cairns. The Hague: Martinus Nijhoff, 1960.

————. *The Crisis of European Sciences and Transcendental Phenomenology: An Introduction to Phenomenological Philosophy,* trans. David Carr. Evanston, Ill.: Northwestern University Press, 1970. Cited as "CES."

————. *Experience and Judgment,* ed. Ludwig Landgrebe and trans. James S. Churchill and Karl Ameriks. Evanston, Ill.: Northwestern University Press, 1973. Cited as "EJ."

————. "Phenomenology and Anthropology," trans. Richard G. Schmitt, in *Realism and the Background of Phenomenology,* ed. Roderick M. Chisholm. Glencoe, Ill.: Free Press, 1960, pp. 129–42.

————. *Phenomenology and the Crisis of Philosophy,* trans. Quentin Lauer. New York: Harper and Row, 1965. Cited as "PCP."

Hyppolite, Jean. *Sens et Existence dans la Philosophie de Maurice Merleau-Ponty.* Oxford, England: Clarendon Press, 1963.

Ihde, Don. *Experimental Phenomenology: An Introduction.* New York: G. P. Putnam's Sons, 1977.

————. *Listening and Voice: A Phenomenology of Sound.* Athens, Ohio: Ohio University Press, 1976.

————. *Sense and Significance.* Pittsburgh: Duquesne University Press, 1973. Cited as "SS."

Ingarden, Roman. "What Is New in Husserl's 'Crisis'," in *Analecta Husserliana,* vol. 2: *The Later Husserl and the Idea of Phenomenology,* ed. Anna-Teresa Tymieniecka. Dordrecht, The Netherlands: D. Reidel, 1972, pp. 23–47.

Israel, Joachim. *Alienation from Marx to Modern Sociology: A Macrosociological Analysis.* Boston: Allyn and Bacon, 1971.

James, William. *The Principles of Psychology,* 2 vols. New York: Dover, 1950.

Janik, Allan and Stephen Toulmin. *Wittgenstein's Vienna.* New York: Simon and Schuster, 1973. Cited as "WV."

Jaspers, Karl. *The Great Philosophers,* 2 vols., ed. Hannah Arendt and trans. Ralph Manheim. New York: Harcourt, Brace and World, 1962–66.

————. *Man in the Modern Age,* trans. Eden and Cedar Paul. Garden City, N.Y.: Doubleday, 1957.

Jay, Martin. *The Dialectical Imagination: A History of the Frankfurt School and the Institute of Social Research, 1923–1950.* Boston: Little, Brown, 1973.

Jonas, Hans. "Acting, Knowing, Thinking: Gleanings from Hannah Arendt's Philosophical Work," *Social Research,* 44 (Spring 1977): 25–43.

————. *The Phenomenon of Life.* New York: Dell, 1968.

Jouvenel, Bertrand de. *The Art of Conjecture,* trans. Nikita Lary. New York: Basic Books, 1967.

Joyce, James. *Ulysses.* New York: Modern Library, 1934.

Jung, Hwa Yol. "A Critique of the Behavioral Persuasion in Politics: A Phenomenological View," in *Phenomenology and the Social Sciences,* ed. Maurice Natanson, 2 vols. Evanston, Ill.: Northwestern University Press, 1973, 2:133–73.

––––––. "Democratic Ontology and Technology: A Critique of C. B. Macpherson," *Polity,* 11 (Winter 1978), forthcoming.

––––––. "Embodiment and Political Action," *Philosophy Forum,* 14 (1976): 367–88.

––––––. "A Hermeneutical Accent on the Conduct of Political Inquiry," *Human Studies,* 1 (January 1978): 48–82. Cited as "HA."

––––––. "Leo Strauss's Conception of Political Philosophy: A Critique," *The Review of Politics,* 29 (October 1967): 492–517.

––––––. "The Life-World, Historicity, and Truth: Reflections on Leo Strauss's Encounter with Heidegger and Husserl," *The Journal of the British Society for Phenomenology,* 9 (January 1978): 11–25.

––––––. "The Place of Valuation in the Theory of Politics: A Phenomenological Critique of Political Behavioralism," *The Journal of Value Inquiry,* 8 (Spring 1974): 17–29.

––––––. "Vico, Hermeneutical Phenomenology, and the Human Sciences: Toward a New Paradigm for the Philosophy of the Sciences." Paper Delivered at "Vico/Venezia": An International Conference Celebrating the 250th Anniversary of the Original Appearance, in Venice, of Giambattista Vico's *Autobiography,* Venice, Italy, August 22–25, 1978.

–––––– and Petee Jung. "The Hermeneutics of Political Ideology and Cultural Change: Maoism as the Sinicization of Marxism," *Cultural Hermeneutics,* 3 (1975): 165–98.

––––––. "Revolutionary Dialectics: Mao Tse-tung and Maurice Merleau-Ponty," *Dialectical Anthropology,* 2 (1977): 35–56.

––––––. "To Save the Earth," *Philosophy Today,* 14 (Summer 1975): 108–17.

––––––. "Toward a New Humanism: The Politics of Civility in a 'No-Growth' Society," *Man and World,* 9 (August 1976): 283–306.

Kantorowicz, Ernst H. *The King's Two Bodies: A Study in Mediaeval Political Theology.* Princeton, N.J.: Princeton University Press, 1957.

Kaplan, Abraham. *The Conduct of Inquiry: Methodology for Behavioral Science.* San Francisco: Chandler, 1964. Cited as "CIM."

Kierkegaard, Søren. *The Concept of Irony,* trans. Lee M. Capel. New York: Harper and Row, 1965.

––––––. *Concluding Unscientific Postscript,* trans. David F. Swenson and Walter Lowrie. Princeton, N.J.: Princeton University Press, 1941.

Klein, Jacob. *Greek Mathematical Thought and the Origin of Algebra,* trans. Eva Brann. Cambridge, Mass.: M. I. T. Press, 1968. Cited as "GMT."

–––––– and Leo Strauss. "A Giving of Accounts," *The College,* Publication of St. John's College, Annapolis, Md. (April 1970): 1–5. Cited as "GA."

Kockelmans, Joseph J. (ed.). *Contemporary European Ethics: Selected Readings.* Garden City, N.Y.: Doubleday, 1973.

———— and Theodore J. Kisiel. *Phenomenology and the Natural Sciences: Essays and Translations.* Evanston, Ill.: Northwestern University Press, 1970.

Kolakowski, Leszek. *Husserl and the Search for Certitude.* New Haven, Conn.: Yale University Press, 1975.

Kosík, Karel. *Dialectics of the Concrete: A Study on Problems of Man and World,* trans. Karel Kovanda with James Schmidt. Dordrecht, The Netherlands: D. Reidel, 1976.

Kroeber, A. L. and Clyde Kluckhohn. *Culture: A Critical Review of Concepts and Definitions.* New York: Random House, 1963.

Kruks, Sonia. "Merleau-Ponty: A Phenomenological Critique of Liberalism." *Philosophy and Phenomenological Research,* 37 (March 1977): 394–407.

Kuhn, Thomas S. "Logic of Discovery or Psychology of Research?," in *Criticism and the Growth of Knowledge,* ed. Imre Lakatos and Alan Musgrave. Cambridge, England: University Press, 1970, pp. 1–23.

————. "Second Thoughts on Paradigms," in *The Structure of Scientific Theories,* ed. Frederick Suppe. Urbana, Ill.: University of Illinois Press, 1974, pp. 459–82.

————. *The Structure of Scientific Revolutions,* 2nd ed., enl. Chicago: University of Chicago Press, 1970. Cited as "SSR."

Laing, R. D. *Knots.* New York: Pantheon Books, 1970.

Landgrebe, Ludwig. "The Phenomenological Concept of Experience," trans. Donn C. Welton, *Philosophy and Phenomenological Research,* 34 (September 1973): 1–13.

Lane, Robert E. *Political Thinking and Consciousness.* Chicago: Markham, 1969.

Leiss, William. "Critical Theory and Its Future," *Political Theory,* 2 (August 1974): 330–49.

————. *The Domination of Nature.* New York: George Braziller, 1972.

————. *The Limits to Satisfaction.* Toronto: University of Toronto Press, 1976.

Levi, Albert William. *Humanism and Politics.* Bloomington, Ind.: Indiana University Press, 1969.

————. *Philosophy as Social Expression.* Chicago: University of Chicago Press, 1974.

Lévi-Strauss, Claude. *Structural Anthropology,* vol. 2, trans. Monique Layton. New York: Basic Books, 1976.

Levinas, Emmanuel. *Autrement qu'Être ou au-delà de l'Essence.* La Haye: Martinus Nijhoff, 1974.

————. *Totality and Infinity,* trans. Alphonso Lingis. Pittsburgh: Duquesne University Press, 1969.

Locke, John. *Two Treatises of Government,* ed. Peter Laslett. Cambridge, England: University Press, 1960.

Löwith, Karl. *Nature, History, and Existentialism and Other Essays in the Philosophy of History,* ed. Arnold Levison. Evanston, Ill.: Northwestern University Press, 1966.

Lukács, Georg. *History and Class Consciousness,* trans. Rodney Livingstone. Cambridge, Mass.: M.I.T. Press, 1968.

MacIntyre, Alasdair. *Against the Self-Image of the Age: Essays on Ideology and Philosophy.* London: Duckworth, 1971.

Macmurray, John. *Persons in Relation.* London: Faber and Faber, 1961.

————. *The Self as Agent.* London: Faber and Faber, 1957.

Macpherson, C. B. *Democratic Theory: Essays in Retrieval.* New York: Oxford University Press, 1973. Cited as "DT."

————. *The Life and Times of Liberal Democracy.* New York: Oxford University Press, 1977. Cited as "LT."

————. *The Political Theory of Possessive Individualism: Hobbes to Locke.* New York: Oxford University Press, 1962. Cited as "PT."

————. *The Real World of Democracy.* New York: Oxford University Press, 1966.

McRae, Robert. *The Problem of the Unity of the Sciences: Bacon to Kant.* Toronto: University of Toronto Press, 1961.

Magliola, Robert R. *Phenomenology and Literature: An Introduction.* West Lafayette, Ind.: Purdue University Press, 1977.

Mandelbaum, Maurice. *The Phenomenology of Moral Experience.* Glencoe, Ill.: Free Press, 1955.

Mannheim, Karl. *Ideology and Utopia: An Introduction to the Sociology of Knowledge,* trans. Louis Wirth and Edward Shils. London: Routledge and Kegan Paul, 1936.

Marcel, Gabriel. *The Mystery of Being,* vol. 1, trans. G. S. Fraser. Chicago: Henry Regnery, 1960.

Marcuse, Herbert. *The Aesthetic Dimension: Toward a Critique of Marxist Aesthetics.* Boston: Beacon Press, 1978.

————. *Counterrevolution and Revolt.* Boston: Beacon Press, 1972.

————. *Eros and Civilization.* Boston: Beacon Press, 1966.

————. "Heidegger's Politics: An Interview with Herbert Marcuse by Frederick Olafson," *Graduate Faculty Philosophy Journal,* 6 (Winter 1977): 28-40. Cited as "HPI."

————. *One-Dimensional Man: Studies in the Ideology of Advanced Industrial Society.* Boston: Beacon Press, 1964. Cited as "ODM."

Marković, Mihailo. *From Affluence to Praxis.* Ann Arbor, Mich.: University of Michigan Press, 1974. Cited as "FAP."

Marx, Karl. *Critique of the Gotha Programme.* New York: International Publishers, 1966.

————. *Grundrisse: Foundations of the Critique of Political Economy,* trans. Martin Nicolaus. New York: Random House, 1973.

————. *Karl Marx: Selected Writings in Sociology and Philosophy,* trans. T. B. Bottomore. New York: McGraw-Hill, 1956.

————. *Writings of the Young Marx on Philosophy and Society,* ed. and trans. Lloyd D. Easton and Kurt H. Guddat. Garden City, N.Y.: Doubleday, 1967.

_____ and Frederick Engels. *The German Ideology,* ed. R. Pascal. New York: International Publishers, 1947.

Marx, Werner. *Heidegger and the Tradition,* trans. Theodore Kisiel and Murray Greene. Evanston, Ill.: Northwestern University Press, 1971.

_____. "In Remembrance of Martin Heidegger," trans. Richard S. Grabau, *Man and World,* 10 (1977): 3–5.

Maslow, Abraham H. *The Psychology of Science.* Chicago: Henry Regnery, 1966.

Mauss, Marcel. "Les Techniques du Corps," *Journal de Psychologie Normale et Pathologique,* 32 (1936): 271–93.

May, Rollo. *Psychology and the Human Dilemma.* Princeton, N.J.: D. Van Nostrand, 1967. Cited as "PHD."

Mehta, J. L. *Martin Heidegger: The Way and the Vision.* Honolulu: University Press of Hawaii, 1976.

Merleau-Ponty, Maurice. *Adventures of the Dialectic,* trans. Joseph Bien. Evanston, Ill.: Northwestern University Press, 1973. Cited as "AD."

_____. *Consciousness and the Acquisition of Language,* trans. Hugh J. Silverman. Evanston, Ill.: Northwestern University Press, 1973. Cited as "CAL."

_____. *Humanism and Terror,* trans. John O'Neill. Boston: Beacon Press, 1969.

_____. "Husserl et la Notion de Nature (Notes Prises au Cours de Maurice Merleau-Ponty)," *Revue de Métaphysique et de Morale,* 70 (July–September 1965): 257–69. Cited as "HNN."

_____. *In Praise of Philosophy,* trans. John Wild and James M. Edie. Evanston, Ill.: Northwestern University Press, 1963. Cited as "IPP."

_____. *Phenomenology of Perception,* trans. Colin Smith. New York: Humanities Press, 1962. Cited as "PP."

_____. *The Primacy of Perception,* ed. James M. Edie. Evanston, Ill.: Northwestern University Press, 1964. Cited as "PPE."

_____. *The Prose of the World,* ed. Claude Lefort and trans. John O'Neill. Evanston, Ill.: Northwestern University Press, 1973. Cited as "PW."

_____. *Sense and Non-Sense,* trans. Hubert L. Dreyfus and Patricia Allen Dreyfus. Evanston, Ill.: Northwestern University Press, 1964. Cited as "SNS."

_____. *Signs,* trans. Richard C. McCleary. Evanston, Ill.: Northwestern University Press, 1964. Cited as "SI."

_____. *Themes from the Lectures at the Collège de France 1952–1960,* trans. John O'Neill. Evanston, Ill.: Northwestern University Press, 1970. Cited as "TL."

_____. *The Visible and the Invisible,* ed. Claude Lefort and trans. Alphonso Lingis. Evanston, Ill.: Northwestern University Press, 1968. Cited as "VI."

Mill, John Stuart. *On Liberty,* ed. David Spitz with Annotated Text Sources and Background Criticism. New York: W. W. Norton.

_____. *Principles of Political Economy,* ed. Sir W. J. Ashley. New York: Longmans, Green, 1885.

————. *A System of Logic: Ratiocinative and Inductive.* New York: Longmans, Green, 1925. Cited as "SL."

Miller, Eugene F. "Leo Strauss: The Recovery of Political Philosophy," in *Contemporary Political Philosophers,* ed. Anthony de Crespigny and Kenneth Minogue. New York: Dodd, Mead, 1975, pp. 67–99.

————. "Political Philosophy and Human Nature," *The Personalist,* 53 (Summer 1972): 209–21.

————. "Positivism, Historicism, and Political Inquiry," *American Political Science Review,* 66 (September 1972): 796–817.

Minkowski, Eugène. *Lived Time: Phenomenological and Psychopathological Studies,* trans. Nancy Metzel. Evanston, Ill.: Northwestern University Press, 1970.

Misch, Georg. *Lebensphilosophie und Phänomenologie,* 2nd ed. Leipzig, Germany: B. G. Teubner, 1931.

Mongis, Henri. *Heidegger et la Critique de la Notion de Valeur.* La Haye: Martinus Nijhoff, 1976.

Morgenthau, Hans J. *In Defense of the National Interest: A Critical Examination of American Foreign Policy.* New York: Alfred A. Knopf, 1951.

————. *Politics among Nations: The Struggle for Power and Peace,* 5th ed. New York: Alfred A. Knopf, 1973.

————. *Scientific Man vs. Power Politics.* Chicago: University of Chicago Press, 1946. Cited as "SM."

Nagel, Ernest. *Logic without Metaphysics.* Glencoe, Ill.: Free Press, 1956.

Natanson, Maurice. *Edmund Husserl: Philosopher of Infinite Tasks.* Evanston, Ill.: Northwestern University Press, 1973. Cited as "EH."

————. *The Journeying Self.* Reading, Mass.: Addison-Wesley, 1970.

————. "The Nature of Social Man," in *Patterns of the Life-World: Essays in Honor of John Wild,* ed. James M. Edie, Francis H. Parker, and Calvin O. Schrag. Evanston, Ill.: Northwestern University Press, 1970, pp. 248–70.

————. *Phenomenology, Role, and Reason: Essays on the Coherence and Deformation of Social Reality.* Springfield, Ill.: Charles C Thomas, 1974.

———— (ed.). *Phenomenology and the Social Sciences,* 2 vols. Evanston, Ill.: Northwestern University Press, 1973.

Nelson, Benjamin. "Scholastic *Rationales* of 'Conscience', Early Modern Crises of Credibility, and the Scientific-Technocultural Revolution of the 17th and 20th Centuries," *Journal for the Scientific Study of Religion,* 7 (Fall 1968): 157–77.

Neurath, Otto. "Sociology and Physicalism," trans. Morton Magnus and Ralph Raico, in *Logical Positivism,* ed. A. J. Ayer. Glencoe, Ill.: Free Press, 1959, pp. 282–317.

Nozick, Robert. *Anarchy, State, and Utopia.* New York: Basic Books, 1974.

Oakeshott, Michael. *Experience and Its Modes.* Cambridge, England: University Press, 1933.

————. "Introduction" to Thomas Hobbes, *Leviathan,* ed. Michael Oakeshott. Oxford, England: Basil Blackwell, 1960, pp. vii–lxvi.

————. *On Human Conduct.* Oxford, England: Clarendon Press, 1975. Cited as "OHC."

Okuda, Kazuhiko. *Hermeneutics and Politics: A Study in Political Symbolism and Communication.* Unpublished Ph.D. Dissertation, Department of Political Economy, University of Toronto, 1977.

O'Neill, Eugene. *A Moon for the Misbegotten.* New York: Random House, 1952.

O'Neill, John. *Making Sense Together: An Introduction to Wild Sociology.* New York: Harper and Row, 1974.

──────. "Scientism, Historicism and the Problem of Rationality," in *Modes of Individualism and Collectivism,* ed. John O'Neill. New York: St. Martin's Press, 1973, pp. 3–26.

Ophuls, William. *Ecology and the Politics of Scarcity: Prologue to a Political Theory of the Steady State.* San Francisco: W. H. Freeman, 1977.

Oppenheim, Felix E. *Moral Principles in Political Philosophy.* New York: Random House, 1968.

Paci, Enzo. *The Function of the Sciences and the Meaning of Man,* trans. Paul Piccone and James E. Hansen. Evanston, Ill.: Northwestern University Press, 1972. Cited as "FS."

Palmer, Richard E. *Hermeneutics: Interpretation Theory in Schleiermacher, Dilthey, Heidegger, and Gadamer.* Evanston, Ill.: Northwestern University Press, 1969. Cited as "HE."

Palmier, Jean-Michel. *Les Écrits Politiques de Heidegger.* Paris: Éditions de l'Herne, 1968.

Petrović, Gajo. *Marx in the Mid-Twentieth Century.* Garden City, N.Y.: Doubleday, 1967.

Pieper, Josef. *Leisure: The Basis of Culture,* trans. Alexander Dru. New York: Pantheon Books, 1952.

Pitkin, Hanna Fenichel. *Wittgenstein and Justice.* Berkeley, Calif.; University of California Press, 1972.

Plessner, Helmuth. *Laughing and Crying,* trans. James S. Churchill and Marjorie Grene. Evanston, Ill.: Northwestern University Press, 1970. Cited as "LC."

Pöggeler, Otto. "Being as Appropriation," trans. Ruediger Hermann Grimm, *Philosophy Today,* 19 (Summer 1975): 152–78.

──────. *Philosophie und Politik bei Heidegger.* Freiburg-München, Germany: Karl Alber, 1972.

Polanyi, Michael. *Knowing and Being,* ed. Marjorie Grene. Chicago: University of Chicago Press, 1969.

──────. *Personal Knowledge: Towards a Post-Critical Philosophy.* Chicago: University of Chicago Press, 1958.

──────. *Science, Faith and Society.* London: Oxford University Press, 1946.

──────. *The Tacit Dimension.* Garden City, N.Y.: Doubleday, 1966.

Polin, Raymond. *La Création des Valeurs,* 2nd ed. Paris: Presses Universitaires de France, 1952.

Popper, Karl R. *Objective Knowledge.* Oxford, England: Clarendon Press, 1972.

Putnam, Hilary, *Meaning and the Moral Sciences.* London: Routledge and Kegan Paul, 1978.

Radnitzky, Gerard. *Contemporary Schools of Metascience.* Chicago: Henry Regnery, 1973.

Rawls, John. *A Theory of Justice.* Cambridge, Mass.: Harvard University Press, 1972.

Reid, Herbert G. "The Politics of Time: Conflicting Philosophical Perspectives and Trends," *The Human Context,* 4 (Autumn 1972): 456-83.

————— and Ernest J. Yanarella. "Toward a Post-Modern Theory of American Political Science and Political Culture: Perspectives from Critical Marxism and Phenomenology," *Cultural Hermeneutics,* 2 (1974): 91-166.

Ricoeur, Paul. *The Conflict of Interpretations: Essays in Hermeneutics,* ed. Don Ihde. Evanston, Ill.: Northwestern University Press, 1974. Cited as "CI."

—————. "Ethics and Culture: Habermas and Gadamer in Dialogue," trans. David Pellauer, *Philosophy Today,* 17 (Summer 1973): 153-65.

—————. *Freedom and Nature: The Voluntary and the Involuntary,* trans. Erazim V. Kohák. Evanston, Ill.: Northwestern University Press, 1966.

—————. *Freud and Philosophy: An Essay on Interpretation,* trans. Denis Savage. New Haven, Conn.: Yale University Press, 1970.

—————. "History and Hermeneutics," trans. David Pellauer, *The Journal of Philosophy,* 72 (November 4, 1976): 683-95.

—————. *History and Truth,* trans. Charles A. Kelbley. Evanston, Ill.: Northwestern University Press, 1965. Cited as "HT."

—————. *Husserl: An Analysis of His Phenomenology,* trans. Edward G. Ballard and Lester E. Embree. Evanston, Ill.: Northwestern University Press, 1967.

—————. "Husserl and Wittgenstein on Language," in *Phenomenology and Existentialism,* ed. Edward N. Lee and Maurice Mandelbaum. Baltimore: Johns Hopkins Press, 1967, pp. 207-17.

—————. *Interpretation Theory: Discourse and the Surplus Meaning.* Fort Worth, Texas: Texas Christian University Press, 1976.

—————. "The Model of the Text: Meaningful Action Considered as a Text," *Social Research,* 38 (Autumn 1971): 529-62.

—————. "New Developments in Phenomenology in France: The Phenomenology of Language," trans. P. G. Goodman, *Social Research,* 34 (Spring 1967): 1-30.

—————. "Phénoménologie et Herméneutique," *Man and World,* 7 (August 1974): 223-53.

—————. *The Rule of Metaphor: Multi-Disciplinary Studies of the Creation of Meaning in Language,* trans. Robert Czerny with Kathleen McLaughlin and John Costello, S. J. Toronto: University of Toronto Press, 1977.

—————. "The Task of Hermeneutics," trans. David Pellauer, *Philosophy Today,* 17 (Summer 1973): 112-28.

Riesman, David. *The Lonely Crowd: A Study of the Changing American Character.* New Haven, Conn.: Yale University Press, 1950.

Riker, William H. and Peter C. Ordeshook. *An Introduction to Positive Political Theory.* Englewood Cliffs, N.J.: Prentice-Hall, 1973.

Roche, Maurice. *Phenomenology, Language and the Social Sciences.* London: Routledge and Kegan Paul, 1973.

Rosen, Stanley. *Nihilism: A Philosophical Essay.* New Haven, Conn.: Yale University Press, 1969.

Rossi, Paolo. *Philosophy, Technology and the Arts in the Early Modern Era,* trans. Salvator Attanasio and ed. Benjamin Nelson. New York: Harper and Row, 1970.

Rousseau, Jean-Jacques. *The Political Writings of Jean Jacques Rousseau,* 2 vols., ed. C. E. Vaughan. New York: John Wiley, 1962.

Royce, Josiah. *The Philosophy of Loyalty.* New York: Macmillan, 1920.

Said, Edward W. *Beginnings: Intention and Method.* New York: Basic Books, 1975.

Sallis, John. *Phenomenology and the Return to Beginnings.* Pittsburgh: Duquesne University Press, 1973.

Sartre, Jean-Paul. *Being and Nothingness,* trans. Hazel E. Barnes. New York: Philosophical Library, 1956. Cited as "BN."

_____. *Critique of Dialectical Reason,* trans. Alan Sheridan-Smith. London: NLB, 1976. Cited as "CDR."

_____. "Faces," trans. Anne P. Jones, in *Essays in Phenomenology,* ed. Maurice Natanson. The Hague: Martinus Nijhoff, 1966, pp. 157–63.

_____. *Search for a Method,* trans. Hazel E. Barnes. New York: Alfred A. Knopf, 1963. Cited as "SM."

Scheler, Max. *Man's Place in Nature,* trans. Hans Meyerhoff. New York: Noonday Press, 1962. Cited as "MP."

_____. *The Nature of Sympathy,* trans. Peter Heath. New Haven, Conn.: Yale University Press, 1954.

_____. *Selected Philosophical Essays,* trans. David R. Lachterman. Evanston, Ill.: Northwestern University Press, 1973. Cited as "SPE."

Schmidt, Alfred. *The Concept of Nature in Marx,* trans. Ben Fowkes. London: NLB, 1971. Cited as "CNM."

Schrag, Calvin O. *Experience and Being: Prolegomena to a Future Ontology.* Evanston, Ill.: Northwestern University Press, 1969.

_____. "Praxis and Structure: Conflicting Models in the Science of Man," *The Journal of the British Society for Phenomenology,* 6 (January 1975): 23–31.

_____. *Radical Reflection and the Origin of the Human Sciences.* Athens, Ohio: Ohio University Press, forthcoming.

Schürmann, Reiner. "The Ontological Difference and Political Philosophy," *Philosophy and Phenomenological Research,* forthcoming.

_____. "Political Thinking in Heidegger," *Social Research,* 45 (Spring 1978): 191–221.

Schutz, Alfred. *Collected Papers,* vol. 1: *The Problem of Social Reality,* ed. Maurice Natanson. The Hague: Martinus Nijhoff, 1962. Cited as "CP."

_____. *Collected Papers,* vol. 3: *Studies in Phenomenological Philosophy,* ed. Ilse Schutz. The Hague: Martinus Nijhoff, 1966.

_____. *The Phenomenology of the Social World,* trans. George Walsh and Frederick Lehnert. Evanston, Ill.: Northwestern University Press, 1967. Cited as "PSW."

―――― and Thomas Luckmann. *The Structures of the Life-World,* trans. Richard M. Zaner and H. Tristram Engelhardt, Jr. Evanston, Ill.: Northwestern University Press, 1973.

Searle, John R. *Speech Acts: An Essay in the Philosophy of Language.* Cambridge, England: University Press, 1969.

Sennett, Richard. *The Fall of Public Man.* New York: Alfred A. Knopf, 1977.

Sibley, Mulford Q. *Nature and Civilization: Some Implications for Politics.* Itasca, Ill.: F. E. Peacock, 1977.

Simon, Herbert A. *The Sciences of the Artificial.* Cambridge, Mass.: M.I.T. Press, 1969. Cited as "SA."

Skinner, B. F. "Behaviorism at Fifty," in *Behaviorism and Phenomenology,* ed. T. W. Wann. Chicago: University of Chicago Press, 1964, pp. 79–108.

――――. *Beyond Freedom and Dignity.* New York: Alfred A. Knopf, 1971. Cited as "BFD."

Skinner, Quentin. "Hermeneutics and the Role of History," *New Literary History,* 7 (Autumn 1975): 209–32.

――――. "Political Language and the Explanation of Political Action." Paper Delivered at the 1977 Annual Meeting of the American Political Science Association, The Washington Hilton Hotel, Washington, D.C., September 1–4, 1977.

Slater, Phil. *Origin and Significance of the Frankfurt School: A Marxist Perspective.* London: Routledge and Kegan Paul, 1977.

Sokolowski, Robert. *Husserlian Meditations: How Words Present Things.* Evanston, Ill.: Northwestern University Press, 1974.

――――. "Husserl's Protreptic," in *Life-World and Consciousness: Essays for Aron Gurwitsch,* ed. Lester E. Embree. Evanston, Ill.: Northwestern University Press, 1972, pp. 55–82.

Spiegelberg, Herbert. "Husserl's Phenomenology and Existentialism," *The Journal of Philosophy,* 57 (January 21, 1960): 62-74.

――――. *The Phenomenological Movement: A Historical Introduction.* 2nd ed., 2 vols. The Hague: Martinus Nijhoff, 1965.

Spragens, Thomas A., Jr. *The Dilemma of Contemporary Political Theory: Toward a Postbehavioral Science of Politics.* New York: Dunellen, 1973.

――――. *The Politics of Motion: The World of Thomas Hobbes.* Lexington, Ky.: University Press of Kentucky, 1973.

Steiner, George. *After Babel: Aspects of Language and Translation.* New York: Oxford University Press, 1975.

――――. *Extraterritorial: Papers on Literature and the Language Revolution.* New York: Atheneum, 1976. Cited as "EX."

Strasser, Stephan. *Das Gemüt: Grundgedanken zu einer phänomenologischen Philosophie und Theorie des menschlichen Gefühlslebens.* Utrecht, The Netherlands: Spectrum, 1956.

――――. *The Idea of Dialogal Phenomenology.* Pittsburgh: Duquesne University Press, 1969.

Straus, Erwin W. *Phenomenological Psychology.* New York: Basic Books, 1966. Cited as "PPS."

――――. *The Primary World of Senses,* trans. Jacob Needleman. New York: Free Press, 1963. Cited as "PWS."

Strauss, Leo. "An Epilogue," in *Essays on the Scientific Study of Politics,* ed. Herbert J. Storing. New York: Holt, Rinehart and Winston, 1962, pp. 307-27.

――――. *Natural Right and History.* Chicago: University of Chicago Press, 1953. Cited as "NRH."

――――. *Persecution and the Art of Writing.* Glencoe, Ill.: Free Press, 1952.

――――. "Philosophy as Rigorous Science and Political Philosophy," *Interpretation,* 2 (Fall 1971): 1-9. Cited as "PRS."

――――. "Political Philosophy and the Crisis of Our Time," in *The Post-Behavioral Era: Perspectives on Political Science,* ed. George J. Graham, Jr. and George W. Carey. New York: David McKay, 1972, pp. 217-42.

――――. *The Political Philosophy of Hobbes: Its Basis and Its Genesis,* trans. E. M. Sinclair. Chicago: University of Chicago Press, 1952.

――――. *Spinoza's Critique of Religion,* trans. E. M. Sinclair. New York: Schocken Books, 1965. Cited as "SCR."

――――. *What Is Political Philosophy? And Other Studies.* Glencoe, Ill.: Free Press, 1959.

―――― and Hans-Georg Gadamer. "Correspondence Concerning *Wahrheit und Methode,*" *The Independent Journal of Philosophy,* 2 (Winter-Spring 1978), forthcoming.

Tawney, R. H. *The Acquisitive Society.* New York: Harcourt, Brace, and Howe, 1920.

Taylor, Charles. "The Agony of Economic Man," in *Essays on the Left.* Toronto: McClelland and Stewart, 1971, pp. 221-35.

――――. *The Explanation of Behaviour.* New York: Humanities Press, 1964.

――――. *Hegel.* Cambridge, England: University Press, 1975.

――――. "Interpretation and the Sciences of Man," *The Review of Metaphysics,* 25 (September 1971): 3-51. Cited as "ISM."

Todes, Samuel J. and Hubert L. Dreyfus. "The Existentialist Critique of Objectivity," in *Patterns of the Life-World: Essays in Honor of John Wild,* ed. James M. Edie, Francis H. Parker, and Calvin O. Schrag. Evanston, Ill.: Northwestern University Press, 1970, pp. 346-87.

Toulmin, Stephen. *Foresight and Understanding.* New York: Harper and Row, 1963. Cited as "FU."

Tran-Duc-Thao. *Phénoménologie et Matérialisme Dialectique.* Paris: Minh-Tan, 1951.

Urmson, J. O. *The Emotive Theory of Ethics.* New York: Oxford University Press, 1968.

Valéry, Paul. *History and Politics,* trans. Denise Folliot and Jackson Mathews. New York: Pantheon Books, 1962. Cited as "HP."

Vico, Giambattista. *The New Science,* trans. Thomas G. Bergin and Max H. Fisch. Ithaca, N.Y.: Cornell University Press, 1961. Cited as "NS."

———. *On the Study of Methods of Our Time,* trans. Elio Gianturco. Indianapolis: Bobbs-Merrill, 1965. Cited as "OSM."

Voegelin, Eric. *The New Science of Politics.* Chicago: University of Chicago Press, 1952. Cited as "NSP."

———. "The Origins of Scientism," *Social Research,* 15 (December 1948): 462 – 94.

Vološinov, V. N. *Marxism and the Philosophy of Language,* trans. Ladislav Matejka and I. R. Titunik. New York: Seminar Press, 1973.

Vygotsky, Lev Semenovich. *Thought and Language,* ed. and trans. Eugenia Hangmann and Gertrude Vakar. Cambridge, Mass.: M.I.T. Press, 1962.

Waismann, Friedrich. "How I See Philosophy," in *Logical Positivism,* ed. A. J. Ayer. Glencoe, Ill.: Free Press, 1959, pp. 345 –80.

Wallas, Graham. *Human Nature in Politics.* New York: F. S. Crofts, 1921.

Walsh, W. H. *An Introduction to Philosophy of History.* London: Hutchinson, 1951.

Watsuji, Tetsuro. *Rinri Gaku* (Ethics), 2 vols. Tokyo: Iwanami Shoten, 1965.

Weinstein, Michael A. "C. B. Macpherson: The Roots of Democracy and Liberalism," in *Contemporary Political Philosophers,* ed. Anthony de Crespigny and Kenneth Minogue. New York: Dodd, Mead, 1975, pp. 252-71. Cited as "CBM."

Weldon, T. D. *The Vocabulary of Politics.* Harmondsworth, England: Penguin Books, 1953.

Weyl, Hermann. *Philosophy of Mathematics and Natural Science.* New York: Atheneum, 1963.

White, Lynn, Jr. *Machina ex Deo: Essays in the Dynamism of Western Culture.* Cambridge, Mass.: M.I.T. Press, 1968.

Whitehead, Alfred North. *Process and Reality.* New York: Macmillan, 1929.

———. *Science and the Modern World.* New York: Macmillan, 1925.

Wiener, Norbert. *Cybernetics.* 2nd ed. Cambridge, Mass.: M.I.T. Press, 1961.

Wild, John. *Existence and the World of Freedom.* Englewood Cliffs, N.J.: Prentice-Hall, 1963. Cited as "EWF."

———. "Existentialism as a Philosophy," *The Journal of Philosophy,* 57 (January 21, 1960): 45 –62.

———. "Foreword" to *Existential Phenomenology and Political Theory: A Reader,* ed. Hwa Yol Jung. Chicago: Henry Regnery, 1972, pp. ix-xi.

———. "Foreword" to Maurice Merleau-Ponty, *The Structure of Behavior,* trans. Alden L. Fisher. Boston: Beacon Press, 1963, pp. xii –xvii.

———. *Human Freedom and Social Order: An Essay in Christian Philosophy.* Durham, N.C.: Duke University Press, 1959.

———. "Interrogation of John Wild," Conducted by Henry B. Veatch, in *Philosophical Interrogations,* ed. Sydney and Beatrice Rome. New York: Holt, Rinehart and Winston, 1964, pp. 119 –78.

Williame, Robert. *Les Fondements Phénoménologiques de la Sociologie Compréhensive: Alfred Schutz et Max Weber.* La Haye: Martinus Nijhoff, 1973.

Williams, Raymond. *Marxism and Literature.* New York: Oxford University Press, 1977.

Winch, Peter. *The Idea of a Social Science and Its Relation to Philosophy.* London: Routledge and Kegan Paul, 1958.

Wittgenstein, Ludwig. *Philosophical Investigations,* trans. G. E. M. Anscombe. Oxford, England: Basil Blackwell, 1953. Cited as "PI."

————. *Remarks on Colour,* ed. G. E. M. Anscombe and trans. Linda L. McAlister and Margarete Schättle. Berkeley, Calif.: University of California Press, 1977.

————. *Tractatus Logico-Philosophicus,* trans. D. F. Pears and B. F. McGuinness. New York: Humanities Press, 1961. Cited as "TLP."

Wolff, Kurt H. *Surrender and Catch: Experience and Inquiry Today.* Dordrecht, The Netherlands: D. Reidel, 1976.

Wolff, Robert Paul. *In Defense of Anarchism.* New York: Harper and Row, 1970.

————. *The Poverty of Liberalism.* Boston: Beacon Press, 1958.

Wolin, Sheldon S. "Political Theory as a Vocation," *American Political Science Review,* 63 (December 1969): 1062–82.

————. *Politics and Vision: Continuity and Innovation in Western Political Thought.* Boston: Little, Brown, 1960. Cited as "PV."

Wood, Ellen Meiksins. *Mind and Politics: An Approach to the Meaning of Liberal and Socialist Individualism.* Berkeley, Calif.: University of California Press, 1972.

Zaner, Richard M. *The Way of Phenomenology.* New York: Pegasus, 1970.

Zetterbaum, Marvin. "Human Nature and History," in *Human Nature in Politics,* NOMOS, vol. 17, ed. J. Roland Pennock and John W. Chapman. New York: New York University Press, 1977, pp. 225–49.

Zijderveld, Anton C. *The Abstract Society.* Garden City, N.Y.: Doubleday, 1970.

Zimmerman, Michael E. "Heidegger on Nihilism and Technique," *Man and World,* 8 (November 1975): 394–414.

Index

action, 6, 13, 18, 19, 26, 27, 59, 60, 78, 103; behavioralist conception of, 96; and body, 30, end and means in, 24; and knowledge, 175 (*see also* theory *and* practice); labor and work compared with, 55; linguistic, 117; meaning and force in, 21 passim, 94; perception as nascent *logos* of, 33; and production compared, 43; as project, 20-29; as projected behavior, 20-40, 96; revolutionary, 28; social nature of, 23-24; and subjective interpretation, 67; temporal dimensions of, 24-25; and text-interpretation, 68; unpredictive and irreversible nature of, 23; and value, 42, 103

Adorno, Theodor W., 13, 182n

adumbration (*Abschattung*), 33, 34, 86, 119

aesthetic, the, 46, 51, 76, 89

aletheia, 7, 72; as disclosure, 6; *physis* as, 150; and thinking, 6. *See also* truth

Almond, Gabriel A., 198n

ambiguity, 4, 27, 38, 117, 119, 122; defined, 21; existential and conceptual, xv; of theory and practice, 10. *See also* dialectic (al)

American political science, 79

analytical politics: defined, 98

anthropology, xiii, 19, 37

Apel, Karl-Otto, xvi, 67, 195n; on analytical philosophy, 219n

Apter, David E.: on approaches in political science, 196n.27

Arendt, Hannah, 5, 13, 54-55, 122-23, 130, 182n, 185n, 189n, 192n, 208n, 214n, 215n, 219n; on action, 23, 123; on anthropocentrism and theriomorphism, 184n; on banality of evil, 61; on Chinese philosophy, 199n; on earth, 41; on "essential," 200n; on Heidegger, 178n, 216n; on labor and work, 54; on natality, 26; on political thinking, 12-13; on promise, 185 n; on thinking, 182n; on unique distinction and plurality, 168; on will, 181n29

Aristotle, 12, 43-44, 69, 145, 147, 150, 156

artifact, 54, 155; as *Zuhandensein*, 20

artificial intelligence (AI), 113, 117, 118, 121, 122; defined, 114-15

artificiality, 114-15; defined, 115

attitude *(Einstellung)*, 79, 105-6

Augstein, Rudolf, 214n

Augustine, St., 12

Austin, J.L., 39, 98-99, 188n, 204n; on descriptive fallacy, 105; performative utterances, exposition of, in, 105, 106

authority: scientific, 88, 90

autopsy *(autopsia)*, 35, 67, 76

Averroism, 101-2

Axelos, Kostas, xiii; on man and nature, 191n

axiology, 17, 171

Bacon, Francis, 85

banality of evil, 48, 141; and thoughtlessness, 6

Barry, Brian, 98, 99, 203n

Barth, Hans, 199n

Beauvoir, Simone de, 24, 25, 184n, 189n; on ambiguity, 21, 27; on existence and temporality, 27; on Hegel, 213n

behavior: and action, 21-22; and meaning, 93-94, 107; overt and covert, distinction of, 95; and self-interest, 99. *See also* action

behavioral pragmatics, 172

behaviorism, 22, 94, 101, 128

Being, 9, 45, 54; as *aletheia*, 6, 7 (*see also* truth); and knowledge, 174; and language, 36; and technology, 111; wild, 32

Being-in-the-world *(in-der-Welt-sein)*, xv, 9, 19-20, 27, 29-30, 34, 68, 69, 72, 73, 116

Bell, Daniel, 42-43, 189n

Bell, David V. J., 67

Beloff, John: on Dreyfus, 207n

Benthall, Jonathan, 187n

Bentham, Jeremy, 94, 130

Berdyaev, Nicholas, 122

Berger, Brigitte, 198n

243